"The values, moral obligations, and stra‿ ╴  ╴  ╴  ╴  ╴
all students graduate from high school ready without remediation to
access opportunity will take political will, a commitment to equity,
and systemic thinking about how to improve whole systems of
schools and not settle for a few more good ones. Hornbeck draws on
successful results from research, policies, and practice to make a compelling case for what must be done to improve school districts and
schools, and the necessary steps to do so for all children." —**Thomas
Payzant**, professor of practice, Harvard Graduate School of Education,
and former assistant secretary, U.S. Department of Education and Superintendent, Boston and San Diego

"As a former member of Congress, I believe that *Choosing Excellence
in Public Schools* is a must-read. Based on his forty years of practical
experience, data, and common sense, Hornbeck spells out what policymakers need to do to make education work for all children. In addition, as president of Common Cause, I am pleased that this book provides powerful reasons about why delivering a quality education to
every child is the responsibility of all Americans, not just parents and
educators. It is the cornerstone of democracy and it is the right thing
to do! Hornbeck tells us how we can act by sharing his own successful experience in building grassroots advocacy efforts." —**Bob Edgar**,
president of Common Cause, and former general secretary, National
Council of Churches

"David Hornbeck reminds us that an abiding, unshakeable belief
that all kids can learn is an essential prerequisite for a successful
educational strategy. This compelling/must-read work details an
experience-based roadmap on how to convert this aspiration into a
reality. This book is about the power of advocacy, the setting and
meeting of high standards, and overcoming the obstacles to education reform." —**Raul Yzaguirre**, presidential professor, Arizona State
University, and president/CEO emeritus, National Council of
La Raza

"*Choosing Excellence in Public Schools* is chock full of evidence on
the steps our schools must take to enable all of our children to participate fully in mainstream American society. Whether you're an educator or simply an interested citizen, it's worth reading for that. But
Hornbeck and Conner's most important contribution may not be in
their recipe to broaden academic success, but, rather, in their analysis
of why—even after more than two decades of 'reform'—we still aren't

there. Fundamentally, their book is about will and the importance of mustering it before it is too late for future generations of young Americans to enjoy the comforts and freedoms their parents took for granted." —**Kati Haycock**, president, Education Trust

"Hornbeck provides a comprehensive framework for urban school reform that is steeped in research, experience, and a set of shared values undergirded by the belief that all children have the wherewithal to achieve high standards given the appropriate supports. This book should be a touchstone for policymakers and practitioners who want to move beyond failure brought by dichotomous choices and silver bullets." —**Warren Simmons**, executive director, Annenberg Institute for School Reform, Brown University

"David Hornbeck draws on extensive research, deeply held values, and forty years of rich experience to demonstrate that we have the knowledge we need to fulfill our dreams of an education system that would equip all our children to become productive and successful adults. In this fascinating tale, Hornbeck is unflinching in identifying both his own missteps as superintendent of the Philadelphia schools, and what it would take to create the conditions in which every American child could receive a quality education." —**Lisbeth B. Schorr**, senior fellow, Center for the Study of Social Policy, and author, *Within Our Reach* and *Common Purpose*

"David Hornbeck speaks 'truth to power' in this hard-hitting urban school reform manifesto shaped through his experience as Philadelphia's outspoken superintendent of schools. He provides an unflinching portrait of the realities and challenges we face if we, as a nation, are to make good on the promise of an education system that is equitable and excellent for all.

Who better than David Hornbeck—leading national reform architect, former Philadelphia superintendent, and Maryland chief state school officer, activist, lawyer, and minister—to deliver an unflinching portrait of the realities and challenges of contemporary, urban school reform? His insights and guidance constitute a handbook for policymakers and school leaders committed to the continuing quest for equity and excellence." —**Paul Reville**, secretary of education, Commonwealth of Massachusetts

"David Hornbeck has earned national respect because he has transformed his lofty ideals into positive results through his work in

Maryland, Kentucky, and Philadelphia, sharing these experiences in this powerful book. Predictably, Hornbeck makes his core values very clear, grounding his work in the high expectation that all children can reach excellence in learning, and he holds adults inside educational institutions and in communities directly responsible and accountable.

Noble ideals are not enough; we must be thoughtful, strategic, and comprehensive, and this is where the book provides unique insight. In a refreshingly open and frank accounting, Hornbeck wrestles with the complex and difficult world of transforming dreams into reality. In true Hornbeck fashion, he leaves this reader with unanswered and troubling questions, bringing me to a point of greater reflection about our efforts to improve public education for all our children, and causing me to appreciate the complexity of this work we are pursuing and what lies ahead." —**Gene Wilhoit**, president, Council of Chief State School Officers, and former chief state school officer in Arkansas and Kentucky

"This book is a must-read for anyone who cares about the education of poor children and knows that the children are not getting the opportunities they deserve and the country is not getting the results it needs. *Choosing Excellence in Public Schools* offers its wisdom nested deeply in the very practical and nitty-gritty experience of reality at the local, state, and national levels." —**Mike Cohen**, president, Achieve

"David Hornbeck brings into clear focus the need to promote equity and excellence for all children, and he challenges educators, community leaders, and policymakers to make the hard decisions—the right decisions—on behalf of our nation's youth. His challenge, succinctly stated, is: We know what to do—now let's get it done!" —**Gerald N. Tirozzi**, executive director, National Association of Secondary School Principals

"David Hornbeck has done it again; he strips us of any comfort in the status quo and challenges us to expect more of our children and ourselves. His piercing analysis and clear moral grounding is informed by a lifetime of innovation, advocacy, and results in public education. Anybody who believes in children and the power of schools should keep this important work close at hand." —**Michael Casserly**, executive director, Council of the Great City Schools

"David Hornbeck has proven that all children can learn and has led a movement to change the schools of America so that they can actualize their potential. In this book, he explains what needs to be done and how to do it. Now, more than ever, we have to take seriously what he has to say." —**Tony Campolo**, professor of sociology, Eastern University, and preacher and founder, Evangelical Association for the Promotion of Education

"Hornbeck's candid reflection on his career as a reformer shows how political will and values shape the character of public education, for better or worse. Grounded in the complexities of the real world, *Choosing Excellence in Public Schools* gives close attention to the wider context of public education. Hornbeck details why providing excellent public education for all our children requires active support from all of us—not only educators and stakeholders, but community members, political, business, faith, and civic leaders, philanthropists, elected officials, and the media. Hornbeck demonstrates that we have the schools we have chosen and the knowledge to do better. This book points the way toward better choices for all children." —**Milbrey McLaughlin**, David Jacks Professor of Education and Public Policy, Stanford University

# Choosing Excellence in Public Schools

*New Frontiers in Education*
A Rowman & Littlefield Education Series
Edited by Dr. Frederick M. Hess

This Rowman & Littlefield Education series provides educational leaders, entrepreneurs, and researchers the opportunity to offer insights that stretch the boundaries of thinking on education.

Educational entrepreneurs and leaders have too rarely shared their experiences and insights. Research has too often been characterized by impenetrable jargon. This series aims to foster volumes that can inform, educate, and inspire aspiring reformers and allow them to learn from the trials of some of today's most dynamic doers; provide researchers with a platform for explaining their work in language that allows policy-makers and practitioners to take full advantage of its insights; and establish a launch pad for fresh ideas and hard-won experience.

Whether an author is a prominent leader in education, a researcher, or an entrepreneur, the key criterion for inclusion in *New Frontiers in Education* is a willingness to challenge conventional wisdom and pat answers.

The series editor, Frederick M. Hess, is the director of education policy studies at the American Enterprise Institute and can be reached at rhess@aei.org, or (202) 828-6030.

# Choosing Excellence in Public Schools

## Where There's a Will, There's a Way

David W. Hornbeck
with Katherine Conner

ROWMAN & LITTLEFIELD EDUCATION
*Lanham • New York • Toronto • Plymouth, UK*

Published in the United States of America
by Rowman & Littlefield Education
A Division of Rowman & Littlefield Publishers, Inc.
A wholly owned subsidary of The Rowman & Littlefield Publishing Group, Inc.
4501 Forbes Boulevard, Suite 200, Lanham, Maryland 20706
www.rowmaneducation.com

Estover Road
Plymouth PL6 7PY
United Kingdom

British Library Cataloguing in Publication Information Available

**Library of Congress Cataloging-in-Publication Data**

Hornbeck, David W., 1941–
  Choosing excellence in public schools : where there's a will, there's a way /
David W. Hornbeck with Katherine Conner.
      p. cm. — (New frontiers in education)
  ISBN 978-1-60709-154-7 (cloth : alk. paper) — ISBN 978-1-60709-155-4
(pbk. : alk. paper) — ISBN 978-1-60709-156-1 (electronic)
  1. Educational equalization—United States. 2. Children with social
disabilities—Education—United States. 3. Public schools—Standards—
United States. I. Conner, Katherine, 1947– II. Title.
  LC213.2.H65 2009
  379.2'6—dc22                                                            2009001995

♾™ The paper used in this publication meets the minimum requirements of
American National Standard for Information Sciences—Permanence of Paper
for Printed Library Materials, ANSI/NISO Z39.48-1992.
Manufactured in the United States of America.

With love to Holly, Tom, Jensen, Fyn, Katherine, Thomas, Natalie,
and any grandchildren-to-be

We covet for you and every child the opportunities of
an excellent education.
When our will equals our knowledge, it will happen.

# Contents

# Foreword

*Richard W. Riley*

*Choosing Excellence in Public Schools* describes a practical path—built on research, good sense, and the experience of one of our nation's education leaders—to fulfilling a vision of an American education system to which many of us have devoted the better part of a lifetime. Imagine an America where every young child sees himself or herself a college graduate. And imagine an America where every child actually graduates from high school with the knowledge and skills to complete college or to be employed in work that results in financial security and personal satisfaction. Imagine an American economy fueled by well-paid women and men in the workforce who have the capacity to compete with fellow workers worldwide. Imagine elections in which 90 percent and more of those eligible to vote *do* vote. Imagine your own community with citizen activism vigilant in its insistence that *all* children—including those of every race, income level, gender, ethnic origin, and first language—can, with hard work, achieve at the level we covet for our own children and grandchildren.

This is a volume based on our values as a nation, laced with experience-based recommendations that can translate our aspirations into reality for all children. It is rooted in lofty ideals transformed into reasonable objectives through doable classroom, community, and system proposals. It is a volume for policy-makers and practitioners; for academics, teachers, principals, and activists. The volume challenges not only educators, but also communities and elected officials, to make choices different than those that have failed huge numbers of children.

Over the past several decades, an unprecedented reform effort has been underway in American education. David Hornbeck and I have been privileged to be part of that effort, with our paths frequently crossing and complementing one another. We are of the same generation; both of us grew up in the South, regrettably went to segregated schools through college, enjoyed the study of law, and decided on careers of public service. Through these experiences, we grew to understand the injustice and waste in policies that hold back many children from achieving high learning standards. We both have devoted our professional lives to trying to make a difference in the lives of children, especially those with whom historically we have failed.

Our efforts in education have substantial parallels. As governor of South Carolina, my passion was early childhood education, comprehensive education reform, and improving funding and other supports for education. David brought those same passions and priorities first to his work as the chief state school officer for twelve years in Maryland, his work in support of education reform with a private law firm, and the Business Roundtable and his pathbreaking design work in shaping the Kentucky system of education in 1990.

Our paths crossed more and more in the 1990s as we contributed in our respective roles to the development of an emerging focus on high academic standards, sound assessment, and fair accountability for educators, students, and fellow citizens. Our work included repeated efforts to develop supports for students and teachers that would result in the achievement of high and challenging standards.

One important example was the reauthorization of Chapter I of the Elementary and Secondary Education Act in 1994. As President Clinton's education secretary, I led the Department of Education's work in shaping that piece of legislation. Outside the government, David chaired an unusual national commission on Chapter I, established under the auspices of the Council of Chief State School Officers, which contributed to the shape of the Administration's proposal. The commission's work was "founded on the conviction . . . that virtually all children can learn at high levels. . . . The challenge . . . was to convert Chapter I from a law designed to teach poor children 'basic skills' to one dedicated to spurring the kinds of educational change that would result in children born into poverty acquiring high-level knowledge and skills." The 1994 Chapter I reauthorization (renamed Title I) made major progress toward that conversion and included many components parallel to the commission's recommendations.

In the early 1990s, David decided to find an urban school district that wanted to make a serious effort to do what no other had ever done—to succeed with virtually *all* of its children. That led to his becoming superintendent of the Philadelphia School District in 1994.

David, coauthor Katherine Conner, and a remarkable array of other talented and dedicated educators embarked on six often-tumultuous years seeking to implement *Children Achieving*, a comprehensive, systemic change strategy. As secretary of education during that time, my work and David's coincided and our efforts were often complementary. Philadelphia pursued imaginative ways to take advantage of the agenda embraced by the Clinton administration, including high standards, expansion of early childhood opportunities that included every child in full-day kindergarten, a very large expansion in after-school programs, lower class size in the early grades, and a serious accountability system.

David and his team left no stone unturned. They met with significant success: a 42 percent increase in achievement in science, reading and mathematics from elementary through high school and a 13 percent rise in on-time high school graduation. However, while they had identified and moved forward with the right set of education strategies, they believe they failed in meeting the full challenge of *Children Achieving* reflected in their mantra, "Now is the time; Philadelphia is the place." This refers to the goal to create learning conditions in which the city would become the first to succeed with virtually all children learning to high levels.

Learning from this rich tapestry of hands-on experience in national and state policy formulation and, even more important, taking on the task at the local level of actually trying to accomplish high-quality education for all children in one of America's large and difficult cities, David and Katherine have put all the pieces together coherently in this volume. They start from the premise of high expectations and affirm the central role of high standards, sound and multiple assessment strategies, and a fair and reasonable accountability system for educators, students, and citizens.

The volume makes clear that quality teachers and school leaders are crucial. It makes practical, though controversial, suggestions about changing the nature of the education, certification, recruitment, continuing development, compensation, and assignment and removal of educators, including the collective bargaining context. It also underlines one of the areas we pioneered in South Carolina—early childhood education—by recommending universal, high-quality early childhood education opportunities for all three- and four-year-old children. This is a prime example that we know *what* to do; we just have not yet chosen to do it anywhere in the nation.

From the same evidence, common sense and experience-based perspective, *Choosing Excellence in Public Schools* addresses the importance of more and different uses of time for students and teachers, effective instructional and school organizational models, health and social service supports, measures to keep students and staff safe, adequate facilities and materials, and the pivotal role technology will play if we are to create the learning conditions in which all students learn to high levels.

Only toward the end does the book address the issue of adequate and equitably distributed funding. The placement of this important chapter on Resources is not accidental. There is much evidence that money is necessary, but not solely sufficient, in bringing all students to high levels of achievement.

*Choosing Excellence in Public Schools* makes a point often missing in commentary on the components of education reform. *There is no silver bullet.* It's not "just" early childhood or "just" good teachers or standards or charters or small schools or any other pet priority. The final policy point is that the change must be comprehensive, simultaneous, systemic and sustained to create enough synergistic power to change the learning conditions for *all* children to succeed.

The last section of this volume moves into the area of the responsibilities of the community and elected leaders, which the book calls "citizen accountability." That our education systems are a product of the choices we make, not preordination, is illustrated through an interesting chapter that compares and contrasts choices made by newspapers, mayors, the business and civic communities, courts, and teacher unions in Philadelphia with very different choices made by those same institutions in other states and cities throughout the country. Whether the authors have correctly interpreted every choice they hold up to illumination is not the point; the point is that the choices we make determine the outcomes and that responsibility for those choices belongs to those of us who make them.

If the knowledge exists to educate all children successfully and we do not do so, that is the result of the choices we make. The good news is that we can make different choices. But those different choices are unlikely to come from inside the system alone. The next-to-last chapter of the book begins with the observation that "many of those in power got there by learning to accommodate the status quo. Even policy-makers of good will are unlikely to change the status quo radically enough from inside; it is too risky and too difficult. Change also requires outside demand."

This could have been the end of the volume, already valuable having laid out the necessary components of a successful system and how they interact with one another. But what of the volume's title, *Choos-*

*ing Excellence in Public Schools*? David stepped down in Philadelphia convinced that the missing ingredient for success with all students is not an educational or technical fix to the education system(s). The missing component is the public will to ensure that political, policy, education, and civic leaders make choices that will result in success by all children.

Therefore, following his superintendency, David founded Good Schools Pennsylvania, a well-funded, professionally staffed, grassroots organization built originally on a faith community base. It played an important role in making education the number one issue in the 2002 gubernatorial campaign. The authors suggest that this organization's activity helped create the climate that resulted in the election of Ed Rendell as governor because his education agenda was the best one. It has continued its citizen activist work, contributing to important changes in Pennsylvania.

Building on that success, David has designed a national model for citizen activism to create the missing public will. Whether that particular model achieves traction is beside the point. The knowledge exists to serve all children successfully. Whether we do rests on whether the wider citizenry insists on it. If we do, in an organized way, elected and appointed policy leaders will get the message and make the choices that pave the way for *all* children to succeed.

*Choosing Excellence in Public Schools* will inspire many readers. Some will declare its proposals unrealistic. Still others will conclude—as do the book's authors and I—that it is unrealistic to believe that we can succeed with all children, even those with whom we have repeatedly failed, *without* the massive changes recommended.

The book concludes: "We know what to do and how to do it. The choices are ours. The consequences of the choices are the legacy we leave to our grandchildren." One of my life's greatest blessings is to have thirteen grandchildren. I join David and Katherine in affirming there is no more important goal for our country than for *all* children and grandchildren to have available a quality public education that equips them for academic and career opportunities, civic success and personal satisfaction.

# Acknowledgments

## DAVID HORNBECK

Work on this book began shortly after I resigned as Philadelphia's superintendent in late 2000. It has taken the better part of a decade to complete due to events and activities that shaped its content in significant ways. Shortly after leaving the Philadelphia superintendency, I founded, and for three years chaired the board of, Good Schools Pennsylvania, a grassroots public education advocacy organization. The effectiveness of that effort (including a significant contribution to changing the Pennsylvania formula for financing education in summer 2008) led to full-time design work on Prepare The Future, a national grassroots public education advocacy organization. This advocacy work delayed completion of the book, but resulted in substantive and evolving contributions as it became clearer that the political expression of America's values and belief systems determine the quality of public education much more than our knowledge about education practices.

I owe much to many. The words and actions of my parents, Johnnie Mae and Holly Hornbeck, shaped my values and worldview as I grew to adulthood. A very special director of Christian Education at the First Presbyterian Church in Longview, Texas, "Zookie" Dyson, provided early leadership opportunities in the work of our church.

Two men were moral beacons as I moved away from home to graduate school and first jobs. One was Bill Webber, my thesis advisor in seminary and, more importantly, the founder of the East Harlem Protestant Parish where my wife Becky and I worked for two years. Almost a half-century later, that worshipping/activist community remains the highlight of our faith experiences. The other was Father Paul Washington, the rector of the Church of the Advocate in Philadelphia and chair of the grassroots organization that I led in the mid-1960s. Paul was one of the only people in Philadelphia who had the quality of character to lead forces of justice forcefully in both the black and white communities. He had great integrity, selflessness, and passion for fairness.

A host of people helped me grow professionally. I offer special thanks to five. The first is John Pittenger, the Pennsylvania secretary of education, who asked Pennsylvania's governor to appoint me executive deputy secretary when I was twenty-nine. Pitt gave me amazing opportunities to develop management and leadership skills while "watching my back." The second is Dick Schifter, a devoted family man, lawyer, and senior foreign policy advisor in both the Reagan and Clinton administrations. Dick, as president of the Maryland State Board of Education, convinced his colleagues to appoint me as Maryland's state superintendent, and then to wait a year for me to assume those duties, while I stayed at home as the principal caregiver for my five- and seven-year-old sons, who were growing up with an absentee father as I was consumed by work.

The third is David Karem, president of Louisville's Waterfront Development Corporation, who, as majority leader of the Kentucky legislature and chair of the curriculum committee, gave me the extraordinary opportunity to shape the design of the new Kentucky education system in 1989–1990. He then played a pivotal role in leading the legislature to enact the proposal, providing a template for standards-based reform throughout the nation.

The fourth and fifth people are Ed Rendell and Ruth Hayre. Ed was the mayor of Philadelphia, whose support was key to my selection and whose maintenance of a 5–4 majority on the school board gave me six years to create the conditions in which achievement and graduation rates improved significantly.

Ruth was the pivotal fifth vote on the board that resulted in the private 5–4 vote for my selection (in public, the vote was 9–0). Ruth, the first African American high school principal and the first African American female board president in Philadelphia, had spent a lifetime of courageous actions. She was the only African American among my initial five supporters and cast that vote in the face of strong pressure to do otherwise. She believed my commitment to accountability was critical to success in Philadelphia. Ironically, within a year the racial alignment of the board had reversed itself, with all the African Americans supporting the agenda and all but one of the white board members in opposition on the most controversial issues.

Space does not permit naming all of those in Philadelphia who helped create the conditions in which student achievement and graduation rates improved significantly. But they include: Clay Armbrister, now managing director of the City of Philadelphia, who served as managing director of the school district with unwavering integrity and commitment; the extraordinary Jeanette Brewer, who served the city's children for over thirty years, retired, and then agreed to come back because she believed in *Children Achieving* and knew that as an outsider, I needed the imprimatur of a lifelong respected district leader; Katherine Conner, my "thought" twin, who has spent a lifetime relentlessly seeking fairness for those children we most often fail, and who has continued to be immensely important in my life as friend and helped me complete this book in only nine years, rather than twenty; Terry Dellmuth, my closest friend for forty-five years, confidant, advisor, and superb problem-solver, who delayed a long-planned retirement to serve as my first chief of staff; Germaine Ingram, my chief counsel, then chief of staff (really deputy superintendent but she didn't have the required superintendent's certificate), public interest lawyer, law professor, professional cake baker, professional tap dancer, and friend, whose commitment to justice and ability to work eighteen hours a day is unparalleled; Vicki Phillips, friend and colleague since we collaborated on educational reform in Kentucky, who agreed to come to Philadelphia to head up the Annenberg Challenge, who understands the features of systemic, comprehensive standards-based education reform better than anyone else I know, and whose advice I sought on anything we did of importance; and Bob Schwartz, education program officer at Pew Charitable Trusts, now academic dean at Harvard School of Education, who encouraged me to apply to be superintendent, helped us receive more than $16 million in grants and, as one of the key architects of standards-based education reform in the United States, was an important source of substantive advice on the content of all we were attempting to do.

There were many, many more—cluster leaders, members of my cabinet, principals, teachers, community leaders, parent leaders, clergy, student leaders from organizations like the Philadelphia Student Union and Youth United for Change—all working tirelessly to make a difference. And make a difference in the lives of Philadelphia's children they did.

There were a number of foundations that were particularly helpful as they invested in *Children Achieving*. These include the Annenberg

Foundation (the late ambassador and Mrs. Annenberg, and Gail Levin); the Ford Foundation (Janet Petrovich); the Annie E. Casey Foundation (Oz Nelson, Doug Nelson, and Ralph Smith); the Pew Charitable Trusts (Rebecca Rimel and Robert Schwartz); the William Penn Foundation (Janet Haas); and the Samuel Fels Fund (Helen Cunningham).

I also thank the foundations that provided financial support for this book. They include: The Eli and Edythe Broad Foundation, Ford Foundation, the Pew Charitable Trusts, and William Penn Foundation. I am particularly grateful to them as they continued to believe that I would produce what I had promised even after the grants had run out.

Finally, I thank my family for their love and encouragement. My wife Becky has been my life's soul mate, partner, source of unwavering support, and my very best critic. Matthew and Mark, our sons, in whom we take so much pride, are products of the Baltimore City school system and now both remarkable principals in that same district. They brought two wonderful daughters-in-law to our family: Ginny, a Baltimore City school psychologist, and Pailin, a member of Baltimore's Park School administration. The four are outstanding parents of fantastic grandchildren—Holly, Tom, Jensen, and Fyn, who are smart, funny, talented, loving, and already, at ages twelve to four, practicing citizens as advocates for justice at demonstrations.

## KATHERINE CONNER

Having begun my career as an elementary teacher in West Philadelphia, urban educational reform became my life's work, and, difficult as it was, I found it enormously rewarding due to the intense sense of mission it engendered and the quality and commitment of the colleagues and friends with whom I worked. I count among them those from the Philadelphia School District that David mentioned above, as well as Hank Kopple, Perry Robinson, and Earline Sloan, colleagues who served as my mentors before David's arrival, as well as the others with whom I worked most closely across the years. They know who they are. And I feel very blessed as having had the privilege of working with David in furthering my long-held values and goals.

Finally, I, too, want to acknowledge the family upon whose love and support I have depended. My parents, Bill and Louise Conner, were elected officials in Delaware who supported such policies as fair housing, the ERA, and the dispersion of public housing beyond Wilmington and into the surrounding county. They instilled in me a passion for fairness, and a sense that our lives were privileged, and thus we had an obligation to give to our community. My husband Marc gave generously of his support and expertise as David and I worked on the book. Furthermore, through all the years, when I was most discouraged he told me that I was his hero for being able to keep faith with our challenging mission; and, when he felt I needed to better pace myself for my own sake and that of our family, he reminded me that this work was not a sprint but a marathon. Our children, Kimberly, Aaron, Kristin, and Ethan, gave us great joy as they grew up, and continue to do so as adults; and our grandchildren (present and future) light up our lives.

# Introduction

## WHERE THERE'S A WILL:
## CORE PREMISES BUILT ON OUR VALUES

School reform has been a front-burner issue in this country for nearly fifty years. Nonetheless, there is no city or state in this nation of any size and diversity in which a large majority of the children have been educated to the level of achievement necessary to succeed in a four-year college, in a job that ensures financial security and personal satisfaction, and as a citizen interested in and able to strengthen the democracy through ongoing participation. This fact is the Achilles' heel of our democracy, our economic power, our capacity to be constructive family and community members, and our yearning to be a moral nation.

This is a book of school reform, but it is more fundamentally a book about values. It has four core premises:

- All children can and must learn to high levels of expectation.
- All education systems—at every level—can and must deliver the learning conditions essential to enable all children to meet rigorous academic, work, and citizenship goals.
- When we leave children behind it is the result of choices made by leaders with either the support or tolerance of the citizens.
- Public will is required to ensure that appointed and elected policymakers provide the necessary policy frameworks for all children to succeed, including adequate and equitable resources, the use of effective instruction, and appropriate accountability systems based on student performance.

The challenges of public education are not technical ones. Determining which standards are appropriate, what accountability system is fairest, what teacher certification credentials are the right ones, and what decisions should be made by whom at what level of the system are relatively easy. The pivotal questions relate to our values, as reflected in the core premises stated above.

Because virtually all students can learn to high standards, *what* students learn in our schools should be the same in that all should meet at least the same high content and performance standards that will equip them to be productive and successful adults. *Where* students learn, *when* they learn, *how* they learn, *who* teaches them, and *how much* support they need should all be variables altered as necessary to achieve the same end goals for all students. Adults, both inside the school and in the broader community, control those variables.

We must get our values straight, and live up to our professed beliefs that all students can learn what they must to be successful in school, work, and the community since the knowledge to teach them successfully already exists. When governments and school boards make policy and resource decisions, when superintendents recommend budget allocations, when principals assign children to classrooms, and when teachers design lesson plans, the same question must be asked: how will this action, this recommendation, this decision help ensure that all children learn to high standards? Every child will learn when, and only when, adults in decision-making positions believe that the children can and make decisions accordingly. We all bear that responsibility. The key question is whether we have the individual and collective values and will to make the choices to do so.

*Choosing Excellence in Public Schools* is, in part, autobiographical. While it is research-based in important ways, it unabashedly reflects values learned from my parents, a strong faith base, and more than forty years of experience in and outside of the education system as a professional.

I attended a segregated elementary school in Texas when *Brown v. Board of Education* was handed down and was in high school when math and science education became the rage as a result of Sputnik. My father, at the time a Republican Barry Goldwater supporter, was responsible for integrating the lunchroom and the changing room of a large division of Eastman Kodak. For months, he was the only white man to eat in the cafeteria. I attended an all-white Presbyterian college (there was one fellow student from the Presbyterian mission in what was then the Belgian Congo).

I always intended to become a pastor in the southern Presbyterian Church—until I went to seminary. In seminary, my wife and I worked in a remarkable parish in East Harlem for two years. I was part of a 24/7 prayer vigil for months supporting passage of the 1964 Civil Rights Act. My first organizing experience in 1966 was leading a boycott of First National City Bank that ultimately resulted in the withdrawal of $40 million because of the bank's investment in South Africa.

Since seminary, I have spent forty-two years working and advocating for children and public education. I have served at the local level (as a Philadelphia community organizer and, nearly thirty years later, as superintendent of schools in Philadelphia), at the state level (twelve years as Maryland's state superintendent of schools, and as founder/organizer of Good Schools Pennsylvania, a Pennsylvania advocacy group), and at the national level (board chair of the Council of Chief State School Officers, Children's Defense Fund, Public Education Network, Carnegie Foundation for the Advancement of Teaching, and the National Title I Commission), and have had many other opportunities to serve.

Over those years, experience led me to a deeper understanding of my values and informed the development of my policy convictions about education. A particularly rich opportunity emerged in 1989–1990 to combine my values and the fruit of my experience in Kentucky when I was chosen to serve as one of the architects of the omnibus Kentucky Education Reform Act. With the same lens, I then worked in twenty states with the governors and CEOs in each state through my work with the Business Roundtable and with another dozen big cities and states as codirector of the National Alliance for Restructuring Education.

I was convinced that there is a parsimonious set of ten components that, if faithfully implemented, would result in all children learning to high standards. I began to look for the opportunity to serve as a superintendent in a big city that wanted to implement this aggressive and comprehensive agenda. Baltimore, Cleveland, and Pittsburgh said thanks but no thanks. Philadelphia at least seemed to say yes to the ten-part agenda.

In Philadelphia, these components were used as the framework for an action plan we called *Children Achieving*. They were:

- High Expectations: Set high standards for everyone.
- Performance Driven: Design accurate performance indicators to hold everyone accountable.

- Local Decision-Making: Shrink the centralized bureaucracy and let the school make more decisions.
- Professional Development: Provide intensive and sustained professional development to all staff.
- School Readiness: Make sure that all students are ready for school.
- Community Services and Supports: Provide students with the community supports and services they need to succeed in school.
- Technology and Instructional Materials: Provide up-to-date technology and instructional materials.
- Public Engagement: Engage the public in shaping, understanding, supporting, and participating in school reform.
- Resources: Ensure adequate resources and use them effectively.
- Comprehensive and Integrated Delivery: Be prepared to address all of these priorities together and for the long term.

This book is not just about Philadelphia. However, my six years as superintendent were pivotal in bringing together the previous thirty years of my professional life and setting the course for the days following.

It was in Philly that I reached a powerful new conclusion. All the effort over the past fifty years of school reform has been important. However, education issues are not the barriers we face in delivering a quality public education. We know what to do. The barriers are ones of values and public will. So far we have not had the courage to do those things that, if done faithfully, would result in all our children—even those who may differ in race/ethnicity, income, native language, and/or disability—succeeding in the way each of us covets for our own children and grandchildren, and those of our friends.

## NOTE

*The interested reader will find further autobiographical reflection in the context of the history of education reform over the past half century at www.childrenachieving.com.

# 1

# The Power of Expectations

Treat a man as he is, he will remain so. Treat a man the way he can be and ought to be, and he will become as he can be and should be.

Goethe

Low teacher expectations set in motion a vicious, self-perpetuating cycle of teacher and student behaviors. The cycle is triggered when low teacher expectations result in inappropriate behaviors on the part of the teacher which ultimately result in the . . . students learning less.

Earline Sloan

The concept of expectations provides a powerful explanation for the poor achievement of many groups of students. Low expectations begin as beliefs, both conscious and unconscious. These beliefs are not communicated by some mystical vapor wafting through the air. They translate directly into behaviors, both individual and institutional. They create a self-fulfilling, downward-spiraling dynamic for student performance. Low expectations influence the policies of schools, districts, and the society, and settle like a blanket on children in classrooms (Sloan, 1977).

There are many individual schools demonstrating that disadvantaged children can learn at high levels. Given how many examples exist, it is remarkable how rarely they are recognized.[1] Below are examples of schools and programs where poor and minority students not only met but also exceeded the expectations we hold for white suburban students.

## EXCEEDING EXPECTATIONS

### Elementary Schools

Two elementary schools in Philadelphia are among the many that began a trajectory of outstanding achievement growth in 1996 under *Children Achieving* and have continued it for a decade. These schools demonstrate that, in the context of the right policies and instruction, poor and minority students can exceed high standards.

Kearny Elementary School is a high-poverty neighborhood school with an enrollment of about four hundred students in grades K–5. Almost all are African American. 80 percent are from low-income families. During the years 1996–2000, Kearny's growth in average scale score on the Pennsylvania System of School Assessment (PSSA) (grade 5) was as shown in table 1.1.

Since 2000, Kearny's PSSA scores have continued to increase. As of 2004, the average fifth-grade math score was 1340. The reading average was 1450. In 2005, 79 percent of the students scored at least at the proficient level in math, and 66 percent in reading. That same year, the state proportion of students scoring at least proficient was only 45 percent in math and 35 percent in reading.

The Welsh School in Philadelphia also reached remarkable levels of achievement in this time period. It has a neighborhood student enrollment of about seven hundred students. About two-thirds are Latino, and the rest black. Eighty-six percent of the students are low-income. Its PSSA scores have increased as shown in table 1.2.

Since 2000, the Welsh PSSA scores have continued to grow at grade 5. The scores in 2004 were 1570 in math and 1450 in reading. The proportion of grade 5 students proficient or better as of 2005 was 93 percent in math and 66 percent in reading, compared with the state figures of 45 percent and 35 percent.

### High School

Hard as it is to achieve remarkable academic growth at the elementary level, achieving such growth for poor and minority students, English-

**Table 1.1.    Kearny School PSSA Average Scale Score Growth**

|             | 1996 | 1997 | 1998 | 1999 | 2000 | Change |
|-------------|------|------|------|------|------|--------|
| Reading     | 1000 | 1070 | 1070 | 1100 | 1130 | 130    |
| Mathematics | 1020 | 1110 | 1170 | 1180 | 1210 | 190    |

Source: Pennsylvania Department of Education, Pennsylvania System of School Assessment, 1966–2000

Table 1.2.  Welsh School PSSA Average Scale Score Growth

|  | 1996 | 1997 | 1998 | 1999 | 2000 | Change |
|---|---|---|---|---|---|---|
| Reading | 1020 | 1120 | 1080 | 1090 | 1120 | 100 |
| Mathematics | 1070 | 1150 | 1160 | 1140 | 1190 | 120 |

Source: Pennsylvania Department of Education, Pennsylvania System of School Assessment, 1966–2000

language learners, and students with disabilities has been even more challenging at the high school level, where cumulative academic deficits and other pressures present greater obstacles. Nevertheless, there are enough examples of dramatic success to let us know that high performance by these students is possible. The best-known example is that of the classes taught by Jaime Escalante, later fictionalized in the movie *Stand and Deliver* (Menendez & Musca, 1988).

Escalante immigrated to the United States as a child and learned English as a second language. He eventually became a math teacher in a high-poverty public school, and created a calculus program that transformed increasing numbers of average students into high achievers who passed the AP calculus test. In 1982, eighteen students passed. This result was so unprecedented for a school of that socioeconomic profile that cheating was suspected. Most of the students were asked to retake the test; they did so and repeated their achievement. The program grew very rapidly. In 1983, thirty-two students took the test and thirty passed. By 1987, seventy-three passed the AB Calculus test, and twelve more passed the even more challenging BC Calculus test (usually given only after Calculus II). The significance of the growing numbers is that the students were not all taught by Escalante.

As Edmonds has written (1979a, p. 32), "How many effective schools would you have to see to be persuaded of the educability of poor children? If the answer is more than one then I submit that you have reasons of your own for preferring to believe that basic pupil performance derives from family background instead of school response to family background." If we can create schools and programs such as these for some poor and minority children, this must greatly raise our expectations for the achievement of the rest. We are left, then, with the responsibility of providing the learning conditions that make this possible.

## EXPERIMENTAL INVESTIGATIONS OF EXPECTATIONS

### Teacher Expectations

Perhaps the best-known study on the impact of teacher expectations is "Pygmalion in the Classroom," conducted in a high-poverty elementary school (Rosenthal & Jacobsen, 1968). After giving an IQ test to all of the children (eighteen classrooms), they randomly selected 20 percent of the students and told the teachers that the test had indicated that these students would experience an intellectual growth spurt during that school year. The students were retested eight months later, at the end of the school year. These so-called bloomers outscored the gains of their classmates by four points overall, and by seven points in reasoning.

Studies like this, in which intelligence test scores are raised by changing the expectations of the teachers, clearly support the importance of environmental factors in the development of performance. An experiment that demonstrates a similar effect in the animal world is described below by Rosenthal (1973, p. 60).

> Fode and I told a class of 12 students that one could produce a strain of intelligent rats by inbreeding them to increase their ability to run mazes quickly. To demonstrate, we gave each student five rats, which had to learn to run to the darker of two arms of a T-maze. We told half of our students that they had the "maze-bright," intelligent rats; we told the rest that they had the stupid rats. Naturally there was no real difference among any of the animals.
>
> But they were certainly different in their performance. The rats believed to be bright improved daily in running the maze—they ran faster and more accurately—while the supposedly dull animals did poorly. The "dumb" rats refused to budge from the starting point 29% of the time, while the "smart" rats were recalcitrant only 11% of the time.

Another clear example of an induced expectancy effect in an experimental setting involved tutors of Head Start children (Beez, 1968). Sixty children were randomly assigned to sixty tutors. Half the tutors were told that they were working with a high-ability child, and the other half that they were assigned a low-ability child. Tutors were told to teach the child as many of twenty word-cards as possible. Children randomly labeled "high ability" learned twice as many words on average as those labeled "low ability." Seventy-seven percent of the "high ability" children learned five or more words, while only 13 percent of the "dull" students did so.

Observations of the tutoring sessions revealed two main differences in tutor behavior. First, the tutors with high expectations tried to teach almost twice as many words as those with low expectations. Second, those with low expectations spent much more time doing activities unrelated to the central task.

## Stereotype Threat

The more recent work of the Stanford psychologist Claude Steele investigates these issues from a different angle (Steele, 1999). Steele has long been interested in issues of stereotyping, and how stereotypes become internalized. Recently, he has worked with colleagues to investigate the well-known test score gap between white and African American middle-class students, using his understanding of the effects of stereotypes to design a set of experiments with dramatic results.

Steele argues that members of groups that are the object of negative stereotypes are subject to a "stereotype threat." He defines this as "the threat of being viewed through the lens of a negative stereotype, or the fear of doing something that would inadvertently confirm that stereotype" (p. 46). His data indicate that whether students experience stereotype threat while taking a particular test depends on a number of contextual cues related to the test itself and/or its administration. For example, when black, middle-class, college sophomores were given a portion of the Graduate Records Exam and told that it was a measure of their ability, they scored much lower than a matched group of white students. However, when a comparable group of students were told that the test was a laboratory task designed to explore styles of reasoning, there was no significant difference between the scores of black and white students.

Steele makes another vital point—*the more important academic performance is to African American students, the more stereotype threat diminishes their performance.* For students who have decided they don't care how well they perform, cuing negative stereotypes does not lower their performance. Ironically, it is those students who care the most about their academic achievement who are most vulnerable to stereotype threat. This is a striking finding, because it offers one explanation for the fact that the lower average scores of blacks on standardized tests do not come because the whole range of scores is lower, but primarily because such small proportions of students score in the very high ranges. This is exactly the outcome that should happen if Steele is right that those who might be expected to score the best are the most handicapped by stereotype threat.

## THE BEHAVIORS THAT CONVEY EXPECTATIONS

We turn now to expectation dynamics in classrooms, schools, and school districts, and the challenges and strategies for changing low expectation practices and policies to high ones.

## Expectations in the Classroom

Several years after his original study, Rosenthal (1987) reviewed the many other studies that had demonstrated the "Pygmalion effect" in order to determine specific behaviors that convey high or low expectations.

He found four categories of teacher behavior that differentiated their treatment of children according to their expectations. The *climate* differed: teachers were less likely to make eye contact with, stand near, or smile at children of whom they held low expectations. These children also received less *feedback*: responses from children of whom little was expected were often ignored, and when they did get feedback it tended to be vague and to provide little guidance about how to improve. Differences in *input* meant that they were taught less material than other students, and at less challenging levels. Finally, these students were given far fewer opportunities for responses, or *output*.

While many individual children suffer the effects of low expectations, it is clear that children in certain groups are far more likely to be victims of low expectations than other children. Especially powerful factors contributing to low expectations are class, race or ethnicity, gender, language, and disability.


### *Class*

Many studies demonstrate that teachers have more positive attitudes, and use more productive teaching behaviors, when dealing with middle-class rather than poor children. In one study, teachers were asked to predict future academic success based on case study reports of four fictional fourth graders. The case studies had clues about each child's social class, but all four students had similar IQs, grades, and behavioral records. The teachers rated the students presented as middle class higher on ten out of the twelve rating scales they had been provided. Another study involved observation of twenty-four fifth- and sixth-grade classes. The middle-class students received significantly more positive reinforcements than the lower-class ones (Miller et al., 1969, p. 806).

In New York City, another study involved middle-class black teachers, who worked with black students (Rist, 1970). By the eighth day of kindergarten, children in these teachers' classes had been sorted into three groups based on what the teachers labeled "indicators of ability." Rist observed that the students at Tables 1, 2, and 3 became [progressively more] dissimilar according to a number of criteria. First of all, students' physical appearances were noticeably different. Students with darkest skin, shabbiest clothes, and worst body odor were all at Table 3. Secondly, students at Table 1 seemed most at ease with their interactions with one another and the teacher, especially when initiating contacts with the teacher. . . . [Third] while students at the first table were most verbal and used more standard English, students at the third table were least verbal and used more dialect. (p. 442)

These observable differences correlated with a set of socioeconomic indicators, which were part of the student records. Students at Table 3 were far more likely to be from families on welfare, to have parents who had not completed elementary or high school, to have many siblings, and to live in one-parent homes. The lowest group, seated farthest from the teachers, received the least instruction over the course of the study. At the end of the kindergarten year, there were measurable differences in test scores among the three groups. By the end of grade 3, a few children had dropped down a group; none had moved up; and the gaps in achievement among them had widened greatly.

### Race

Race is another key factor affecting expectations. In one study, black students tended to receive lower grades than white students who had the same academic performance record (Good, 1981). In another, teachers listened to a tape of a student responding to an open-ended question. They were then shown a picture that was supposedly of the child, and "asked to rate the taped responses for personality, quality of the response, current academic abilities, and future potential. . . . There was a highly significant relationship between the race of the student in the picture they were shown and their estimation of the student's response and academic abilities" (Ferguson, 1998). Other studies show that teachers tend to attribute achievement-oriented behavior of white students to factors that can be affected by good instruction, such as effort and motivation, while they attribute the same behavior in black students to parental encouragement or heredity, which teachers regard as beyond their control (Scott-Jones & Clark, 1986).

### Language

Language also affects expectation levels. Bikson (1974) found that even if the speech performance of African American or Hispanic students is equal to or better than that of white students, teachers still perceive them as inferior. Tharp describes the consequences for students:

> At-risk students, particularly those of limited Standard English proficiency, are often forgiven any academic challenges, on the assumption that they are of limited ability; or they are forgiven any genuine assessment of progress, because the assessment tools don't fit. Thus both standards and feedback are weakened, with the predictable result that achievement is handicapped. While such policies may often be the result of benign motives, the effect is to deny many diverse students the basic requirements of progress: high academic standards and meaningful assessment that allows feedback and responsive assistance. (Tharp, 1997)

### Other Factors

In addition to class, race, ethnicity, and language, other factors including religion, appearance, disability, gender, and even temperamental styles all can influence expectations (Baird et al., n.d.). Teachers will tend to prefer students who are adaptable, persistent, and approachable, and tend to reject those who are overly active and distractible (Carruthers, 1994). Furthermore, low expectations can exist even in schools in which children are lovingly nurtured.

An examination of expectations-related behaviors at a Philadelphia school populated by low-income white students and a small percentage of Latino students revealed the pervasive attitude that the students were "sweet, but dumb." Teachers in the school had become unaware of the grade level of the readers the students were using. They were genuinely shocked to find out how far behind grade level their students were. They were equally surprised when a survey of parental aspirations showed that the parents had high goals for their children's future, if little sense of how those goals might be achieved. A caring school with hard-working, dedicated teachers was, thus, unintentionally contributing to the ongoing cycle of low expectations and achievement (Sloan & Schwartz, 1980).

### Multiple Factors

The factors related to teacher expectations do not occur independently of each other. They are often present in combination, as in the case of poor students who are also black, or are English-language learners. The overrepresentation of poor black boys among students labeled "disabled" is a telling example. For children in more than one of these categories, the low expectations they experience can lead to devastating effects.

### Doing "Too Well"

Also chilling are the studies showing the dynamics when children of whom teachers have low expectations actually do *well*. In the early 1980s, Rosenthal (1987) did a further analysis of data from the original Pygmalion study, focusing on the control students—those who had not been labeled as likely to have an intellectual growth spurt. "We looked at the control-group children, who had also gained in IQ, as to whether the teachers liked them as much as the bloomers. To our astonishment, the more the control group students increased in IQ, the *less* well adjusted, interesting, and affectionate the teachers thought them. . . . This was especially true, we discovered, for children in 'Low ability' classes."

A study by Eleanor Leacock (1969) refines this finding by distinguishing between the factors of race and class. Having already reported that teachers were more positive about middle-income than low-income children, and about white children than black children, Leacock then went on to relate the children's IQ scores to the teacher's feeling toward them.

> IQ scores of the middle-income students, both black and white, were clearly related to the positive attitudes of their teachers. This relationship did *not* hold for the low-income children; in fact it was reversed. That is, lower-income children who had *higher* IQs tended to have teachers who viewed them *negatively* and this *was especially true for lower-income children who were black* [author's italics]. The children who surpassed their teachers' expectations got resentment and complaints for their pains.

Later studies have shown that this finding is especially true for black boys.

## EXPECTATIONS AND POLICIES

The connection between expectations and performance is not just an aggregate of the biases, conscious or unconscious, of teachers. They also find their way into school and district policies. The tracking of students by skill or "ability" level, which occurs in most school districts, including at the high school level, is a good example. Proponents of tracking believe that a bell curve of achievement is inevitable, and see no sense in grouping students heterogeneously. They believe that heterogeneous grouping wastes the time and talent of the top students, and does not meet the needs of the students with weaker skills.

There are two key arguments against tracking. First, the evidence is that all but the highest group students do worse in tracked situations than in heterogeneous ones. Robert Slavin (1981, 1983a, 1983b) and others further assert that the highest-achieving students perform equally well in tracked or nontracked settings if the teachers receive and make use of appropriate professional development. Thus, if we want all students to achieve, it follows that tracking is not instructionally sound. The second and equally important reason to oppose tracking is that its negative impact is not random. Those who suffer its ill effects are disproportionately poor, children of color, or students who are nonnative English-speakers or have disabilities.

Jeanne Oakes's research has repeatedly made clear how insidious the practice of tracking is. She writes, "Throughout the grades, race, social class, and track assignments correlated consistently with low-income students and non-Asian minorities disproportionately enrolled in low track academic classes and advantaged students and whites more often enrolled in high tracks" (Oakes, 1992, p. 2). These students in the lower tracks drop out disproportionately; they engage in higher levels of risky behavior. It is not the tracking system alone that leads to these results; other factors are also at play. However, the tracking system greatly exacerbates learning gaps.

A system that sorts human beings on the basis of test scores and grades without attention to the factors that systematically depress the scores of certain groups is immoral, and serves to perpetuate the centuries-old practice of sorting people into first- and second-class status. Against a backdrop of students coming from communities in which there has been generational discrimination in education, housing, jobs, health, safety, and other conditions, affirmative measures are required. Simply being "color blind" won't do the job. *Color blindness is, in effect, affirmative action for whites* because of all the elements of white privilege with which a white person is born. Our efforts to reduce high school tracking in Philadelphia provide a clear illustration of how difficult the issue is.

### Expectations and Tracking: Philadelphia

*Context*

In 1994 in Philadelphia, tracking was widespread at the high school level. In addition to twenty-two comprehensive high schools and four vocational-technical schools, we had a top track of eleven special admission high schools. Some were considered among the best schools in the United States. The student body of these schools was admitted on the basis of test scores and grades; other qualities in a student were not considered. That process disproportionately excluded racial and language minorities, as well as low-income students and those with disabilities.

The argument is not that students who could not do the work should have been admitted. However, the student selection process should develop a range of criteria to identify all those students who could productively take advantage of advanced study, be proactive about being sure that all students are aware of the opportunities to attend these schools, and conduct a lottery to determine which of the qualified students should be admitted. School districts with special admission schools and programs also have the obligation to give special help to students who may not quite measure up but with extra help could get into the pool of eligible students, and then ensure that students who do get in have the necessary supports to succeed once they are there.

Beyond the special admissions high schools described above, thousands more students throughout the city were tracked within the comprehensive high schools. In each "comp" there was at least one program for high achievers. At the bottom of the in-school hierarchy, there were programs targeted for students whose skills were well below grade level.

An interesting feature of Philadelphia's system was the place of vocational-technical high schools in the spectrum of tracked programs. All the vo-tech schools were, informally, ranked above the average program in most comprehensive high schools. Students selected them, not because of a particular interest in their vocational focus, but because they wanted to escape their neighborhood high school.

### Our Attempt to Reduce High-School Tracking

From the beginning of *Children Achieving*, we began to work to broaden opportunities for students to attend the special admission schools and programs and to ensure that other programs in the comprehensive high schools would become more heterogeneous. There was never any intent to fully open admission to the citywide special admission schools; resistance from alumni groups and the public would have been so strong that it would have compromised the rest of our efforts.

We believed that over time, as the rest of the *Children Achieving* agenda was implemented, more and more applicants would be able to meet the standards for competitive admission to these schools. Thus, as part of the settlement of a lawsuit against tracking policies and a civil rights commission directive, the administration committed to gradually eliminating tracking within the comprehensive high schools and for admission to the vocational-technical schools.

There was serious opposition from parents, students, and faculty who enjoyed the perceived advantages of the special treatment embedded in the status quo. There was also push-back from those who had advocated for, worked with, and taken credit for the successes of the programs for high achievers. The public opposition to our efforts made the City Council nervous and, more significantly, led to the only public disagreement Mayor Rendell and I ever had. He decided that the "special admits" and the programs for high achievers in the comprehensive high schools were politically crucial to his attempts to attract and to keep middle-class residents in Philadelphia.

He was wrong. The solution to middle-class flight is not to cling desperately to the handful of youngsters who attend the elite public high schools. The solution, the only solution, is to improve the bulk of the schools in the city, so that wherever someone lives, they can send their child to the local school and feel confident that he or she will be well served. This would never be possible in the balkanized, tracked system that Philadelphia had when I arrived.

A committee was formed to address these issues; it included members of City Council, a state legislator, local advocates, and a small number of school district personnel. In the first meeting, we received a surprise visit from the mayor, who entered the room, stood behind me with his hands on my shoulders, and told the group that I had his total support—and that I would produce a solution to the problem that would help prevent the flight of middle-class families from the city. Clearly, this body language was less a "laying on of hands" than a signal that he would "keep" me in my place. The message was unmistakable: his support was contingent on the solution being *his* solution—keeping tracked programs in place.

The political compromise that was finally reached restored special programs in the comprehensive high schools, and allowed these programs and the vocational-technical schools to set some admissions standards. However, using the lawsuit[2] as leverage, we secured a policy for these standards to set a "floor" of what knowledge and skills were required to qualify for admission, rather than permitting a ranked selection from among all applicants. This policy required that every student who met the minimum requirement be placed in the pool of qualified applicants, who were then granted admission based on a lottery system. The policy also called for a student's interest in the school's specialized program offerings to receive substantial weight in the admission process. As part of this compromise, the special admission schools were required to set goals for admission of students with disabilities and English-language learners, with central office monitoring their progress toward these goals, and intervening as required. This process, as well as the implementation and monitoring of all the district's admission policies and practices, was overseen, both firmly and fairly, by Gwen Morris, within the Office of Equity.

**Reflections**

Tracking is only one example of policies that institutionalize low expectations for some students. For many years, federal Title I regulations actually encouraged low-scoring students in high poverty schools to be taught in pull-out programs with curricular materials and assessments that stressed remediation, and were required to differ from those used in the regular classroom. This well-meaning policy was intended to ensure that needy students were getting services above and beyond the regular to meet their special needs. Instead, it had the perverse result of denying these students exposure to the content being taught to the rest of the students, thus ensuring that they would never achieve as well as their colleagues in the regular classes.

## GETTING TO HIGH EXPECTATIONS

The greatest barriers to success with all students are not technical or educational. They are attitudinal, cultural, historical, and emotional. There are two general approaches to removing these barriers: working directly to change attitudes, and working to change behaviors, in the belief that the results produced by the changed behaviors will eventually change attitudes as well. If we look to the civil rights movement for strategic guidance, we see that the movement clearly sought to do both. Many of its actions were a symbolic call to conscience, making explicit the injustices inherent in segregation and its legacy—eloquent appeals to the hearts and minds of America. But at the same time, the movement sought legal changes, to expand the rights of blacks and set requirements for the behavior of the general population, whatever their attitudes. As Martin Luther King said on numerous occasions, "Laws cannot change the heart, but they can restrain the heartless."

The rest of this chapter explores four strategies for combating low expectations—acknowledging the problem, changing classroom behaviors, changing school practice and policies, and strategically using the leadership of the superintendent and school board.

## Acknowledging the Problem

Like most serious problems, the issue of low expectations is unlikely to be resolved unless we are willing to acknowledge it. Denial prevents us from admitting how widespread and important low expectations are, and from identifying the specific ways in which they are transmitted in the context of our classrooms, districts, and individual behaviors. As the phrase "the soft bigotry of low expectations" implies, low expectations are similar to racism in that they are ingrained in our thinking and behaviors and require conscious awareness and resolution to change. Admitting to them, or labeling them, can create guilt, anger, and controversy. It is important to understand that low expectations are not necessarily intentional. They have been hundreds of years in the making. Their undoing will not happen overnight. However, the good news is that we can begin immediately, through individual resolve and institutional policies, to eliminate the symptoms.

## Changes in Classrooms

High expectations not only reflect a belief system, but also ground specific and effective instructional strategies. The behaviors associated with high expectations are integral components of the very best teaching and the very best pedagogy. These behaviors will produce increased student achievement whether or not the behaviors reflect the teacher's personal beliefs; these gains will then begin to change the attitudes of teachers, students, and the public, resulting in an upward, self-fulfilling spiral of increasing expectations and increasing achievement.

### Content Knowledge

When principals and teachers behave as if all children can learn to high levels, they are clearer about the content and level of performance for which they are responsible, and understand that the content and expected performance levels apply to virtually all students. Teaching different content for different students is wrong if the difference arises from "dumbing down" the content for some students. Different content is acceptable only if the level and complexity of the content is the same, and the difference arises from an assessment of what works best with a given child, or from a clear program of teaching prerequisite skills that lead directly to teaching the more complex ones.

A corollary to clarity about the content and expected level of performance is that teachers must have the necessary knowledge and skill to teach the content. To teach a subject, one must understand it at a significantly higher level of competence than the level at which one is expecting the student to learn.

### Pedagogy

Table 1.3 provides a concise summary of behaviors that convey high expectations and contrasts them with behaviors that do the opposite.

**Table 1.3.    Teacher Behaviors that Convey High or Low Expectations**

| Teacher Behavior | High Expectations | Low Expectations |
| --- | --- | --- |
| Use of time | Start on time; limit outside interruptions; keep students on task; specific, challenging time limits | Start late; end early; allow interruptions; allow students of be off-task; open-ended time limits |
| Goal-stating, summarizing | Frequent, clear, specific, challenging goal statements; frequent summaries | Infrequent, unclear, general, unenthusiastic; summaries infrequent |
| Input | Lots of input; much new material; challenging work | Little input; little new material; much review; easy work |
| Type of questions | Many questions; frequently higher-order | Few questions; many of them rote |
| Wait time | Wait three to six seconds after a question; pursue if answer is wrong or incomplete | Wait under one second; move on if answer is wrong or incomplete |
| Encouraging Students to express confusion | Set climate in which students are not afraid to ask questions | Set climate in which students are afraid of looking stupid if they ask questions. |
| Feedback | Frequent, immediate, differentiated, specific | Infrequent, delayed, undifferentiated, vague |
| Nonverbals | Facial expression engaged, warm; frequent eye moves around room; contact; uses names often | Dull or negative expression; little eye contact; stays in one area of classroom; little use of names |

Source: Conner, K., & Kopple, H. (1980). *The Mastery Learning Manual.* School District of Philadelphia, 108.

"Wait time" is a good example of whether a teacher exhibits high or low pedagogical expectation behavior (Rowe, 2004). When a teacher calls on a student to answer a question, how long does she or he wait before either prompting the student or moving to another student? Many studies have shown that the amount of time a teacher waits reflects the teacher's expectation as to whether the student is likely to come up with the answer. After three seconds of no response from a strong student, the teacher assumes the student is thinking about the answer and continues to wait; after three seconds without response from a weaker student, the teacher assumes the student will not get the answer, and moves on. But if the teacher consciously extends the wait time to six seconds, the "slow" student becomes more likely to answer, and more likely to provide an answer at a complex level.

Thus, wait-time behavior is self-fulfilling—a teacher who expects poor performance produces it, and a teacher who expects good performance (or at least behaves as if she or he does) produces a good performance.

The nature of the feedback a teacher gives is also a self-fulfilling prophecy. Students of whom teachers expect little tend to get little feedback, and what they get is general rather than specific. The teacher might say, "thank you," or "good try," or move on to another student without comment. Students of whom teachers expect a lot tend to receive a lot of feedback that specifically lets them know how to improve.

There are many more examples of high-expectation teaching behaviors. Principals and teachers with high expectations know that to reach all students they must have a broad range of instructional strategies, must continue to learn new approaches, and must collaborate with other teachers to maximize the progress of individual students and groups. If a teacher knows content, but does not have a repertoire of instructional strategies that are responsive to different learning styles and backgrounds, it is far less likely that all of that teacher's students will learn to high levels.

### School Policies and Practices

In the United States, the idea that achievement is governed by student ability (as measured by IQ) rather than by a student's effort is deeply ingrained. Many industrialized nations believe the opposite, structuring their educational systems on the assumption that effort matters more than aptitude. Jeff Howard, president of the Efficacy Institute, expresses this view as, "Smart is not something you are—smart is something you become" (1992, p. 22). In other words, through effort we can learn how to learn more effectively. Lauren Resnick argues eloquently that if we wish to ensure that all children achieve high standards, we must structure our schools on this assumption (1995).

Are high expectations for students communicated among staff members, to students, and to parents? Researchers cite the following (Cotton, 1989):

- Setting goals which are expressed as minimally acceptable levels of achievement rather than using prior achievement data to establish ceiling levels beyond which students would not be expected to progress (Good, 1987).
- Developing and applying policies that protect instructional time, for example, policies regarding attendance, tardiness, interruptions during basic skills instructional periods, pullout programs, which cause the weakest students to miss key class instruction, etc. (Murphy et al., 1982).
- Developing policies and practices that underscore the importance of reading, that is, written policies regarding the amount of time spent on reading instruction daily, use of a single reading series to maintain continuity, frequent free reading periods, homework that emphasizes reading, frequent sharing of student reading progress with parents, and strong instructional leadership (Hallinger & Murphy, 1985; Murphy et al., 1982).
- Establishing policies that emphasize the importance of academic achievement to students, for example, minimally acceptable levels of achievement to qualify for participation in extracurricular activities, regular notification to parents when academic expectations aren't being met, etc. (Murphy & Hallinger, 1985).
- Having staff members who hold high expectations for themselves as leaders and teachers, taking responsibility for student performance (Brookover & Lezotte, 1979; Edmonds, 1979a; Murphy & Hallinger, 1985; Murphy et al., 1982).
- Using slogans that communicate high expectations, for example, "academics plus," "the spirit of our school," etc. (Newberg & Glatthorn, 1982).
- Establishing a positive learning climate, that is, the appearance of the physical plant and the sense of order and discipline that pervades both noninstructional and instructional areas (Edmonds, 1979b; Newberg & Glatthorn, 1982; Murphy et al., 1982).
- Insistent coaching of students who are experiencing learning difficulty (Good, 1987; Taylor, 1986–1987).

**School District Initiatives in Support of High-Expectations Pedagogy**

Every decision a district makes, from developing standards, assessments, and accountability systems, to hiring quality teachers and providing them with first-rate professional development, should be connected to the effort to improve pedagogy. Philadelphia focused this work in a number of ways.

### Identification of Best Practices

With all the effort that goes into educating our students, schools and teachers cannot by themselves stay on top of local and national progress in identifying the strategies that are most effective. A central office can play a valuable role in keeping abreast of these developments, examining and recommending programs, materials, and strategies that have proven their value and effectiveness with students. The dissemination of identified strategies must include ways for schools and teachers to understand which programs meet the needs of their own population, and must be coordinated with school planning and budget processes.

### Curriculum Supports

Informed and dedicated educators disagree on the amount of curriculum guidance and the number of mandates that should be provided to teachers. Some believe that, once provided with standards, teachers and schools should be free to design daily lessons and select materials as long as they are aligned with those standards. Others argue for a mandated and highly specific curriculum, with consistent materials, pacing, and measures for all students in all classrooms. Like most districts, Philadelphia has swung back and forth between these views many times in the past forty years.

The approach *Children Achieving* took to curriculum was to provide strong support, including the identification of best practices described above, but to avoid mandating specific curriculum except in schools that consistently failed to make achievement progress. However, many felt that this left individual teachers with too much leeway to determine what students were taught, especially given the challenges of high teacher turnover, high numbers of new teachers, and high student mobility. That led, over the years of *Children Achieving*, to our providing additional specific curriculum and even lesson plans for new teachers to fill in perceived gaps in the standards and the curriculum frameworks that we had first provided.

### Equity Supports

As we work to ensure that *all* children achieve high standards, three key strategies must be differentiation of strategies, equity, and monitoring of progress.

There is a strong tendency among even the best-intentioned educators to focus on strategies, materials, and lessons that are appropriate for a hypothetical average student, without the differentiation needed to help each student become successful. We must instead learn the nuances of bringing students with a range of achievement levels, needs, and learning styles to the same high standards. Furthermore, there is an instinct to believe that fairness dictates that all students should have the same level of supports. If all students are to meet high standards, we must recognize that some will require more support than others. In education, this concept is captured by the word "equity." We must also monitor closely the progress of the groups who have suffered most from low expectations, constantly consider whether central office policies and strategies support equity, and monitor progress. Several *Children Achieving* initiatives explicitly supported these efforts.

### Equity Office

An important way to ensure that the district and schools are working toward high achievement for all students is to have an office that, with the full support of the superintendent, sets common standards, monitors the progress of the groups that have historically been the least well served, and reviews policies and practices to make sure they are equitable. The Office of Standards, Equity, and Student Services (OSESS) housed the development of standards (both for outcomes and for equitable inputs), assessments, and accountability, as well as the support for various students from historically poorly served subgroups, from low-income students to those with learning disabilities.

The office assessed the academic progress of various groups, based on disaggregated data, and monitored whether other offices were providing services designed to meet the needs indicated by these data. It ensured that curriculum and assessment materials were diverse, and that professional development and best-practice identification dealt explicitly and routinely with approaches most effective for various subgroups of students. OSESS reviewed admissions and deselection policies of magnet schools and other selective programs. They ensured that school funding and budgets took into account differing poverty rates at each school, since we were committed to an equitable distribution of funds within the district even though we did not enjoy that equity between districts within Pennsylvania.

OSESS had the responsibility and authority to examine any issue within the district that contributed (or failed to contribute) to leveling the playing field so that all could meet high standards. Within OSESS, key leadership was provided by Allie Mulvihill and Gwen Morris, long-time district educators whose careers were devoted to equity, and whose skill at coaxing old district norms closer and closer to the principles and practices of *Children Achieving* was remarkable.

### Equity Support Coordinators

Key to the effectiveness of the equity process was the role of the Equity Support Coordinator (ESC). An ESC was housed in each cluster office and functioned as part of the cluster team, but reported directly to the associate superintendent for OSESS. The creation of these positions led to substantial push-back on the part of many cluster leaders, but I was convinced that ensuring equity was one of the most critical functions of the central office. The ESCs had to be the front line in helping clusters and schools recognize and address equity needs. They also provided the central office with a mechanism for tracking progress on an ongoing basis. Most of the ESCs were sufficiently skilled, dedicated, and savvy to be able to walk this political tightrope. They provided an important conduit of equity influence, information, and leadership across the various levels of the organization.

### Comprehensive Student Support Process (CSSP)

The CSSP was a way to institutionalize teacher collaboration to support struggling students. The basic structure of CSSP was a weekly meeting of groups of teachers, usually organized by grade level, in which students of concern were discussed. The teachers described what they saw as problems and what they had tried. Fellow teachers made suggestions based on their experience with the same student or similar students. If the identified needs included out-of-school supports, the counselor or another member of the Family Resource Network (see chapter 12) became part of the process. Teachers were expected to try out alternative approaches, and report back on progress. The CSSP was often the key safety net for student achievement, as principals used it to identify groups and individuals with problems, and to help teachers identify and implement approaches to help.

### School to Career Office

Most school district programs involving the transition between school and work concentrate on the students who are not regarded as college-bound, preparing them for hands-on jobs through a mix of coursework (almost always less demanding than that of the other students) and work experience. The Philadelphia School to Career Office, under the leadership of Executive Director Mary Jane Clancy, was an exemplary exception. Mary Jane and her key staff, Cassandra Jones and Melissa Orner, understood that we are now preparing students for the new economy. That requires that all students achieve at high levels, and each student should graduate with qualifications that would give her a choice between going to college and starting a career.

The office was a prime mover in involving the business community in standards-setting. It also provided leadership in ensuring that every student was given the supports to achieve to the same standards. They gave special attention to students who were poor, minority, disabled, and/or English-language learners, and whose educational and career prospects were therefore most at risk. The office worked to reform our high schools, leading our efforts to move to rosters that supported better instruction, to implement small learning communities, and to build work and service opportunities into the curriculum. Their considerable success, and expertise, and energy made them a model program nationally, and led us to receive large amounts of grants toward these efforts.

## Leadership Strategies for the School Board and Superintendent as Tools for Raising Expectations

Teachers and principals, working with parents, have enormous power to raise expectations in their own school. However, such results cannot be brought to scale without leadership from the superintendent and the board of education. Only they have the opportunity to make decisions that will create a climate of high expectations throughout the district and throughout a student's school career. Their leadership must send the signal that a new era of high expectations for all students is needed, and that this will require the participation of administration, teachers, political leaders, and citizens. No one bears individual blame for the low expectations that are endemic in our society, but each must participate in changing them. This section describes three key strategies for exercising that leadership.

## A Clear Agenda as a Strategy toward High Expectations

The superintendent and the board must articulate an agenda that lays out strategies that exemplify and support high expectations, and are clear, compelling, and based on either proven practice or sensible hypotheses drawn from research. The district's commitment to ensuring achievement for all students should be transparent.

The agenda described here grew directly out of my experiences with the Kentucky Educational Reform Act, the Business Roundtable, the National Alliance for Restructuring Education, and the Chapter I Commission. It was evident that there was no need to reinvent education: there were many practices that had proven effective in the classroom. What was needed was to combine these practices into a coordinated strategy and implement them with careful attention to culture and context of the district.

The *Children Achieving* Agenda

1) Set high expectations for everyone.
2) Design accurate performance indicators to hold everyone accountable for results.
3) Shrink the centralized bureaucracy and let schools make more decisions.
4) Provide intensive and sustained professional development to all staff.
5) Make sure that all students are ready for school.
6) Provide students with the community supports and services they need to succeed in school.
7) Provide up-to-date technology and instructional materials.
8) Engage the public in shaping, understanding, supporting and participating in school reform.
9) Ensure adequate resources and use them effectively.
10) Be prepared to address all of these priorities together and for the long term—starting now. (*Children Achieving Action Design*, 1995, p. i ff.).

The first point deals directly with expectations at the attitudinal, behavioral, and policy levels. The importance of setting high expectations was a cross-cutting belief, strategy, and way of framing and evaluating all that we did. Point 10, which underlines that this agenda is a recipe rather than a menu, was included explicitly to preempt the predictable, low-expectations question, "Which of these could we do without, if we had to make choices?"

Long before my first day on the job, the agenda was a matter of public record. It was widely disseminated. Every speech focused on it.

There were many, many implementation details to fill in, and those details would be critically important, but the basic shape of the agenda was a given, a condition of my going to Philadelphia in the first place.

The first order of business was to customize the agenda for Philadelphia. To that end, the district assembled seven task forces with a total membership of over three hundred educators, business leaders, elected officials, and community leaders. They were coordinated by the city's key child advocate, Shelly Yanoff, who took a four-month leave from her job as executive director of Public Citizens for Children and Youth to work on this project. These hundreds of people worked prodigiously hard, making use both of local knowledge and data and of national expertise. Their recommendations were then framed as the *Children Achieving Action Design*.

The action design was widely shared. It was the starting and stopping place for everything the administration did. Policies and organizational decisions were based on it. Every budget request was explicitly justified against it. Programs were cut if they were not a part of it. Grants were sought and accepted only if they were integral to it. Without this kind of disciplined focus, we could not hope to find the time, energy, and resources to implement a complex and ambitious agenda focused relentlessly on all children achieving.

The particular methods for making the agenda clear will vary in different contexts. The overarching point is that having a clear agenda is a vital part of communicating high expectations, and that the agenda must provide criteria for operational decisions, and for deciding what to stop as well as what to initiate, rather than existing simply as rhetoric.

## The Accountability System as a Strategy for Setting High Expectations

A second key leadership strategy to raise expectations is to ensure that the accountability system of the district is one that makes it clear that the district accepts responsibility for historically underserved students. The chapter on accountability details this strategy, but the point I wish to make here is that it must always be evident that all students count, including students of color, low-income students, English-language learners, and students with disabilities. It must be clear that rewards and sanctions of the accountability system are based on rapid improvement toward the goal of meeting the needs of these students while continuing success with the students already better-served.

## Philadelphia's Accountability System

An accountability system built on high expectations will be immediately controversial for those who believe that many students—whether for reasons of heredity or because of their home environment—cannot learn to high levels. In Philadelphia, the second of these beliefs was frequently expressed by officials of the local teachers union in the context of discussing accountability.

During the 1990s the national American Federation of Teachers leadership, through the voices of people like Al Shanker and Sandy Feldman, was frequently eloquent in support of high expectations for students and teacher accountability. In a dramatic departure from this position, the Philadelphia Federation of Teachers took the position that teachers could not be held responsible for student achievement because they could not have significant impact on it.

Their general counsel was quoted in the *Philadelphia Inquirer* as saying that, "Teacher performance and student achievement are not related" (Mezzacappa, *Inquirer*, Sept 1, 1996, p. E03). This sentiment was echoed by both union president Ted Kirsch and vice-president Jack Steinberg (Merrow Report, 2000a). Their view, considered charitably, was that students brought such overwhelming poverty-based problems to school that teachers could not be expected to be able to intervene powerfully enough to make a difference. As a consequence, they sent an oft-repeated message to Philadelphia teachers that if students did not do well, environmental conditions were to blame rather than school culture, teacher content knowledge, pedagogical skills, low expectations of the children, or any other factor within the teachers' control. Thus, in the hands of union leadership, low expectations of children turned into low expectations of faculty—a lethal combination for student achievement.

## Identifying and Fighting for Resources as a Strategy for Raising Expectations

A third key element to create a climate of high expectations within the district is that the superintendent and the board must make clear what resources are necessary to implement the agenda, and must fight for those resources.

## Expectations and Philadelphia Funding

In 1977, the state had paid for over 55 percent of all education costs in the state. By the time I became superintendent in 1994, the state share had dropped to about 35 percent. Both the Democrats and the Republicans in Pennsylvania had taken steps that reduced the adequacy and equity of state financial support. Philadelphia, with a weak local tax base and taking all taxes into account, taxed itself *more than double the state average.* Nevertheless, our available resources averaged $1,500 less per pupil per year than the average of the sixty-one neighboring districts—and some districts were spending more than twice what Philadelphia could afford.

What was striking was that there was a general assumption on the part of the citizens of the state, including Philadelphia and its suburbs, that Philadelphia spent much more per child than the suburban districts, and paid its teachers better. The reality was the reverse. Acknowledging this reality removed what had been perceived as "evidence" that the students couldn't learn, the teachers couldn't teach, and the administration was some mix of the incompetent and the lazy. The degree of resistance to this new information showed just how strong and pervasive the community's low expectations of both students and staff actually were.

The district staff was also caught up in a low-expectations culture. Having for years been exhorted to "do more with less" and not to "alienate Harrisburg," the district had been largely passive for years in the face of the growing inequities. Furthermore, staff and parents had become accustomed to responding to budget reductions by wringing their hands—and then fighting one another over which programs would go and which would be saved. Rather than mobilizing together, they had been cannibalizing one another.

## CONCLUSION

A district and community with high expectations has a very different attitude, and very different behaviors, from those I found in Philadelphia. If one has high expectations about what all children can achieve, it seems natural that all children should receive supports sufficient to ensure that they achieve high standards (including adequate funding). That includes the fact that if some children need more supports than others, the definition of adequacy for them is greater than that of other children.

Fighting for necessary resources is an expression of high expectations about both the students and the community. It emphasizes that the students are a worthwhile investment, and expresses the belief that the community will see the children as valuable and will be prepared to fund their education. It also helps leadership send a message that convinces local educators that an ambitious agenda like the one laid out here is doable, thus making it more likely that they will change their own expectations in the classroom.

However, as important as the battle for resources is, I must make two cautionary comments. First, it must be clear that adequate funding is essential, but by no means sufficient, to promote student achievement. Many examples show us that without the other points of the *Children Achieving* agenda, substantial increases in funding will have little effect on achievement. Second, unless there has been recent court action or another circumstance that makes additional funding possible in the short run, it is likely that the fight for resources will take time, and it will be essential that the district spend the funds that are available in the best possible ways.

## NOTES

1. The Education Trust has been particularly aggressive in identifying schools at all organizational levels in which students outperform the traditionally expected level.

2. The district had been sued several years before by the Education Law Center, which had a long history of defending the right of students historically badly served, asserting that our competitive school-admission practices discriminated against students with disabilities. Of course, they did. We entered into an agreement with the ELC to make the process fairer.

# 2

# The Origins of Low Expectations

> Man often becomes what he believes himself to be. If I keep on saying to myself that I cannot do a certain thing, it is possible that I may end by really becoming incapable of doing it. On the contrary, if I have the belief that I can do it, I shall surely acquire the capacity to do it even if I may not have it at the beginning.
>
> Mahatma Gandhi

All children can and must learn to high levels of expectation—as high as we hold for white, suburban students, and high enough to succeed in postsecondary education, support a family, and be productive citizens. Many have contended that in the civil rights struggle to ensure full rights of citizens to all groups, quality education of all students, including those who are of color, are poor, have disabilities, and/or are English-language learners, is the new frontier. The widespread belief that many groups of students are incapable of learning to high standards is the biggest obstacle to taking the next steps toward conquering that frontier.

## THE ORIGINS OF LOW EXPECTATIONS

As we develop the premise that all children can and must learn to high levels of expectation, a key question is why we as a society have such low expectations of so many of our children. The answers go far back into our history, and into the ways our behaviors and social policies have continued over time to give some people a head start while holding others back.

From the time the first Europeans arrived in what was to become the United States, people of color and people who lacked power and wealth have been oppressed in many ways, including force, discriminatory laws and behaviors, and lack of educational and economic opportunity. The legacy of this treatment remains not only in the lower income and educational status of many of these groups, but also in the belief that those who have been held back the most must have inherent traits of character or mind that make their unequal participation in our society inevitable. People of color and the poor suffer not only socioeconomic and educational inequalities, but also a cycle of self-fulfilling low expectations that are still used to justify our society's historic and current failure to recognize their full potential.

All of us have been exposed to some of the history of people of color, as well as those who are poor, or have disabilities, or are English-language learners. We know that Native Americans were virtually destroyed by the immigration that created the United States (rs6.loc.gov/learn/features/immig/native_american.html), suffering as a result not only from rifles, disease, and broken treaties, but also of forced removal from their land, and the denial of their citizenship by the same Fourteenth Amendment that ensured citizenship to African Americans. We know that African Americans suffered the horrors of the passage to America and generations of slavery, that after the Civil War they were denied their promised "forty acres and a mule," even as former slave owners were compensated at the rate of $300 for each former slave, and that Jim Crow laws (originally created in New York) crippled their lives and life chances.

We know also that Asian immigrants have been faced with violence, with legal exclusion from immigrating, with the appropriation of the land, and with relocation camps. We also know that Hispanics have suffered from low-paying jobs, violence, poor educational opportunities; we may not, however, be aware that if current demographic trends continue, "the grandchildren of poor [Mexican] immigrants may lose ground economically, disengage politically, and end up with poorer health, higher rates of crime, or greater family instability than their ancestors or counterparts in their native country" (Hochschild, 2005, pp. 74–75).

However, most of us know much less of the history of European immigrants, which differs in striking ways from those we now consider to be people of color. It is important to remember that groups of European ancestry, who arrived in waves of poor immigrants after the colonial period, also suffered significant oppression. Indeed, their very "whiteness" was in question. Benjamin Franklin worried as early as

1751 that the United States, "founded by English, [would] become a colony of aliens, who will shortly be so numerous as to Germanize us, instead of our Anglifying them, and will never adopt our language or customs any more than they can acquire our complexion" (quoted in Daniels, 2002, p. 110).

In an essay on human population, he wrote,

> The number of purely white people in the world is proportionally very small. . . . All Africa is black or tawny; Asia, chiefly tawny; America [meaning the English], exclusive of the newcomers, wholly so. And in Europe, the Spaniards, Italians, French, Russians, and Swedes are generally of what we call a swarthy complexion; as are the Germans also, the Saxons only excepted, who with the English, make the principal body of white people on the face of the earth. I could wish their numbers were increased. (quoted in Daniels, p. 110)

## Examples

### "Polluting" the Population

Despite such simmering concerns, the 1790 naturalization law permitted "free white persons" to become citizens. However, after the 1840s, as large waves of German, Irish, and Italian immigrant groups came to the country, concerns about their "polluting" effect on the population began to echo those expressed by Franklin almost one hundred years earlier. These immigrants were believed to have low intelligence, with significant physical differences that led scientists to consider them as different races, or as lower subclasses of whites. There were even court decisions that questioned their "full whiteness." There were frequent references to "the Irish race" and "the Italian race." The Irish were particularly stigmatized and racialized; a *Harper's Weekly* piece in 1851 described the "Celtic physiognomy" as "distinctly marked" by, among other things, "the small and upturned nose and the black tint of the skin" (Jacobson, 1998, p. 48).

### Transition to White versus Black

As more restrictive laws limited further immigration, as economic factors helped those immigrants already in the country improve their education and incomes, and as people of yet darker colors became more visible across the United States, the emphasis on different "shades of whiteness" faded. Color dynamics became polarized on a continuum of black and white, with Irish, Italians, and other "swarthy" peoples now considered whites, and Native Americans, Hispanics, and Asians viewed, functionally, as black (Jacobson, 1998, pp. 13, 14).

The European immigrants are important to this discussion for two reasons. First, their history makes it clear that race is a fluid social construct, defined in ways that are used to justify barriers to full participation in society. Second, it demonstrates that, despite the difficult struggles of the European immigrant groups, they experienced the privilege of being able to enter the United States and become citizens at much higher rates than those of darker skin, and that the wavering color line was adjusted to include them in a way that it has not been for other groups.

## THE LEGACY

The history described above created a legacy that has deeply affected both people and policies in the not-so-distant past. This plays out in the present in many ways; underlying all of them is the belief that certain groups of people are inferior to others, in ability and/or character.

### Race

Since the civil rights era of the 1960s and 1970s, racism has become more subtle and complicated. Overt acts of prejudice are much less frequent—there are no longer "whites only" signs over drinking fountains. Whereas discrimination used to be required by laws, laws now prohibit it. Instead, racism has become less explicit and more insidious.

We tell ourselves that inequalities between groups are the consequence of nonracial factors, that resegregation of schools occurs because of the nonracially based neighborhood configurations, that economic factors result in the concentration of blacks in some neighborhoods and whites in others, that disparities in income result not from race but from hiring practices that emphasize qualifications, and that the disparities in qualifications result from differential school performance, which in turn result from differences in preparation at home, dysfunctional families, the absence of fathers, and low levels of parent participation.

Two important and controversial aspects of the continuing influence of race are white privilege and the prejudice against people of darker skin that occurs both on the part of racial and ethnic group members, and on the part of those outside those groups.

## WHITE PRIVILEGE: AFFIRMATIVE ACTION FOR WHITES

This country's history of racial and ethnic discrimination does not live only in the past. The price paid by people of color goes far beyond the historical effects of slavery, poverty, disenfranchisement, and lack of access to education and to good jobs. It goes beyond the effects of explicitly racist attitudes. As a result of all of these factors, for generations, people of color have been prevented from having both real capital (money, goods, property) and social capital (education and connections with the mainstream power structure). The fruits of their labors have been denied them, whether through slavery, low pay, or legal or illegal stealing of their property and savings—creating the roots of the economic disparities that persist today.

**Examples:**

*Racial Wealth Gap*

> Almost 40 years after the passage of the 20th century's major civil rights legislation, huge wealth disparities persist. However, the myth that those laws leveled the playing field is widespread. For anyone who accepts the myth, it follows that if families of color are not on an economic par with whites today, the problem must lie with them.
>
> But the racial wealth gap has nothing to do with individual behaviors or cultural deficits. Throughout U.S. history, deliberate government policies transferred wealth from nonwhites to whites—essentially, affirmative action for whites. (Lui, 2004, p. 43)

*Transfer of Wealth*

We are all aware of examples of transfer of wealth from people of color to whites, such as slavery, Jim Crow laws, and the systematic pillaging of the resources of the Native Americans. Many Americans are also aware of the effects of immigration, land ownership policies, and outright discrimination toward Asians and Hispanics. However, all these circumstances are often regarded as too far in the past to create current problems. Less discussed are the many ways in which government policy entrenched the economic differences that discrimination created, benefiting whites and leaving people of color behind.

### Social Security Act of 1935

This act provided an income after retirement for millions of Americans, but excluded agricultural workers and domestic servants—occupations in which blacks, Hispanics, and Asians were overrepresented. These workers were left to depend on their children to support them in their old age. Parents of color were left with no choice but to drain their children's financial resources, while white parents, with their government-funded retirement assistance, were able to provide their children with a financial head start.

### 1935 Wagner Act

This act created the right to collective bargaining, which facilitated the move of millions of white workers into the middle class. However, these benefits did not extend to minorities, because for many decades the unions could, and did, exclude people of color or deny them access to the pay and benefit levels of whites (Adelman, 2003, p. 1).

### New Deal

> But it was another racialized New Deal program, the Federal Housing Administration, that helped generate much of the wealth that so many white families enjoy today. These revolutionary programs made it possible for millions of average white Americans—but not others of color—to own a home for the first time. The government set up a national neighborhood appraisal system, explicitly tying mortgage eligibility to race. Integrated communities were ipso facto deemed a financial risk and made ineligible for home loans, a policy known today as "redlining." Between 1934 and 1962, the federal government backed $120 billion of home loans. More than 98 percent went to whites. (Adelman, 2003, p. 1)

### Two Steps Forward

People of color were able to benefit from the G.I. bill following service in World War II, from programs of the Great Society in the 1960s and 1970s, and from affirmative action programs. However, as the "last hired and first fired," and as those whose hold on wealth is most precarious, they still suffer most from any economic downturn. The wealth gap between whites and people of color has recently widened. Tax policies that redistribute money to the rich, and reduce services to the poor, both vigorously pursued during the first years of the twenty-first century, further increase gaps.

> One result of the generations of preferential treatment for whites is that a typical white family today has on average eight times the assets, or net worth, of a typical African American family, according to economist Edward Wolff. Even when families of the same income are compared, white families have more than twice the wealth of Black families. Much of that wealth difference can be attributed to the value of one's home, and how much one inherited from parents.
>
> But a family's net worth is not simply the finish line, it's also the starting point for the next generation. Those with wealth pass their assets on to their children—by financing a college education, lending a hand during hard times, or assisting with the down payment for a home. Some economists estimate that up to 80 percent of lifetime wealth accumulation depends on these intergenerational transfers. White advantage is passed down, from parent to child to grandchild. As a result, the racial wealth gap—and the head start enjoyed by whites—appears to have grown since the civil rights days. (Adelman, 2003, p. 1)

### White Privilege: The Subtle Dimensions

Peggy McIntosh has written, "I was taught to see racism only in individual acts of meanness, not in invisible systems conferring dominance on my group" (1990, p. 1). McIntosh emphasizes a view of white privilege as "an invisible package of unearned assets that I can count on cashing in each day, but about which I was 'meant' to remain oblivious. White privilege is like an invisible weightless knapsack of special provisions, maps, passports, codebooks, visas, clothes, tools, and blank checks."

She continues with a long list of conditions on which "my African American coworkers, friends, and acquaintances with whom I come into daily or frequent contact cannot count." Some examples:

- I can go shopping alone most of the time, pretty well assured that I will not be followed or harassed.
- I do not have to educate my children to be aware of systemic racism for their own daily physical protection.
- I can swear, or dress in second hand clothes, or not answer letters, without having people attribute these choices to the bad morals, the poverty or the illiteracy of my race.

• I can be sure that if I need legal or medical help, my race will not work against me. (McIntosh, 1990, pp. 2, 3)

In summary, low expectations of groups of color in the distant past created long-term conditions that continue to feed low expectations in the present, and provide whites with systematic advantages, both social and psychological. Thus, the suffering, rather than the iniquities, of the fathers and mothers of color are visited on their children over many generations. And iniquities of the white and powerful are visited on other people's children.

### *"Light Privilege"*

"Colorism," discrimination within a racial or ethnic category against those whose skin is darker, also contributes to low expectations. Colorism is practiced both by light-skinned members of groups against the darker-skinned group members, and by members of other groups, who practice different degrees of discrimination according to darkness of skin. This prejudice is not new; it exists across many cultures and continents, and has done so for centuries.

> Surveys from the 1990's show that lighter-skinned African Americans and Hispanics continue to enjoy higher incomes and more education than their darker counterparts. They are more likely to own homes and to live among white neighbors, and less likely to be on welfare. Darker Blacks and Latinos have higher rates of incarceration; dark-skinned Mexican Americans speak less English and are less likely to be unionized if they are workers. Dark-skinned black men convicted of a crime receive longer sentences than lighter-skinned counterparts. Both blacks and whites attach more negative and fewer positive attributes to images of dark-skinned, compared with light-skinned, blacks. (Hochschild, 2005, p. 79)

This reality, which is not frequently discussed in the wider society, is likely to become less closeted as more blacks, Latinos, and Asians enter the middle and upper classes, and the dark-skinned are increasingly left behind, not just by their lighter-skinned counterparts, but by all of us.

## POVERTY

Poverty, regardless of (though often compounded by) color, also contributes to low expectations. It brings with it poorer schools, poorer health, less family stability, more susceptibility to emergencies, and a host of other problems that make it very hard to "bootstrap" out, despite our cherished myths about opportunity. Yet the poor are often treated as if they brought these conditions on themselves. While few would blame an infant from an impoverished family for its living conditions, most seem ready to declare that same child culpable by the age of eighteen, if not earlier. We seldom ask ourselves how we as a society contribute on a daily basis to the conditions that have reduced that child's life chances.

Poor whites, as well as minorities, often suffer major inequalities; white privilege is less great for some than for others. This impact is seen most prominently among the rural poor. Nationally, while those receiving welfare are disproportionately of color, the numerical majority is white. The test scores, and life chances, of these students are depressed and depressing, and the low expectations we hold of them are a self-fulfilling prophecy. Disaggregated data of many kinds show us the disadvantage of being poor as well as being of color.

## LANGUAGE

Level of English fluency also affects our expectations of children. Today, immigration laws favor those with high skills and high incomes. Such immigrants are far more likely to have entered the country fluent in English than immigrants of previous generations, or poor immigrants today. Immigrants and their children who arrive with neither economic resources nor knowledge of English are doubly disadvantaged—a circumstance compounded by their usually darker skin. Those who are not fluent are often regarded as stupid, and have less access to the social capital (as well as economic capital) that would permit all of them to advance. Within the school systems, despite growing evidence that bilingual programs are most effective in helping them not only to learn English but also to learn the academic content that they need, there are strong pressures toward "English only."[1]

## DISABILITY

Approximately 11 percent of the children across the United States have documented disabilities. Due to lawsuits and parental pressure during the past forty years, these children are for the most part no longer hidden from view, but are attending our public schools. There is a lot of good news. The numbers of students served are up, more children with disabilities are included in regular classrooms, there are programs for 0–2-year-olds, more students are included in testing, graduation rates are up, college enrollment among those with disabilities has grown from 3 percent to 9 percent, and there are more well-trained teachers for children with disabilities.

Public school systems have learned to comply with the federal and state laws governing the education of students with disabilities. Sometimes we provide these students with excellent instructional programs that meet their needs. But much too often, despite our technical compliance with the law, our expectations of most students with disabilities are inappropriately low. We assume that their disabilities limit their eventual achievement levels, rather than that they need to be taught in a different manner. The net result is that the academic achievement of students with disabilities—even the vast majority who have learning differences for which good instruction can teach them to succeed—is on average dramatically lower than that of other students. Their graduation rates are significantly lower, their rate of employment is 60 percent of that of adults without disabilities, and those who work are in lower-wage jobs.

## CONCLUSION

I have attempted in this chapter to continue to lay the groundwork for the most important point of the book. The biggest challenge of those who hold power in public education is to eliminate the low expectations of students with whom we have historically failed, the legacy of exclusion and domination that has persisted from Columbus to the present. The first and most difficult step is acknowledging the problem and resolving to change it.

History and personal experience provide many examples of the power of belief systems and public will. We know the power of belief systems from the fierce resistance to the ideas that the earth is not the center of the universe; that the world is not flat; that germs can cause disease; or that humans evolved from other species. Experience reminds many of us of the more recent resistance to the idea that people of color, and women, can perform with excellence in jobs and roles once limited to white men. Acceptance that it is desirable and possible that all of our students learn to high standards requires a similar sea change in public beliefs—or at least a change in behavior.

In calling for a change in our beliefs and values as they impact on children of color, English-language learners, low-income students, and young people with disabilities, we need not wait for hearts and minds to change before we insist on changes in behavior. We learned that with the Civil Rights Act of 1964. Many argued at that time that we cannot legislate morality. True! But as Dr. King observed, we can and should legislate behavior. We can do that in the area of education just as we did it with civil rights. Belief systems can and do change as a result of new experiences that arise from changes in behavior.

In addition, we must make it unacceptable to tolerate bad education for poor children. We need to make it an embarrassment to a state, a city, a superintendent, a principal, teacher, or neighborhood to have schools with children of color or poor children disproportionately not succeeding. Political correctness is often castigated especially by those on the right, and in some quarters has received a bad name, because it demands that people speak and/or act in a way that is inconsistent with their underlying beliefs. Political correctness is feeling embarrassed to say that blacks are just not as smart as whites while really believing that to be the case; it is feeling we must only talk of poor people as disadvantaged while really believing that they are lazy; it is feeling pressure to say that all children should have an adequate and equitable education while really believing that some children are a very poor investment. Political correctness is acting in ways that are more inclusive than some are prepared to act.

That is not a bad thing. Rather, despite the cynicism implied by the term "PC," it is a good first step. It means that there exists in this country a social mechanism, a kind of collective conscience that operates in the space between legislated collective behavior and individual beliefs. Political correctness need not stem either honest discussion and debate or the naming of real problems, but it is good to have norms that create discomfort when we behave or speak in ways that reflect old prejudices and stereotypes.

Through lawsuits, labor contracts, legislation, and the fostering of constructive social norms, we must create the conditions of justice and opportunity. The federal government, states, school districts, and schools must act like they believe that all children can learn to high standards. This means not only stating high expectations, as the No Child Left Behind (NCLB) legislation does, but also providing the necessary resources and intelligent regulations, which NCLB does not.

We cannot end the soft bigotry of low expectations without ending the hard bigotry of unequal and inadequate funding and other discriminatory behavior such as the assignment of teachers according to seniority rather than need, or not providing quality early childhood learning opportunities to three- and four-year-olds or using single tests to fail students without providing proper supports; but if we do both, the resulting behaviors will become a self-fulfilling prophecy, and the outcomes will turn "PC" behaviors into sincere and routine ones.

## NOTE

1. It should be noted that bilingual education was common for the waves of German-speaking immigrants arriving between the late nineteenth century and the approach of World War I; it was then eliminated for political reasons.

# 3

# All Children Can Learn
# to High Standards

If the misery of our poor be caused not by the laws of nature, but by our institutions, great is our sin.

Charles Darwin

## ALL CHILDREN CAN LEARN TO HIGH
## LEVELS OF EXPECTATION

Some people would disagree that high achievement by all children is desirable, but there are many who believe it is not possible. The phrase "All children can learn" is too often understood to mean either that "Most children can learn more than they are learning now" or that "Most children can meet standards if we don't set them too high." My message is very different. These other interpretations accept substandard learning on the part of large proportions of our children who are, for the most part, poor, of color, nonnative English-speakers, or disabled. The evidence is strong and growing that, with appropriate supports, 95 percent or more of our children can learn at the levels now expected of well-off suburban white students.

The statement that all children can learn to high levels does not imply that there are no differences in learning styles. Differences in the way students learn are clear to any parent or teacher, and are well supported by research. A key part of helping all students learn to high levels is addressing these differences. There is also strong evidence for the existence of meaningful differences in children's potential learning level, and in their speed of learning. However, the effect of these differences is greatly increased by the beliefs, behaviors, and policies that guide our educational practice (especially those related to class, race, language, and disability). Students' individual differences would not prevent most of them from learning at high levels if, as a society, we have the will to teach them effectively. There are simply too many examples of success by so-called low potential students to permit us to behave as if the current wide range in achievement is natural and inevitable.

## LIMITS VERSUS POTENTIAL

The greatest challenge to accepting the evidence that all children can learn to high levels is the continuing and widespread belief in the myth of a fixed and innate IQ, distributed according to a bell curve (Gould, 1981). The debate about human intelligence—what it is, what determines it, and who has how much of it—goes back centuries, and is always shaped by the scientific techniques and political context of the moment. Scientists fall into two major camps on this issue. One group believes that intelligence is determined by heredity and fixed at birth—a theory of limits. The other group views intelligence as a complex set of processes, and believes that both heredity and environment play critical roles in shaping the intelligence of individuals and groups. Stephen Jay Gould, to whom we are idebted for many of the ideas that form the foundation of this chapter, characterizes this interpretation as a theory of potential (Gould, 1981). There is a great deal of evidence suggesting that the theory of limits is wrong. More important, it is wrong in ways that have enormous social consequences if we base social policy on it. Given how much evidence there is that (1) supports a theory of potential, and (2) supports how much better students do if they are taught based on that theory, we would be negligent if we did not base our schooling on the assumption that almost all students can learn to high standards.

## THEORIES OF LIMITS

The key propositions of the theory of limits framework are: (1) that differences between groups and between individuals are inborn, and (2) that intelligence is measurable by IQ tests, and is unchangeable.

### Studies of Brain Size

*Prior assumptions can bias research.* Much of the early work in the theory of limits tradition was based on the assumption that brain size determines intelligence. Samuel Morton conducted a classic study in 1850. A firm believer that whites had larger skulls and more intelligence than other groups, Morton had an enormous collection of skulls from around the world, which he used to measure the brain size of people from a variety of racial/ethnic groups. To determine brain size, he filled the brain cavities of the skulls with sifted mustard seed, then poured the seed out and measured its volume. The seed measure produced inconsistent results. Therefore, he later switched to lead BB shot, which produced much more reliable measurements.

The conclusions of Morton's work, in Gould's words, "matched every good Yankee's prejudice—whites on top, Indians in the middle, and blacks on the bottom; and, among whites, Teutons and Anglo-Saxons on top, Jews in the middle, and Hindus on the bottom" (1981, pp. 53–54). However, Gould demonstrates that Morton's conclusions resulted from his prior assumptions. When, almost 150 years later, Gould returned to Morton's research notebooks and reanalyzed the raw data, Gould found no significant differences in brain size by racial group. Instead, he found a pattern of data manipulation and miscalculation. In Gould's view, this pattern did not reflect any intention to cheat; instead, it resulted from Morton's unconscious need to support his prior beliefs about racial ranking (1981, p. 54).

One of the clearest examples is shown in Gould's comparison of the results Morton found when using the mustard seed versus those he found with the more consistent BB shot. While almost all brains measured larger with the BB shot, the change for Caucasian skulls was an increase of one and eight-tenths cubic inches for shot over seed, but for African skulls the increase using shot was three times as large—five and four-tenths cubic inches. Says Gould, "Plausible scenarios are easy to construct. Morton, measuring by seed, picks up a threateningly large black skull, fills it lightly and gives it a few desultory shakes. Next, he takes a distressingly small Caucasian skull, shakes hard, and pushes mightily at the foremen magnum with his thumb. It is easily done, without conscious motivation; expectation is a powerful guide to action" (1981, p. 65).

The Morton example is enormously relevant to education today. The kind of unconscious bias it demonstrates is widespread among many in educational and policy circles who believe that they are advocates of children, but whose low expectations are a key part of the vicious downward spiral that traps the very students for whom they advocate. Gould's image of Morton "pushing mightily" to cram more seed into a Caucasian skull is a vivid example of how a belief translates into a behavior.

## The IQ Test

*Misuse of IQ testing produced results that seem laughable, but were used as the basis of social policy.* In the early years of the twentieth century, similar biases appeared in the context of immigration studies and army tests of World War I recruits. These studies made use—or misuse—of a tool for measuring intelligence referred to as the IQ test. It was developed in France by Alfred Binet for the purpose of identifying at an early age children who were in need of special help in order to do well in school. Binet was insistent that his test was developed for children, for the purpose of maximizing their learning—not to declare anyone unfit to learn. However, it was soon adapted for very different purposes.

Soon the test was used to test immigrants as they left the boat on Ellis Island. Although the test was translated into the languages of the arriving immigrants, the test subjects had just endured an exhausting trip, they were dazed by the experience of being "processed," and they were totally unused to tests of the sort they were being given. The results, in 1913, indicated that 79 percent of arriving Italians, 80 percent of Hungarians, 83 percent of Jews, and 87 percent of Russian were "morons" with a mental age under twelve (Gould, 1981, p. 166). The data were interpreted as meaning that intelligence is inherited—that there is an "intelligence gene," which is either normal or defective. The findings were widely accepted at the time. They provided a rationale, not only for discriminatory behaviors, but, also, for such social policy as restrictive immigration laws.

## The IQ Bell Curve

*The IQ test did not reveal a bell curve of IQs—it was designed to create it!* Lewis Terman further popularized the IQ test with his development of the Stanford-Binet test. This test increased the number of tasks, and the item selection and statistical procedures were carried out so as to guarantee that the test results would create a bell curve, with a normal score of 100 points and a standard deviation of fifteen to sixteen points. In effect, what he did was a fancy version of what teachers do when they "curve" a classroom test.

These were not invalid or unethical procedures, but the result they produced did not in any way "prove" that no other distribution of scores could have been possible. As Ken Richardson explains it, "the 'normal' distribution . . . is achieved in the IQ test by the simple device of including more items on which an average number of the trial group performed well, and relatively fewer on which either a substantial majority or a minority of subjects did well" (Richardson, 2002).

Thus, the bell curve of IQ was and is an artifact of the way the test was designed. Richardson writes, "it needs to be stressed that, if the bell-shaped curve is the myth it seems to be—for IQ, as for much else—then it is devastating for nearly all inference and discussion around it" (2002, pp. 35, 36).

Having created the bell-curve distribution, however, Terman went on to treat it as a biological reality. He argued both that the distribution of scores arose from genes rather than environment and that the social class of individuals was a result of IQ. "It is safe to predict that in the near future intelligence tests will bring tens of thousands of these high-grade defectives under the surveillance and protection of society. This will ultimately result in curtailing the reproduction of feeble-mindedness and in the elimination of an enormous amount of crime, pauperism, and industrial inefficiency" (quoted in Gould, 1981, p. 179).

### The Army Tests

*World War I army tests of IQ again produced laughable results that were used to support destructive social policies, including segregation.* Robert M. Yerkes, a Harvard psychologist, was made a colonel in World War I and supervised the intelligence testing of 1.75 million recruits. The results, interpreted by Carl Brigham, indicated that the average mental age of white American recruits was thirteen—just above the moron range of eight to twelve; the average mental age of Russians was eleven and thirty-four hundredths; of Italians, eleven and one-hundredth; and of Poles and African Americans, ten and forty-one hundredths (Gould, 1981, p. 197).

Again, content of the test questions meant that the tests measured familiarity with American culture rather than any underlying intelligence. The testing procedures were inconsistent with Yerkes's instructions. Inappropriate statistical procedures further depressed scores. Says Gould,

> The army mental tests could have provided an impetus for social reform, since they documented that environmental disadvantages were robbing from millions of people an opportunity to develop their intellectual skills. Again and again, the data pointed to strong correlations between test scores and environment. Again and again, those who wrote and administered the tests invented tortuous, ad hoc explanations to preserve their hereditarian biases. (1981, p. 221)

The tests provided a powerful tool for those wishing to maintain segregation. They also became a tool in the successful battle to restrict immigration, culminating in the Restriction Act of 1924. Wrote Henry F. Osburn, president of the American Museum of Natural History, 1923:

> I believe those tests were worth what the war cost, even in human life, if they served to show clearly to our people the lack of intelligence in our country, and the degrees of intelligence in different races who are coming to us, in a way which no one can say is the result of prejudice . . . we have learned once and for all that the negro is not like us. So in regard to many races and subraces in Europe we learned that some which we had believed possessed of an order of intelligence, perhaps superior to ours were far inferior. (quoted in Gould, 1981, p. 231)

The similarity to the ways in which present-day IQ and achievement test results are used by some to defend the status quo, rather than to fuel educational reform, is striking.

### Second Thoughts: Too Little, and Far Too Late

Later in their careers, Terman and Brigham changed their interpretations of their own data in ways that recognized the large influence of environment on test results. Brigham, for example, wrote in 1930, "Comparative studies of various national and racial groups may not be made with existing tests. . . . One of the most pretentious of these comparative racial studies—[my] own—was without foundation" (Gould, 1981, p. 233).

## MID-TWENTIETH-CENTURY PERSPECTIVES

From the late 1940s through the end of the twentieth century arguments that intelligence is hereditary were made much less loudly, undoubtedly made less acceptable by the horrors of the Nazi extermination policies and by the values spread by the U.S. civil rights movement. However, significant heredetarian voices still argued for genetic bases of differences in intelligence related to race and class. There has always been a strong undercurrent of support for their ideas.

### Herrnstein and Murray—The Bell Curve

In the early 1990s, Richard Herrnstein and Charles Murray's *The Bell Curve* (1994) opened the debate. This book and responses to it were fascinating in the degree to which they rehashed issues we have already discussed in this chapter. The book argues that innate differences in intelligence exist both between races and between social classes. It argues further that the educated must save themselves from the poor—and save the poor from themselves.

The book argues that "a general intelligence exists, is accurately reflected in IQ scores, and can be measured across all cultures," that "it is predominantly inherited, independent of schooling," that "racial and ethnic differences—including a 15 point difference [in I.Q] between whites and African-Americans—are genetic," and that "socially undesirable behaviors (poverty, divorce, crime, illegitimacy) are associated with low intelligence" (Sternberg, 1995, p. 116). Like their predecessors in the theory of limits, Herrnstein and Murray spell out the contemporary social implications of the theories of limits. In Robert Sternberg's words:

> The authors conclude that American society is being stratified into a self-segregated "cognitive elite" of wealthy, successful business and technical professionals and a rapidly breeding, disproportionately black underclass of the stupid, who are becoming incapable of dealing with the ever-more-complex world around them. . . . "For many people, there is nothing they can learn that will repay the cost of education." While this process cannot be reversed, they argue, its effect—especially the anger of the cognitively advantaged over all of the money and rhetoric being wasted on the incurably dumb—can be mitigated. First, the authors suggest, social policies that have exacerbated the "dumbing down" of America must change. . . . Second, a moral transformation of society must occur, so that all people, even those with minimal intelligence earn a "valued place" in the world. . . . If not, they argue, the cognitive elite will handle the underclass by consigning it to an authoritarian "custodial state." (Sternberg, 1995, pp. 116–17)

The theory of limits may seem extreme when its societal implications are shown, but we must bear in mind that the history is, except in the case of Herrnstein and Murray, a report on the mainstream of psychological, social, and educational thinking of the day. These ideas re-cycle frequently, even in the face of opposing evidence. Even those of us most resistant to this approach have been, too often, deeply socialized into accepting its premises.

Clearly those who buy the arguments of the theory of limits, even in its milder forms, do not accept the proposition that all children can learn to high levels if given the appropriate supports. They regard such thinking as a fantasy that, while perhaps well intentioned, is at best foolish and misguided and at worst wasteful of resources and a cause of unnecessary frustration and social dissent.

## THEORIES OF POTENTIAL

For years, theories of potential have competed with theories of limits. As we weigh the evidence for and against them, we need to remember that we do not yet know enough about human intelligence to fully prove one theory or another. Rather, we look for the convergence of many kinds of evidence to suggest which theory is most plausible. Recent work in biology, neurobiology, psychology, and educational research has provided strong evidence that contradicts the basic premises of the theory of limits and supports instead theories emphasizing human potential.

There is no evidence of any gene for intelligence that differs from group to group. Furthermore, neurobiology indicates that the key feature of the human brain is its enormous flexibility and plasticity. The very nature of brain cells, the size and number of cells, and the specialization of parts of the brain are all profoundly influenced by an individual's environment. In addition, it is now clear that intelligence is not a unitary thing, but a set of capabilities. These capabilities derive from interaction between the brain and the environment, and will vary greatly depending on a person's experience.

### The Nature of Intelligence

Those working in the tradition of the theories of potential have addressed a series of key issues about the nature and origins of intelligence.

#### Intelligence: Nature or Nurture?

Generations of researchers and educators have struggled over the origin of intelligence. Does it have a genetic basis, or is it the result of environmental influences? The shorthand for this is the "nature or nurture" debate. Clearly, both heredity and environment influence intelligence, just as both influence walking and talking and most other major human activities. Those who advocate theories of limits argue, however, that environmental factors play a very small role. Those who support theories of potential argue that while genes may set some parameters, enviroment has greater influence across both individuals and groups. Interaction with the environment is critical in building intelligence, accounting for most of the variation from person to person and from group to group (Gould, 1981; Nesbit, 2009).

Several bodies of research provide support for the effect of environment on intelligence. Here we provide examples from two of these: studies of adoption, and changes in average IQ over generations. Ironically, most of the studies reported here make use of the very IQ tests that we have been challenging throughout this chapter. Because the measure and the beliefs underlying the theory of limits are so tightly entangled, there is really no other choice when trying to attack that theory's basic assumptions. It is only when those assumptions have been proven false that other ways of measuring intelligence—if, indeed, it is necessary to measure it—can be taken seriously.

Studies of adopted children demonstrate the crucial role of environment: These studies provide a way to partially untangle the effects of heredity from those of environment. Because there is no opportunity to pretest adopted infants, the method compares the average IQs of the adopted children at or around adolescence to that of their birth parents and of their adoptive parents. In many of these studies, the children show gains of approximately fifteen points over their parents. Typically, these are cases in which the birth parents are less well-off and less educated than those who adopt the children, and score substantially lower on IQ (Howe, 1997, pp. 41–42).

These changes can, of course, be interpreted in at least two ways: first, that the "better" environment provided the children actually increased their intelligence, or second that the lower scores of the birth parents reflected their life experience much more than any basic intellectual capacity. It's likely that both are true. In any case, it should be noted that, according to Howe, "even *The Bell Curve*'s authors, Richard Herrnstein and Charles Murray, agree that the findings imply that moving to a good home environment (sic) can produce a benefit of almost twenty IQ points" (Howe, 1997, pp. 41–42).

Changes in average IQ over generations demonstrate the crucial role of environment: A comparison of changes in IQ averages over time provides one of the most interesting and compelling arguments for the role of environment in the development of IQ. These comparisons are based on raw scores, since IQ tests are constantly rescaled to maintain a mean of 100. They show that in many groups and countries, as illustrated in the table below, IQs have increased at least fifteen points every generation or so (Sowell, 1995; Howe, 1997 ).

Basically, someone who just twenty or thirty years ago received the average score of one hundred on an IQ test would today receive

**Table 3.1.    IQ Growth Across Generations**

| Population | Time Period | Dates | IQ Increase |
| --- | --- | --- | --- |
| U.S. Soldiers | 25 years | WWI vs. WW II | 12 points |
| France | 25 years | 1949–1976 | 21 points |
| Netherlands | 18 years | 1964–1982 | 15.6 points |
| Average of U.S., Britain, Japan, Germany, Austria, Spain | 30 years | 1950–1980 | 15 points |
| Ashkenazi Jews | 80 years | 1918–1998 | From "moron" To "above average" |

only an eighty-five for the same answers. We can either believe that our ancestors were genetically "dumber" than we are, or we can appreciate that our improved environmental and educational conditions have done much to improve intelligence (as measured by IQ) over the past several decades.

## Studies of Race, Class, and Intelligence

One of the most damaging effects of this controversy about intelligence and heredity has been the widespread belief in the existence of differences in intelligence grouped by race and/or class. IQ scores are almost always the evidence called on to support this view. Although racial dynamics in the United States are profoundly complex, we will focus our analysis here on the most discussed and studied area, black-white dynamics.

From the 1930s to the 1980s, there was about a fifteen-point difference in IQ scores between blacks and whites in the United States. During that period, however, each group's overall scores increased by fifteen points. Given that genetic arguments cannot account for the speed of these score improvements, even Herrnstein and Murray conclude in *The Bell Curve* that "Given their size and speed, the shifts [in scores of blacks and whites] over time necessarily have been due more to changes in the environment than to changes in the genes" (quoted in Sowell, 1995, pp. 75–76).

A number of studies suggest that genes play no role in IQ score differences. For example, a study of German children fathered by World

War II GIs showed no differences in IQ between those whose fathers were black and those fathered by whites (Flynn, 1980). A study of three thousand young black people in Philadelphia used blood composition to estimate the proportion of Caucasian and African genes in an individual's DNA. The study showed no correlation between IQ and race (Sowell, 1995). In fact, in a different study of black children with high IQs, the children actually had a higher proportion of African to European ancestry than the black population as a whole.

All this evidence points to the conclusion that differences in IQ scores between blacks and whites stem from environmental rather than genetic causes. The good news is that race-based score differences have declined over the past twenty-five years, from twelve points in 1980, to ten points in 1990, to seven to ten points in 1995 (Martinez, 2002). Grissmer et al. (1998) have correlated this trend with changes in U.S. social policy designed to overcome effects of race and poverty. Gains were greatest in places where the policies and practices changed the most.

Similarly, since 1970 the math and verbal scores of black students have increased by approximately a standard deviation (the equivalent of a fifteen-point jump in IQ) on tests standardized across the United States. From 1971 to 1996, the score gap between blacks and whites dropped from one and twenty-five hundredths to sixty-nine hundredths of a standard deviation in reading, and from one and thirty-three hundredths to point eighty-nine hundredths of a standard deviation in math. Scores on the National Assessment of Educational Progress also show long-term closing of achievement scores disaggregated by race. From 1971 to 2004, average reading scale scores of black and Hispanic students increased by substantially more points than those of white students, at all ages measured. From 1973 to 2004, the same was true in mathematics. It should be noted, however, that despite faster progress, the differences in scores between the white students and those of the black students remain substantial. In no case have the minority group scores caught up by 2004 to the levels achieved by whites back in 1971 or 1973 (U.S. Department of Education Center for Educational Statistics, 2001). Despite the progress in closing racial/ethnic gaps, we should remember that socioeconomic and educational status still plays a persistent and powerful role in determining measured IQ as well as tests of achievement. Class has been a major theme in the discussion about intelligence for generations. Those who believe in the theory of limits see class differences in IQ as evidence of the impact of genes; those who support the theory of potential see the changes in the IQ of adopted children and changes across generations as part of the evidence that class differences are environmental, and thus will change depending on social policy.

## CONCLUSION

If we believe that intelligence is hereditary and unchangeable, the goal of schooling is to determine who has the most potential, concentrate resources there, and provide to others whatever basic skills are helpful to the economy. However, if we believe that intelligence, while having some genetic parameters evenly distributed throughout the population, is developed mostly through interaction with the environment, then the policy implication is that both individuals and the society will be best off if we do all we can to provide the environment that maximizes its growth for everyone. Either approach will be self-fulfilling. The policies and practices described throughout the rest of this book rest on the theory of potential.

**4**

# All Children Must Learn to High Levels

> The illiterate of the twenty-first century will not be those who cannot read and write, but those who cannot learn, unlearn, and relearn.
>
> Alvin Toffler

Some would argue that even if all children *can* learn to high levels, there is no reason why they *must*. The premises of this argument are (1) that there will always be jobs that take little skill, and we need people to fill them; and (2) that, given this, providing adequate resources to those children who face the most obstacles is a waste of money. I disagree.

## ECONOMIC CHANGES

Once upon a time, a worker could earn enough to support a family without a high school diploma. That has changed in the past century as the country transitioned from an agrarian economy to an industrial economy to today's information and service economy. In 1901, the U.S. census showed that only 6 percent of the nation's eighteen-year-olds were high school graduates, and only 2 percent of the country's population earned a BA in the subsequent four years. By 2005, 73 percent were high school graduates and 35 percent had earned a BA within four years (U.S. Census Bureau, 1901–2000). In the past century, this educational growth made possible the development of America's information and service economy. In the next century, education will be required to survive in it.

According to a 1999 National Democratic Leadership Council (NDLC) report, characteristics of the new economy include

> an increase in knowledge-based jobs, higher levels of entrepreneurial dynamism and competition, reduced delays between design and production, faster times to market, increased product and service diversity, constant technological innovation, the advent of the Internet and the information technology revolution, globalization, the replacement of hierarchical organizational structures with networked learning organizations, and relentless economic churning. These are more than economic fads or passing trends; they go to the heart of how the New Economy works. (1999, p. 1)

In 2006, the National Center on Education and the Economy (NCEE) wrote, "This is a world in which a very high level of preparation in reading, writing, speaking, mathematics, science, history, and the arts will be an indispensable foundation for much of the workforce" (2007, p. xviii). Our students score between the middle and the bottom on the major long-term comparative studies across the industrialized nations in literature, mathematics, and science. Meanwhile, as technology allows employers to mechanize more and more tasks, ever fewer jobs require routine work, and those that persist are increasingly outsourced. Because "the jobs that are most vulnerable are those that require routine work," (NCEE, 2007, p. xvii) the people who are and will be most vulnerable will be those doing these routine jobs.

## Growing Income Inequality

Americans have become so used to large income disparities between groups in our society that we have forgotten how much more egalitarian the economy was in decades past. These disparities are increasing by occupational or class groups, by educational level, and by race/ethnicity.

### Class Groups

As average salaries grew rapidly in the 1950s, 1960s, and early 1970s, the relative gap between white collar and blue collar remained stable—incomes more than doubled for families at all rungs on the economic ladder. However, *between 1979 and 1999, the poorest 20 percent of American families saw their inflation-adjusted incomes dwindle by 4 percent, while the middle 20 percent gained 11 percent, and the richest 20 percent gained 42 percent* (The State of America's Children, 2001, p. 2).

### Educational Levels

Similarly, education attainment makes a huge difference in income. As of 2007, the average salary for someone without a high school diploma was $22,256 with an unemployment rate of 7.1 percent. For those with a high school diploma, the average salary was $31,408 with an unemployment rate of 4.8 percent. Those with a BA averaged over $50,000 with unemployment at 2.2 percent, and those with a doctorate or professional degree earned over $75,000 with unemployment at 1.4 percent (Bureau of Labor Statistics, 2008).

### Race, Ethnicity, and Gender

The fault lines are not limited to class and education. Racial, ethnic, and gender gaps also persist. The table below shows the median annual earnings of black, Hispanic, and white men and women as a percentage of white men's annual earnings over time. While there has been considerable improvement in the income of women, particularly white women, there has been no such improvement for black men and Hispanic men. Furthermore, the income of white men is still 25–50 percent higher than that of all other groups.

If our nation wishes to increase productivity enough to maintain high wages, then we have a strong economic incentive to ensure that significantly larger numbers of people have a great deal more knowledge and skill. Today's young people will, on average, hold at least six jobs and have three different careers during their lifetimes. This makes it essential that they have the tools to continue to learn. We must develop a workforce that is resourceful, imaginative, self-confident, flexible, creative, and entrepreneurial. These workforce requirements demand an educational system that produces high levels of achievement through strategies that require the intellectual capabilities suggested above. We must build our education system on these principles.

Table 4.1.    The Wage Gap, by Gender and Race

| Year | White Men | Black Men | Hispanic Men | White Women | Black Women | Hispanic Women |
|------|-----------|-----------|--------------|-------------|-------------|----------------|
| 1975 | $1.00 | $0.74 | $0.72 | $0.58 | $0.55 | $0.49 |
| 2004 | $1.00 | $0.74 | $0.63 | $0.76 | $0.68 | $0.57 |

## DEMOGRAPHIC SHIFTS

The makeup of the American population is radically different at the start of the twenty-first century than it was at the start of the twentieth century, and these demographic shifts will continue. In 1900, 90 percent of the population was white, and 10 percent was black.[1] In 2000, America's white population had dropped to 69.1 percent of the total, 12.1 percent were black, 3.7 percent were Asian, and 12.5 percent Hispanic (Kent et al., 2001, p. 14). The Census Bureau has announced that by 2050, the current majority group of the country will have become the minority (U.S. Census Bureau, 2008). Already at 44 percent, when my great-grandchildren enter elementary school around 2030, minority children will constitute the majority of the school children of this country. Given present practices, these children are the most likely to be poor, and the least likely to be well educated of our future workforce.

Furthermore, "retiring baby boomers take with them valuable skills derived from work experience. A younger work force—particularly the immigrant component that is younger on average than the native-born work force—will necessarily have less of this type of human capital" (Feagin, 1996, p. 14). Some may argue this is a reason to limit immigration. That's not a feasible solution even if it were a moral one. We need the workers. Thus, it is essential that we increase our efforts to provide a quality public education for immigrants and native born alike. A quality education cannot entirely replace the experience of the retiring workers but it will diminish the negative impact.

As our nation's population ages, each worker will have to support a growing number of those who do not work. In 1990 there were sixty dependents for every one hundred workers, but by 2040 that ratio will be closer to seventy-four per hundred. "By that time, other things being equal, each worker will have to produce on average almost 20 percent more for the population at large than one of today's workers to sustain the same standard of living we enjoy now" (Marshall & Tucker, 1992, p. xv). That's not possible if the children whose numbers are growing are also those whom we underserve educationally.

Family income is highly correlated with college success. Kati Haycock reports that while 75 percent of students from high-income families graduate from college by age twenty-four, only 9 percent of students from low-income families do (2008). That's not surprising given income-related secondary school experiences. Low-income students are disproportionately relegated to vocational programs.

Low-income students and minority students are significantly less likely to take algebra in the eighth grade than white students or more affluent students. Classes in high-poverty high schools are more often taught by underqualified teachers, as are math and science classes with a high percentage of minority students (Education Trust, Inc., 2006, p. 12).

We are doing an exceptionally poor job of educating those who, in a very short time, will be the majority of the country. We are failing to educate the groups of children who, as baby boomers retire, will form the bulk of our nation's workforce and the backbone of our economy. America's remarkable economic prosperity, and therefore its high standard of living, will continue only if we have an innovative, intelligent, well-educated labor pool. Unless America acts, the poor quality of its public schools will have dire repercussions for the entire country. As demographic shifts continue, it becomes more and more clear that we *must* educate *all* our students to high levels, including (and especially) those with whom we have historically failed as they become the majority.

## CIVIC REQUIREMENTS

The third reason we must educate all children to much higher standards is to enable our citizens to meet the duties of citizenship and participate meaningfully in our democracy. Several years ago in a lawsuit related to funding adequacy and equity, a New York court, remarkably, held that one of the things education must address is citizenship (*CFE v. State of New York*, 2001) The court said,

> A sound basic education instills the skills students need to become productive citizens. . . . Productive citizenship means more than just being qualified to vote or serve as a juror, but to do so capably and knowledgeably. It connotes civic engagement. An engaged, capable voter needs the intellectual tools to evaluate complex issues, such as campaign finance reform, and global warming, to name only a few. . . . jurors may be called on to decide complex matters that require the verbal, reasoning, math, science, and socialization skills that should be imparted in public schools. Jurors today must determine questions of fact concerning DNA evidence, statistical analyses, and convoluted financial fraud. . . . In sum, the court finds that a sound basic education consists of the foundational skills that students need to become productive citizens capable of civic engagement and sustaining competitive employment.

As John F. Kennedy said, "There is an old saying that the course of civilization is a race between catastrophe and education. In a democracy such as ours, in an age such as this, we must make sure education wins the race" (1960).

## PERSONAL WELL-BEING

Other important returns on education that bear separate mention are the benefits that bring personal well-being and satisfaction to the individual. Better-educated persons enjoy better health (Bentley et al., 2004, p. 10). They have the knowledge that helps them to choose better doctors and insurance plans and technologies that result in better health (Lichtenberg & Lleras-Muney, 2002, p. 2). The bottom line seems to be that education attainment has a positive impact on mortality (Lleras-Muney, 2005). Moreover, the health gap between the more and less educated appears to be rising. The better educated have fewer problems in child-rearing and are less likely to suffer from depression. Education increases motivation to achieve, and results in greater problem-solving skills, which result in more ability to manage radical changes such as being laid off, divorce, or the loss of a spouse (BBC, 2001).

## THE MORAL IMPERATIVE

For centuries, a central part of our national identity has been the concept that we are a land of opportunity. As the importance of education has grown over time, equality of educational opportunity as a core value has grown; this idea was central to the *Brown v. Board of Education* decision. It is immoral to create and maintain a system of education in which one can predict with a high degree of accuracy the quality of a child's education based on his or her zip code. It is immoral that about 50 percent of the children who are income-eligible for Head Start have no access to it because there are no more slots available in their community. It is immoral for an urban school district to have thirty or more students in a first-grade classroom, when, in a well-off suburb less than a mile away, student teacher ratios are more than a third better. Despite our core value of equal opportunity, the reality is that the schools in which we educate poor children far more often replicate social inequalities than serve as a stepping stone to better life chances.

The need for change is clear, and it is urgent. We are a nation that pledges justice for all. Even if it were not so clearly in our economic, demographic, and civic interest, providing equity of opportunity for all children, as we do for our own children and grandchildren, is at the most basic level of morality. It's the right thing to do.

**NOTE**

1. At the time, Hispanics were not counted (and indeed would not be counted until 1970), and Asians and Native Americans together were significantly less than 1 percent.

5

# We Know How to Make All Schools Effective: *Children Achieving* and Philadelphia Outcomes

> We can, whenever and wherever we choose, successfully teach all children whose schooling is of interest to us. We already know more than we need in order to do this. Whether we do it must finally depend on how we feel about the fact that we haven't so far.
>
> Ron Edmonds

All children can learn to high standards! Pipe dream, or reality? By 1994, there was no district of any size and diversity, much less any state, in which virtually all students succeeded. However, many individual children, classrooms, and schools had demonstrated that fulfilling this vision was doable. Based on these examples, theoretical evidence regarding high expectations, research, a passionate and moral commitment to the proposition, and early signs of success in Kentucky, we defined our conviction in 1994 in Philadelphia with the mantra "Now Is the Time; Philadelphia Is the Place." We called our action plan *Children Achieving*.[1]

## THE *CHILDREN ACHIEVING ACTION DESIGN*

*Children Achieving* was not a pick and choose menu of separate components. It consisted of a limited set of features designed as a system. It was crafted on the premise that each feature was essential, but, by itself, insufficient. Like any effective system, it was designed to achieve specific results—defined, measurable high achievement by all children, that would equip them for appropriate postsecondary education, work sufficient for financial security and personal satisfaction, and the skills for good citizenship.

We envisioned an accountability system based on student performance that resulted in rewards and penalties: for educators in the central office and in the schools; for students aspiring to promotion and graduation; and for a citizenry that was dissatisfied with the performance of the city system. For educators and students struggling to meet the required results, the design provided for substantial help and support before penalties were imposed.

We were clear that our vision would be difficult to achieve. Wishful thinking would not be enough. High expectations, standards, assessment, and accountability would be essential. Teachers and school leaders were going to need a lot of help, including deeper, more intense staff development.

It was clear that our children were coming to school in kindergarten well behind children in more financially privileged communities. Thus, quality, developmentally appropriate, early-childhood initiatives, beginning at age three, and full-day kindergarten were a priority.

If a significant measure of accountability was to rest at the school level, authority, decisions, and relationships at the school level had to change; the size of classes, especially in the early years, had to be reduced; the bureaucracy had to shrink significantly.

While convinced that poverty and its social and health impact on education must not be an excuse for failure, we were fully aware that poverty and its consequences made the challenge of succeeding with all children much more difficult. Thus, it was imperative that we construct specific ways to address the health and social service needs of our children. It was unacceptable to simply observe that schools cannot do everything and that these challenges were someone else's responsibility.

We rejected the perspective embraced by too many that our children should "make do" with what is given them. Given their challenges, it was more important than ever they have up-to-date technology, instructional materials, and facilities. If our children start school behind and our teachers have bigger challenges, they require more help, not less.

*Children Achieving* never identified money as the only or even the first requirement of success. We started from the premise that we had an obligation to demonstrate good stewardship of the funds we had as a first order of business. We always placed money next to last in the litany of system requirements. Nevertheless, as with the other re- quirements, adequate money was essential, and we were clear that what constitutes "adequate" was not the same for all students. Stu- dents with greater needs required greater support.

The *Children Achieving* design described a vision that had not been realized in any city or school district with a diverse population. Philadelphia had no one to emulate—we were on the frontier.

## Accomplishments

We successfully implemented important parts of all of the core ele- ments of *Children Achieving* with one major exception: we never con- vinced Harrisburg that it was its moral, economic, political, and legal responsibility to provide districts with high concentrations of poor and minority children with fair and adequate funding.

The greatest accomplishment of all was the dramatic achieve- ment gains made at all levels, and especially in the early grades, dur- ing the years when I served as superintendent—and beyond. It is im- portant to underline the measure of our children's success to make clear that when a comprehensive systemic agenda like *Children Achieving* is fully implemented in a sustained manner, it will result in the achievement we expect for our own children and need for the nation's children.

### *Children Achieving* Outcomes, 1996–2004

The baseline measurement for *Children Achieving* occurred in the spring of 1996. This summary of the impact of *Children Achieving* thus starts with the period from 1996–2000, through the end of the *Children Achieving* administration. For two prior years we had de- signed the details of the program and begun implementation; the first test score results available at either the state or district level are from the spring of 1996.[2]

### Summary: 1996–2000—During the *Children Achieving* Administration

#### *Overall Results*

Prior to *Children Achieving*, the school district had several years of stagnant test scores. During the *Children Achieving* administration,

Philadelphia students showed dramatic gains on the Stanford-9 Achievement Test (SAT-9) and other measures.

- The percentage of students participating in the testing program increased from 71.5 percent to 88.1 percent. Since this expansion included many students who were poor attenders, students with disabilities, and English-language learners, and students who had previously avoided the test or refused to take it, it made the testing pool much more weighted toward low-achieving students. Thus, it depressed the gains in achievement scores—making them all the more impressive.
- The percentage of all students enrolled in grades 4, 8, and 11 scoring at or above the basic level[3] on the Stanford Achievement Test, ninth edition (SAT-9), across grades and subjects (reading, math, and science) increased from 29.9 percent in 1996 to 42.6 percent in 2000—nearly thirteen percentage points—for an increase of 42 percent, as shown in table 5.1.
- The four-year on-time high school graduation rate increased from 48.9 percent to 56.9 percent, an increase of 16 percent.

**Table 5.1. Percentage Growth of All Students Enrolled in Grades 4, 8, and 11 Scoring at Or above the Basic Level on the Stanford Achievement Test across Grades and Subjects, 1996–2000**

| 1996 | 2000 | % Point Change | % Growth |
|------|------|----------------|----------|
| 29.9 | 42.6 | 13 points | 42.6% |

Source: Harcourt Brace, reports to School District of Philadelphia, 1996–2000

### Early Grades

Increases in achievement were greatest in the early grades, where *Children Achieving* was most fully implemented.

- In fourth grade, the SAT-9 percentage points increase in students at or above basic was *eighteen* points over the four years, as shown in table 5.2.
- Elementary students also showed *strong gains on two other indicators*: the SAT-9 national percentile rankings, and the Pennsylvania System of School Assessment (PSSA) scores, as shown in tables 5.3 and 5.4.

**Table 5.2.   Grade 4 Percentage Point Growth in Students at/above Basic, Stanford Achievement Test, 1996–2000.**

| Reading | | | Math | | | Science | | |
|---|---|---|---|---|---|---|---|---|
| 1996 | 2000 | Change | 1996 | 2000 | Change | 1996 | 2000 | Change |
| 43.7 | 59.7 | +16 | 38.3 | 51.5 | +13.2 | 39.9 | 63.8 | +23.9 |

Source: Harcourt Brace, reports to School District of Philadelphia, 1996–2000

**Table 5.3.   Grade 4 Change in Stanford Achievement Test National Percentile Ranking**

| Reading NPR | | | Math NPR | | | Science NPR | | |
|---|---|---|---|---|---|---|---|---|
| 1996 | 2000 | Change | 1996 | 2000 | Change | 1996 | 2000 | Change |
| 32nd | 41st | +9 | 23rd | 31st | +8 | 24th | 38th | +14 |

Source: Harcourt Brace, reports to School District of Philadelphia, 1996–2000

**Table 5.4.   Growth in Pennsylvania State System of Assessment, Grade 5 Mean Scale Scores; Philadelphia Scores vs. Average State Scores**

| Population | Reading | | | Math | | |
|---|---|---|---|---|---|---|
| | 1996 | 2000 | Change | 1996 | 2000 | Change |
| Philadelphia | 1090 | 1140 | +50 | 1100 | 1140 | +40 |
| Pennsylvania | 1300 | 1320 | +20 | 1300 | 1310 | +10 |

Source: Pennsylvania Department of Education, 1996–2000

These results show that the *Children Achieving* reform agenda resulted in strong achievement gains at all levels from 1996 through 2000, with the strongest gains occurring in the early grades, where implementation had been most concentrated. Such substantial growth—especially in light of the fact that a higher and higher proportion of the students were being tested each year—is encouraging evidence for the impact of high expectation strategies on the children whom schools have served least well over time. The overall levels remained far too low to ensure fair life chances for most of our students. Nevertheless, these results, achieved with no increased funding from the state or city, point powerfully toward the combination of factors that will result in high achievement for all students with the resources and public will needed to fully implement the *Children Achieving* agenda over an extended period.

**Summary: 2001–2004—Long-Term Effects of *Children Achieving***

Most analyses of the academic impact of educational reform programs are based on the achievement results for the time period of implementation—in the case of *Children Achieving*, the period from 1994 through 2000. While such an approach may seem logical, it ignores the fact that if student cohorts have shown learning gains, those gains should provide a base for higher future achievement as the students move up the grades. Furthermore, if reforms that have contributed to achievement gains are kept in place, they should continue to have positive effects on achievement for classes that benefit from them beyond the administration that implemented the reform. For these reasons, an analysis of program impact should go beyond the period of initial implementation to determine whether there is evidence that the reforms had a lasting effect.

The elementary student cohorts who benefited from the *Children Achieving* reform from 1996 to 2000 continued their higher achievement as they progressed through higher grades from 2000 through 2004.

### Grade 8 Scores

We begin with the scores in grade 8, from 2001 to 2004, because they show the progress of the student groups who had been in grades K–4 *during* the implementation of *Children Achieving*. During that period

- As each cohort reached grade 8, PSSA scores consistently increased.
- Average increases of these eighth-grade classes almost doubled compared to the eighth graders of earlier classes who had not been in K–4 during *Children Achieving*.

### Grade 5 Scores

From 2001 to 2004 new groups of students experienced the *Children Achieving* reforms that were kept in place, including in particular full-day kindergarten and a much lower pupil-teacher ratio, and they, also, enjoyed higher achievement. The classes that had been in first through fourth grades in the years *following* the implementation of *Children Achieving* reached fifth grade in 2001 to 2004.

- Across the period, grade 5 student test scores *increased each year*.

- The average increase was *twice as great* as that of earlier students who had not experienced these programs.
- Thus, students who had benefited from the *Children Achieving* program in their early years, both during and after the Hornbeck administration, later showed achievement increases, at both grade 5 and grade 8, that doubled those of earlier classes.

### Kindergarten Class of 1995–1996

For the first time in the fall of 1995, all high-poverty schools offered full-day kindergarten. The group of students who entered kindergarten that year benefited from the full range of *Children Achieving* reforms throughout its elementary school experience, and from some institutionalized reforms in fifth through eighth grades.

- This cohort made the *largest overall gains* of the grades tested, across both of the above time periods.
- It also produced the *greatest reductions in the gap*s between the city scores and the state scores, and among racial/ethnic groups.
- Its *gains were sustained*, and often built on, by the cohorts that followed it that experienced the same reforms.

## CONCLUSION

The results laid out in this chapter provide strong evidence of both the short- and longer-term impact that *Children Achieving* reforms had on student achievement. Of course, it cannot be assumed that effects that go beyond the original implementation period of an educational reform are due *solely* to the ongoing impact of that program. Steps are usually taken by new administrations to build on many of the program elements and implement additional changes.

However, given that (1) many elements of the reform were kept in place from 2001 to 2004, and (2) the new superintendent was not in place until the 2002–2003 school year; and, given the pattern of the gains described above, it is reasonable to conclude that a substantial part of the 2001–2004 gains were due to longer-term effects of *Children Achieving*. This explanation is particularly compelling given the outcomes of the kindergarten class of 1995–1996, which is the group that experienced the most intensive program supports, and shows the strongest and most consistent patterns of gains as it moved across the grade levels from 1996–2004.

## NOTES

1. A full copy of the *Children Achieving Action Design* can be found at www.childrenachieving.com.

2. Methodology and more detailed data underlying the accomplishments summary may be found at www.childrenachieving.com.

3. The performance levels for the test were advanced, proficient, basic, and below basic. Because very few of the students were achieving at the proficient level at that point, our summaries focused on the proportion for students at or above the basic level. However, our public reporting included the percent of students at every level.

# 6

# Standards

If you don't know where you're going, any road will get you
there.

*Alice in Wonderland*

There are three crucial goals of public education: equipping all students to meet high standards and continue their education beyond
high school, preparing students for employment that is both sufficient for financial security and personally fulfilling, and providing
the students the knowledge and skills to function as good citizens
and constructive participants in their communities. To meet these
goals, it is crucial to set standards so we know when students have
reached them and how educators can and have assisted in that
process.

Standards, assessment, and accountability should be considered as
a unit. All three proceed from, and must be designed to support and
circle back to, the goals. Achieving the promotion and graduation
standards should result in the knowledge and skills required by the academic, work, and citizenship goals. The assessment system must
measure student, school, and district performance. The accountability
system and incentives must be correlated to the standards and assessments and hold students, educators, and citizens responsible for performance.

Standards define the "contract" between children, educators,
schools, and the larger society. They include both content standards,
which specify what should be learned, and performance standards,
which define how well students must learn it. Any contract must

include not only what a party (in this case, community and parents) will get, but also what they will give in return. The social contract between the community and the schools must include the resources sufficient to create a successful learning environment. These learning conditions or inputs have been designated as opportunity to learn standards.

Content and performance standards—in other words, outputs—should be set first. Then, standards for students' opportunities to learn—inputs—should be defined by what will be required to create the learning environment that results in students meeting the content and performance standards. The unsatisfactory but more often embraced alternative is for a community to determine the maximum it is prepared to provide in terms of resources, and then define the outcome standards that can be achieved with that level of support.

Thus, academic standards are set with little regard to required resources, and then parents, students, educators, schools, and districts are blamed when the standards are not met. A good example of putting the cart before the horse is that what students learn is very often governed by time, rather than by learning goals or standards. How much learning can take place in 180 days with six-hour school days, within which as few as three or four are devoted to real instruction, determines student performance.

The federal No Child Left Behind (NCLB) legislation has continued, and escalated, this tradition. Since 1990 we have gone from no state having learning standards to nearly all having NCLB standards, many of which are low enough that they can be met with little change in instruction—or in outcomes. As a result, the powerful call to end the "soft bigotry of low expectations" is being mocked by the cruel realities of continuing the "hard bigotry" of inadequate resources.

The determination of standards is negotiated between the schools and society, whether this occurs formally or informally. Outside the United States, most industrialized nations have national standards; typically, the national government defines the academic standards and provides schools with most of their resources, including more supports for children with greater needs. In the United States, however, the state is the level of government responsible for public education, as made clear both by the Supreme Court (*Rodriquez v. Edgewood*, 1973) and by every state constitution. We tend to take this practice for granted and to defend it in the name of local control, despite the fact that it results in huge variations in the quality of education, and in much duplication of effort in the definition of the standards and the measurement of outcomes.

## DEVELOPMENT OF ACADEMIC STANDARDS IN PHILADELPHIA

Prior to NCLB, the standards in most states "sat on the shelf." On my arrival in Philadelphia in 1994, Pennsylvania was a good example. The state had had standards for several years, but as far as local school districts could tell, they were available for anyone who wanted to use them but were not required.[1]

Given the weaknesses of the state standards, we chose to develop our own in Philadelphia. The *Children Achieving* Task Force on Standards and Assessments, which included district staff, parents, community leaders, and the union, set forth the content domains: the arts, health and physical education, language arts, mathematics, science, social studies, technology, and world languages. In addition, their charge included the drafting of a set of competencies cutting across disciplines that were to be integrated with the academic or discipline-based standards. These were: communication, reasoning and problem-solving, citizenship and service, multicultural competence, and workplace and higher education readiness. We wanted them built into the subject matter courses to change what was taught. We also wanted to change how learning and teaching was done.

District staff,[2] in collaboration with the Philadelphia Education Fund, assembled teams of teachers, principals, curriculum specialists, community leaders, and central office personnel. These experts drafted comprehensive standards. Their draft standards then underwent extensive review by school faculties and communities and were revised based on these reviews prior to their ultimate adoption by the board of education.

Beyond that level, we developed very specific criteria within each standards area, as well as a curriculum framework to assist teachers in implementing the standards. Standards are a reflection of the values of a community or state in the context of its goals for public education. They, in combination with the assessment and accountability systems, will define what is and is not important in our schools.

## PRINCIPLES FOR DEVELOPMENT OF ACADEMIC STANDARDS

There are five key principles to follow when building a standards-based program.

## All Students Must Be Held to One Standard

If we want all students to have the opportunity to meet the goals of public education, we must have one universal standard of proficiency to connect excellence to equity. Our history is not positive. Tiered diploma systems abound. A common structure involves one diploma for college-bound students, another for those labeled "vocational," and a third that is individualized for students with disabilities. The different standards put a low ceiling on what the non-college-bound will be taught.

## The Standard Must Be High

Low minimum standards are insufficient. A meaningful standard is one that will equip a student to succeed in postsecondary education,[3] in the workforce, and as a citizen. To create such standards of proficiency in no way limits achievement beyond that level of proficiency for those with the interest and willingness to exert the effort to reach higher levels. However, if the pattern of higher achievement begins to reflect race, language, income, gender, or other characteristics that should be unrelated to performance, the district must closely examine their practices for the reasons behind such a pattern.

## The Standards Must Reflect Choices and Priorities

Our standards must connect to and help guide our priorities. First, developing meaningful standards requires selectivity. Standards should be limited to a small range of content that, in the aggregate, adds up to sustained meaningful understanding of the discipline and forms the basis for further learning over a lifetime. In addition, the disciplines must extend beyond reading and math to include a range of learning appropriate to the goals of public education.

Second, our priorities should be driven by depth, not breadth, of knowledge in any given discipline. We must identify and include what facts and figures students absolutely need to know, but the most important choices in each discipline area are the choices of core concepts and processes. Within a U.S. history course, for example, universal suffrage would be a concept within the core concept of democracy, and learning to do research would be a core process. Moreover, in selecting the facts, concepts, and processes that lie at the heart of any disciplinary standards, it is important to state them in ways that encourage the use of critical thinking and problem-solving skills and the prospect of community-based learning and real-world application.

### Standards and Assessments Must Be Aligned

Assessments must measure the chosen standards. If they do not, at best children and teachers will receive mixed signals about what they are to learn and teach. If the incentive system is built around un-aligned assessments there will no longer be much in the way of am-bivalent signals. Teachers and students will quickly determine that the assessed (and rewarded) standards are the real ones.

### The Process of Standards Development Must Involve Both Professional Expertise and Community Participation

Standards are too important to be left just to the experts—or just to the community. Their development must be a collaborative process.

## OPPORTUNITY TO LEARN STANDARDS

Our country is not doing a very good job of providing the necessary support to make the academic standards achievable. The point is a simple one: setting outcome standards is not a silver bullet, even if one attaches accountability to their achievement. It will be possible to squeeze some improved teaching and learning performance out of a flabby system that had been operating in a culture of low expectation. We were able to do that in Philadelphia. However, if the goal is achievement for all students at high levels, far more will be required, particularly in those settings where educational resources are inade-quate and inequitable and have been so historically.

To date, few have been willing to acknowledge the necessity of, or to implement, meaningful opportunity to learn standards. In the 1980s many major American cities adopted ambitious promotion and gradu-ation requirements, a crude form of learning standards, and promised to accompany them with remedial supports, a crude form of opportu-nity to learn standards. In city after city, the supports did not materi-alize at any meaningful level. The standards-related policies were dropped within a few years as repeated failures began filling the late el-ementary grades with adolescent students.

In the early 1990s, as the subject of academic standards again be-came prominent, the subject of opportunity to learn standards became a hot topic at the national level. Congress established the National Council on Education, Standards, and Testing (NCEST). The council seriously considered recommending opportunity to learn standards as a necessary corollary to content and performance standards. At the last moment, however, the council lost its nerve and simply included the report on opportunity to learn standards (produced by the council task force I had the honor of chairing) as an appendix to its full report.[4]

In addition, many dedicated educators are again calling for eliminating the accountability system under NCLB instead of seizing the moment to insist on the opportunity to learn provisions that would result in all students achieving at high levels. It is easy to develop the standards, assessment, and accountability provisions but not the supports; it's equally easy to "rail" against the standards, assessments, and accountability provisions rather than dig in hard advocating for the supports. Neither approach will help poor, black, brown, and students with disabilities.

## Principles for Development of Opportunity to Learn Standards

### Opportunity to Learn Standards Must Be Adequate to Support the Academic Standards

As Marshall Smith[5] noted during the deliberations of the aforementioned NCEST, content and performance standards are a hoax absent sufficient support to allow students to learn to the standards and teachers to teach to them.

### Opportunity to Learn Resources Must Be Distributed in Proportion to Need

Since the point of opportunity to learn supports is to ensure that *all* students meet standards, we cannot ignore the reality that some students—and schools, and communities—will need more supports than others. Thus, a definition of adequacy that may be appropriate for more affluent suburban white native English-speakers will not be sufficient for many other groups. Equal is not adequate; rather, resources must be equitable.

### Opportunity to Learn Standards Must Be Developed Together with the Academic Standards

Since development of academic and opportunity to learn standards is a mammoth task, it is very tempting to get the academic standards into place, and leave the delivery standards for later. However, this is almost certain to result in the opportunity to learn standards being treated as an afterthought to which policy-makers often do not return.

*Both "Content Domains" and Performance Levels Must*
*Be Established for Opportunity to Learn Standards*

Frequently, when opportunity to learn standards do make it onto the public agenda, they do so at levels that are so vague as to render them meaningless. They must include not only the identification of key supports drawn from the best of practice and research, but also specifically the amount of those required supports and the resources. Examples are provided in the accompanying chart (table 6.1).

As with performance standards for academic content, more specific measures would then be developed for each performance standard. The distinguishing feature of these standards is that each is measurable.

**Table 6.1.   Examples of Opportunity to Learn Standards**

| Content Standard or Domain | Performance Standard |
| --- | --- |
| Early childhood education | Quality, developmentally appropriate full-day programs for three-, four-, and five-year-olds |
| Qualified teachers | Certified teachers in all classrooms, with the best teachers assigned to the neediest students and schools. |
| Teacher-pupil ratio | 1:17 in K–3, below 25 in upper grades |
| Safety | Classrooms without frequent disruptions; safe passage to and from school |

Source: *Children Achieving Action Plan*, School District of Philadelphia

*Accountability Must Be Contingent on the Timely*
*Fulfillment of Opportunity to Learn Standards*

Once opportunity to learn standards have been developed and the cost of the supports has been quantified, a timeline must be established for phasing in the implementation of the supports. That timeline should be aligned with the timeline for accountability for academic standards. If supports are provided first in the earliest grades, then those should be the first to be held to significantly higher standards. Similarly, if the supports are not provided in a timely manner, then the social contract has been broken, and accountability must be suspended until the supports are on track.

## MAKING THE STANDARDS REAL: ASSESSMENT AND ACCOUNTABILITY

While academic standards are achievable only with commensurate opportunity to learn standards, they are meaningless without assessment and accountability resources to ensure that the standards are at the core of the school mission. The next two chapters will focus on these topics, but first let us look at how some of the tradeoffs and interrelationships of standards, assessments, and accountability were handled in Philadelphia.

## Philadelphia: A Balancing Act

### Deciding Which Standards to Measure

In any system with accountability, meaningful standards are measured standards. What is going to count? In Philadelphia, we started with reading, math, and science. We chose to do this for three reasons. One, we felt that focusing only on reading and/or math, as some would recommend, was too narrow. Two, given how far students had to go in those three areas, we thought that taking on all the academic disciplines at once was foolhardy. Third, the assessment instruments in areas other than reading, math, and science were not of the quality that we wanted to use for high-stakes purposes. Nevertheless, the debate persisted from the beginning around whether what we had chosen to count was too much given the high levels of the standards and the time span we had laid out. Was that a valid criticism or was it simply the "carping" of people with low expectations of themselves and the children? It may have been some of the latter, but it was a valid question and one with which we struggled constantly. There were also those who were concerned about the content areas that were left out—social studies, the arts, and others. There is no one right answer to these questions, which must be thoughtfully examined from all angles.

### Determining the Level of the Standards

In establishing the accountability system for educators, we defined the end goal as 95 percent of the students reaching the proficient level of performance on standards derived from the recommendations of the various national professional groups. These standards were truly "world class." They were not beyond what American students need to learn in order for our nation to reach the highest level of productivity in the current and future world economy, nor were they beyond what the students of Philadelphia are capable of learning, given the necessary supports. However, at the upper grade levels they were far beyond the level at which most U.S. students—including suburban, more affluent, native English-speaking, white students—were performing.

*Establishing the Long-Term Timeline for Proficiency*

The issues of level and scope of standards are inextricably intertwined with the issue of time—how much time is available for teachers to teach to the standards and students to learn to the standards, and the time period in which schools and students can fairly be expected to reach the expected levels of high achievement.[6]

In Philadelphia, we set the long-term goal as achieving proficiency for 95 percent of the students in reading, math, and science in twelve years, or one student generation (grades 1–12). We had been aware from the start that the proficiency levels for the older students were enormously difficult to reach by the end of the twelfth grade, even if far more resources had been made available immediately. These standards were much higher than what most suburban students were achieving, and our upper grade students were even farther behind than those in the lower grades, as a result of many years of inadequate education.

We were faced with a dilemma. Our primary message at that point was that our students were capable of learning to world-class standards. While we would have preferred to have eighteen years rather than twelve for the upper grades, the public made it clear—in the voices of even the politicians who were truly supportive—that twelve years was as long as they were willing to tolerate. Faced with the alternative of settling for lower standards for the upper grades, and then trying to explain that these lower standards didn't mean that we didn't believe in the long-run capacity of these students, we chose to stay "on message" with high expectations in the hopes that we could make modifications down the road.

When I left in 2000 we were still on a trajectory of improvement that if maintained would have resulted in our meeting our very rigorous goals. However, we had achieved this improvement by raising a very large number of students from the very bottom of the performance ladder to the basic level of achievement. Furthermore, the greatest progress had been made at the elementary levels. The performance of our students, while having improved a great deal, had a very long way to go.

Had I stayed, I would have recommended to the board that we extend the upper grade timeline, taking into account actual resources available and longitudinal progress of students, as well as the time that can be "made up" in the upper grades through higher expectations, and better instruction. Kentucky made the shift from twelve years to eighteen for the same reasons even though, there, performance improvement had been sustained for the better part of a decade.

However, such a decision is politically very difficult. Even twelve years represents several terms for most state legislators and city council persons. In the same way that corporate people have difficulty in thinking beyond the next corporate quarter, elected officials define lifespan in the framework of the next election. Thus, they want results yesterday. Boards and superintendents, with informed support from the wider community, must educate them to the realities of changing whole cultures.

### Sequencing Standards and Assessments

The test that the district was using on my arrival in Philadelphia in 1994 was an out-of-date version of a norm-referenced test developed prior to the development of the standards by the national professional groups. Thus, it was not useful for either baseline or outcome data. Therefore, as soon as it became clear that the committees working on developing the district's standards would be recommending use of standards developed by national professional groups, we chose off-the-shelf assessment instruments based on the national standards. This permitted us to move ahead with collecting baseline data in 1996, while we carried out the process of tailoring the national standards to meet needs in Philadelphia. Was this ideal? No. Was it good enough? We thought so, especially since we had already decided, based on the experience of other states, that using an off-the-shelf test and aligning it to our standards was more credible and cost-effective than developing our own assessments from scratch.

### Making Accountability Contingent on Implementation of Opportunity to Learn Standards

Most accountability systems—including the one required by NCLB—hold schools and students accountable for progress on academic standards even if the opportunity to learn standards don't exist or are not being met. We were unwilling to do this. We made the connection between academic and opportunity to learn standards by building into the accountability system the condition that the opportunity to learn supports be implemented at increasing levels if the increasing levels of accountability were to be enforced.

It would be unfair to impose high stakes on students and staff if we did not provide them the tools we knew were necessary for them to get the job done. Significant opportunity to learn standards developed in Philadelphia were put into place, including full-day kindergarten, more professional development, development of schools within schools, additional health and social service support, more technology and instructional material, upgrade of facilities, many more school volunteers and increased participation by the business community, new administrative structures, and practices that were more productive. These were made possible not by increased state or city funds, but by our fundraising success and aggressive stewardship through our administrative and noninstructional cost reductions. All of this, together with high standards and an increasing sense of accountability, resulted in our achieving the large improvement in student performance described in chapter 5.

However, we were clear that growth could not continue to the level of desired proficiency absent our ability to provide far more supports. The most critical additional opportunity to learn supports needed in the year 2000 included: pre-kindergarten for all three- and four-year-old children, class size no larger than seventeen through the third grade, extra academic assistance (significantly more time) for one-third of our students, and twenty days per year of professional development for the teachers. In 2000, when the defined necessary support was not forthcoming, we made good on the decision as it related to high stakes for students. After a rigorous discussion within the board, we suspended the new and higher promotion requirements for the eighth graders, while focusing the resources we had on the fourth graders, maintaining their accountability; we also would have suspended the educator accountability system had the resources for opportunity to learn standards continued to be unavailable.

## STANDARDS AND THE FEDERAL GOVERNMENT

Other than the standards that were developed pursuant to the Kentucky Education Reform Act, there was no state in the nation that had established rigorous academic standards in a broad array of disciplines when the Clinton administration came to office in 1992. With presidential commitment and Secretary Richard Riley's leadership through the Goals 2000 Act, every state had academic standards by 2000.

The 2002 reauthorization of the Elementary and Secondary Education Act (the so-called No Child Left Behind Act) then moved us forward toward a national standards and accountability system. It requires each state to set standards for students. Like the original Kentucky system and our system in Philadelphia, the federal law expects students to meet the standards within twelve years. Progress is to be measured each year from grades 3–8 in literacy and mathematics. Science is to be added later.

Much like the Texas system of accountability, student performance is to be disaggregated based on categories including race and language. Low-performing schools are to be identified and extra assistance provided by the state. When satisfactory student performance does not occur, sanctions are to be imposed, up to and including school reconstitution. Some extra money is provided. There are even some opportunity to learn requirements, such as one that requires every class to have a quality teacher.

This act goes significantly beyond any other federal initiative historically. That said, the act has many problems. It requires that states have standards, but does not specify what they should be. The NCLB assessment requirements reinforce multiple choice, short answer testing, which is incompatible with high standards that involve problem-solving and critical thinking. The act creates perverse incentives to keep standards low to ensure that it is as easy as possible for students to pass.

The increased dollars under NCLB are trivial compared to the remaining resource inequalities between and within states. There is nothing in the law that requires adequacy or equity within a state. Supports and sanctions for struggling districts and students are wholly inadequate both in design and implementation. There is no provision that penalizes a state for inadequate supports so long as they set the standards and have some sort of punitive system in place for districts and schools who fall short.

## NOTES

1. Ironically, Pennsylvania did have a crude accountability system that identified the districts in which at least 50 percent of the students scored in the lowest quartile on the state reading and math tests. However, the testing program predated the standards; any connection was accidental. Moreover, the testing system, like that of most states, was built on a norming basis. Thus, if large numbers of low-scoring students showed dramatic progress in absolute scores, they were likely to remain in the bottom quartile because their own higher scores would simply raise the cut-off score or norm.

2. The standards work was led by the school district, under the direction of Katherine Conner and Joseph Jacovino, in collaboration with Warren Simmons, then head of the Philadelphia Education Fund. Warren had previously been codirector with me of the National Alliance for Restructuring Education, and he is now head of the Annenberg Institute at Brown University. Warren

sat on my executive committee, as did Vicki Phillips, the head of the Annenberg Challenge at Greater Philadelphia First, who has since served as superintendent in Lancaster, Pennsylvania, secretary of education for the Commonwealth of Pennsylvania, superintendent in Portland, Oregon, and director of education at the Gates Foundation. Both brought intellectual leadership and an outside perspective to our work. They were part of the effort to create major reform within the district and serious partnerships with people and groups beyond it.

3. I feel compelled to note that this point is not that all students are expected to attend college, a criticism leveled by those wanting to take issue with a call for one high standard. It does assert that all students should have the option by virtue of preparation to an appropriate form of postsecondary education.

4. The reader can find the intriguing saga of opportunity to learn standards in the council at www.childrenachieving.com.

5. Mike was then dean of Stanford's College of Education; he later was undersecretary and acting deputy secretary of education in the Clinton administration. Until recently he held the education portfolio for the Hewlett Foundation. He is now a senior adviser to Secretary of Education Duncan. Mike has long been one of the most astute education policy-makers and analysts in America.

6. *Education Week* reported in 2000 that "70% of teachers say they have 'somewhat too little' or 'far too little' time to cover what is required by state standards." These figures are presumably even higher now that NCLB requires all students to be moving steadily toward the proficient level.

# 7

# Assessment

All students will count only when all students are counted.

David Hornbeck

A second learning condition essential to ensuring that all students learn to high standards is assessment. Academic standards are impotent without it. The feedback that assessment provides is critical to knowing how well implementation of other learning conditions is proceeding. We can claim success only if all students have the knowledge and ability to succeed in pastsecondary education and function as good citizens and productive workers. We can know that only through assessment that measures progress toward our standards, and does so in ways that captures what all of our students know and can do.

## CREATING AN ASSESSMENT SYSTEM: THE IDEALS

Reams of excellent work on assessment have been published elsewhere. Rather than review this literature, we will address the practicalities of implementing an assessment system. The following is a summary of the functions, characteristics, and challenges of standards-based assessment (Educational Commission of the States, 2002).

### Functions

- Communication of the standards of what students need to know and do.

- Measurement of what students know and can do.
- Shaping of instruction.

## Differences from Traditional Tests

- Tight alignment to standards and curriculum.
- Comparison to an absolute standard rather than a norm.
- A system that uses multiple types of assessment conforming to the nature of each standard and modeling good instruction—for example, multiple choice or performance-based tests, depending on the standard in question.

## Challenges

- Consensus building—Creating a real consensus about what students should know and should be able to do, and at what level.
- Standards-writing—Creating standards that are clear, detailed, and measurable.
- Alignment of assessment and instruction—Providing teachers with the curriculum and supports to teach toward the standards effectively, and the tools to assess what is taught.
- Use of off-the-shelf versus locally developed tests—Weighing alignment, expertise, and credibility.
- Balance of levels of assessment—Refusing to allow system-wide testing to get in the way of classroom assessment.
- Definition of progress—Determining how to define achievement and track it over time.
- Use of results—Helping school staff, parents, students, and the wider community understand and use the results; determining the importance of national comparisons.
- Inclusion of all students—Ensuring that all students, including those with disabilities and those whose first language is not English, participate in testing and are validly assessed.
- Satisfaction of legal requirements—Providing appropriate learning opportunities before consequences are enforced for students, especially those who have been historically underserved by our schools.

Importantly, the last bullet brings us full circle to the issue of opportunity to learn standards.

## CREATING A GOOD-ENOUGH ASSESSMENT SYSTEM: THE REALITIES

Philadelphia is not the ultimate model of curriculum and assessment alignment. The ideal process is one in which the content and performance standards are built first. Then, a curriculum framework is designed, so that when the assessment system is built, it can be embedded in the curriculum. A system of testing should be built as a direct derivative of the standards and curriculum framework. Field tests for the new assessments should include multiple choice, constructed responses, and portfolios of student performances, all conducted along with the implementation of the curriculum framework.

The test items should be designed from the outset to be appropriate for different kinds of learners. An iterative process should unfold in the development of an actual curriculum and the assessment. Throughout, an independent expert panel—comprised either of individually chosen experts or of a recognized group[1] should monitor and critique the process. The problem, of course, with such a development process is that it takes more time and more money than any school district or state[2] operating in a real-time political environment can count on.

### Children Achieving: Assessment

Several of our earliest decisions about implementation of *Children Achieving* related to assessment issues, because we could not create a baseline for measuring our progress, or create an accountability system, without a sound testing program.

### Selecting an Off-the-Shelf Test

While part of the motivation for using an off-the-shelf assessment system was to save several years of test development, there were other compelling reasons as well. Previous experience with assessment in Maryland and Kentucky and knowledge of the pioneering portfolio work in Vermont (all three states built their own) led to the decision to use the best off-the-shelf assessment system that we could find, rather than develop our own. The three states had done an outstanding job, but each encountered many challenges, both psychometric and political.

It is extremely time-consuming to build an assessment system, requiring a number of years to establish the level of validity and reliability that must accompany the use of tests for high-stakes purposes, which we intended as part of our system. We needed to move more quickly.

Furthermore, when a state or district develops its own assessment system, if student performance improves, critics contend that the tests were designed to make the jurisdiction look good. In addition, test errors, such as misprinted booklets or scoring mistakes, will be tolerated more readily if the test is produced by a major company than if the state or district has developed it. An off-the-shelf test has a layer of credibility and mystique that reduces self-serving charges from critics.

Any test that is used for high-stakes purposes will be justifiably under particularly close scrutiny for educational, moral, and legal reasons. Beyond that, those who object to accountability in the first place will target the tests as a way of undermining the credibility of an accountability system. We hoped that choosing a testing program that was already widely used elsewhere and that had been field tested for reliability, validity, and bias by an independent institution would make such criticism less strident. This strategy was only partially effective. The Philadelphia Federation of Teachers leadership, for example, repeatedly characterized the SAT-9 as an experimental assessment instrument when, in fact, it had been fully field-tested and was used by the state of California and the city of Houston among other places. This criticism, largely a symptom of resistance to accountability, persisted even after the leadership was informed of the facts.[3]

### Aligning with Standards and Curriculum

Given the need to obtain, as soon as possible, an achievement baseline on a measure we could use over time, our challenge became to find a way to ensure alignment between still-to-be-developed standards and a still-to-be-purchased testing program, and then to develop curriculum aligned to both. The vehicles that made this possible were the national standards in various discipline areas, which had been the basis for the SAT-9. We built local standards, chose these assessment instruments, and wrote a curriculum framework that as tied to the standards that had been created by national English, mathematics, and science professional organizations.

### Comparing to Absolute Standards

Criterion-referenced assessment, rather than norm-referenced assessment, was essential to our standards-based approach. Criterion-referenced tests tell us how a student performs against a predetermined desirable standard. Norm-referenced tests tell us only how a student performs in relationship to other students. This can be very misleading. If the other students (the norming sample) perform at a low level, it would make it appear that high-performing students know more than they really do. The opposite would be equally true.

### Providing National Comparisons

While committed to an assessment system built on standards not norms, we also wanted to be able to measure how well our students were doing against those in other states and cities. Thus, we needed an assessment system that was in sufficiently widespread use that we could examine how students in other states and cities performed on the same instrument, administered and scored in the same way, compared to Philadelphia student performance.[4]

Comparative data are important for four reasons. First, use of comparative data provides context both for the level of performance in a district and for the rate of improvement. When standards are high and scores are low, this can help the public to be patient about the time needed for serious reform. For example, Philadelphia could demonstrate that the very low proficiency levels of our high school students were part of a national pattern in other cities using the same test. This did not reduce the urgency of improving these scores, but it contextualized the scores in terms of a long-term national reality rather than a recent local failure.

Second, use of comparative data permits a district to identify other districts and schools whose performance is better and to study them for identification of "best practices." Third, it acknowledges that students in any given district or state must compete in the same workforce environment (and for entry into postsecondary education institutions) as students in other districts and states.

Finally, use of comparative data provides a monitoring checkpoint. When a district chooses to equate its own tests with a second test battery, this can have the advantage of assuring the district that the results they have been getting are valid. In the case of Philadelphia, we emphasized the SAT-9 because we felt, with its performance-based items and greater rigor, it was a good instrument. Nevertheless, it was important that Philadelphia's performance on the SAT-9 paralleled our performance on the state-required Pennsylvania System of School Assessment (PSSA). The ability to make such a comparison was a useful political tool as well. It permitted us to use the test we thought best and, simultaneously, show our critics that we had not manipulated our test results to make ourselves look good.

### Including Performance-Based Items

Our assessment system could not rely exclusively on multiple choice questions. Multiple choice tests have the advantage of being easy to score by computer, and can therefore be scored quickly, cheaply, and consistently. More complex assessments need to be scored by human beings. Multiple choice tests may be able to measure what information students know, but are unable to sufficiently measure what students can do. They cannot measure a student's written and oral communication skills. Alone, they cannot assess the nuances of problem-solving and critical-thinking skills. Good citizenship cannot be captured by a multiple choice test. For all these reasons, we wanted Philadelphia's assessment system to include performance-based components, including writing samples and constructed-response questions.

### Facing Financial Limits

Given the crucial role that assessment plays in a standards-based system, we would have liked to use the best off-the-shelf system available at the time—in our judgment the New Standards Reference Exams. These exams embodied high expectations, assumed students can excel through hard work, and measured higher-order thinking and problem-solving skills. More than other assessment systems, they were designed to be embedded in the curriculum.

However, there were two problems with the New Standards Reference Exams when we were choosing our assessment system. First, the only exam that had been fully validated was the English reference exam. We also needed mathematics and science assessments. Having been involved throughout the development of the New Standards project, I knew their commitment to quality. The difficulty of popularizing a whole new idea of assessment had resulted in several delays. We felt that Philadelphia schools could not wait.

The other problem was that the New Standards exams were prohibitively costly at that time, at least in the Philadelphia context. We would not have been able to afford to give them in their complete form to every child. While they would have been useful for gauging the overall performance of a grade, school, or the district, they could not have been used to chart a student's individual progress, which we felt we needed.

*Ensuring Validity: Inclusion and Fairness*

Given our premise that 95 percent of students can attain academic proficiency, and our belief that students who aren't "counted" in testing are too often treated like they "don't count," we devoted a lot of energy to ensuring that virtually all students would be included in the testing program, and that the assessments would be valid.

A test is valid when it measures what it claims to measure. While this seems obvious, the principle is often violated. This is true, for example, when a child taking a mathematics test has an excellent understanding of the concepts being tested, but does poorly because he cannot read well enough to understand the problems. Tests are invalid when test-takers, such as English-language learners or students with disabilities, don't have the background experiences assumed by those who designed the exam.

Efforts to create items that are more accessible to such students are often labeled as issues of inclusion, cultural sensitivity, and fairness; ironically, those who don't understand their "accommodation" purpose too often consider them "unfair." Tests that don't allow students to show all that they know about a given content mask student's actual competence, and are invalid for those students.

The cultural fairness or bias of standardized tests has been an issue that has justifiably received a lot of attention. In 1996 the cultural framework for the SAT-9 was clearly white and middle-class. Given the numbers of black, Hispanic, and Asian students in the United States, we were amazed that Harcourt Brace and other companies had not developed tests that were more reflective of the experiences of these groups; this seemed particularly odd given that the SAT-9 was the test of choice in California and in a number of large districts in Texas, including Houston. We approached Harcourt and offered to provide site-based input for their development of test items that reflected a broader community.[5] They initially resisted, but after we exerted pressure to the point of threatening to choose another test, Harcourt finally responded positively. Under the skilled and sensitive leadership of Rich Maraschiello in our research office, we developed a number of items with Harcourt's participation, which became more enthusiastic as they began to understand what we meant and appreciate the need for improved tests.

We also worked to ensure the inclusion and fair treatment of our students who were English-language learners. For discipline areas other than English, it is desirable to test students who lack facility with English in their native language. If a student who does not have adequate English-language skills is tested on mathematics or science in English, their English-language prowess will be measured more than their mathematics or science knowledge. Unfortunately, there are relatively few tests available in languages other than English—and the situation was worse in 1995. The SAT-9 was available in a Spanish version for reading and mathematics. We used this version. In addition, because Harcourt Brace did not have a Spanish version of the SAT-9 in science, we had the English version of the test translated into Spanish. That was not ideal, because our translated version had not been through the same rigorous field tests as the Apprenda versions of the other tests. However, we felt that it would provide a better assessment than the English version. Similar accommodations were not possible at the time for other languages.

## VALIDITY, ACCESSIBILITY, AND FAIRNESS BEYOND PHILADELPHIA

Bond et al., 1996, make the central point that bias occurs when a test is not equally valid for all groups who take it. If it is not equally valid for all groups, then the scores of the individuals in the group will be too high or too low to reflect their true performance (p. 117).

This chapter has used Philadelphia as a case study in the creation of a good-enough assessment system. However, the issues of test validity, accessibility, and fairness merit further discussion, especially in light of the policies of inclusion and high-stakes assessment required by No Child Left Behind.

For generations, tests have been constructed to differentiate and rank the achievement of students regarded as "normal"—that is to say, students who were from the mainstream culture, who were native speakers of English, and who did not have disabilities. English-language learners and students with disabilities were not included in norming samples, and did not usually take the tests. Poor students and African American students were part of the norming sample, but for generations their concentration in the lowest percentiles was thought to reflect their inherent abilities, rather than the shortcomings or biases of the test. These practices grew largely from the view that these groups could not be expected to learn like, or as much as, other students.

In the past decade, new research and evidence has changed our knowledge of how students learn and what historically underserved students are capable of knowing and doing. This has begun to affect our values surrounding inclusion and expectations. Educational policy has moved rapidly from the requirement that these students be measured separately and differently (or left out of testing altogether), to the mandate that they be measured by the same standards and measures as other students. This change is one of the most positive features of NCLB, and the spotlight this legislation has put on universal test validity may well speed up progress on these issues. However, as positive as the policy changes are, the assessment methods have not kept pace with them.

However, we know far more about test validity and fairness than we have put into practice. A 1999 Pennsylvania Department of Education (PDE) document titled "Principles, Guidelines and Procedures for Developing Fair Assessment Systems" demonstrates this (Delgado et al.). PDE staff wrote it with substantial input from our Philadelphia staff in the offices of Research and Assessment, Language Equity, and Special Education, with additional input from national experts, other state educators, and community members. Ironically, this excellent document was largely ignored in Pennsylvania until 2003, with the arrival of a new governor (Rendell) and secretary of education (Phillips). The document included a set of test fairness principles developed by the National Center for Fair and Open Testing (Delgado et al., 1999):

- Assessment systems are fair to all students in order not to limit students' present education and future opportunities.
- Assessment results accurately reflect a student's actual knowledge, understanding and achievement.
- Assessments are designed to minimize the impact of biases on the student's performance, including: biases of persons developing or conducting the assessment, evaluating the performance, or interpreting or using the results; biases caused by basing assessments on the perspectives or experiences of one particular group; and biased format or content, including offensive language or stereotypes.
- Educators and assessment and content experts construct assessment systems that support learning by all students in a diverse population with variety of learning styles.
- Assessment systems allow for multiple methods to assess students' progress toward meeting learning goals and for multiple but equivalent ways for students to express knowledge and understanding.

The Fairness Task Force added another important principle (Delgado et al., 1999, p. 16):

- Assessment systems require the participation of every student.

This last recommendation, far ahead of its time, grew out of a belief in full inclusion for all students in programs and services, giving everyone the opportunity to acquire and demonstrate academic abilities. It was consistent with the view that with the onset of high-stakes testing, *all students will count only if all students are counted.*

## BEYOND ASSESSMENT ACCOMMODATIONS TO UNIVERSALITY

Most of the work that has been done on student inclusion in assessment has focused either on accommodating and adapting previously developed tests, or on developing separate tests that are for purposes other than measuring the mainstream standards. However, standards-based assessment will never really be inclusive if we continue to rely on "retrofitting" items developed with the "regular" child in mind (Dolan & Hall, 2001). Instead, we need to rely on the research that shows us that children learn and show knowledge in a wide variety of ways. There is no such thing as a "regular" child, and all children will benefit if tests are developed with this in mind. James Pelligrino observes,

> Current assessment systems are the cumulative product of various prior theories of learning and methods of measurement. Although some of these foundations are still useful for certain functions of testing, change is needed. The most common kinds of education tests do a reasonable job with certain limited functions of testing, such as measuring knowledge of basic facts and procedures and producing overall estimates of proficiency for parts of the curriculum. But both their strengths and limitations are a product of their adherence to theories of learning and measurement that are outmoded and fail to capture the breadth and richness of knowledge and competence. The limitations of these theories also compromise the usefulness of the assessments. Assessment systems need to evolve to keep pace with developments in the sciences of learning and measurement if we are to achieve the learning goals embedded in many of our current standards. (Pelligrino, 2001)

Technology will help spur the creation of many universal test designs, but many low-tech approaches will also be necessary and are important for large numbers of students. On written tests, issues to address include the language, format, kind of stimuli, and kinds of response required. There are important issues in passage selection when students are to read (or listen to) a passage as part of the test process. Oral testing, hands-on testing, portfolios, performances, and systematic observation and analysis of class work will sometimes be appropriate.

It should be noted that at this time no test can meet all of the criteria outlined in this chapter. Some would argue that this fact eliminates the possibility of any high-stakes assessment. In reality, in our imperfect world we do not have the luxury of permitting large groups of children to suffer the effects of low expectations and lack of accountability that have been the norm in the absence of accountability. Rather, in designing assessment systems, we need to do all we can to address these issues, to continue to make progress in developing and implementing instructional strategies that are effective with historically underserved groups, and to provide maximum supports to those most handicapped by our failure to meet all of our testing standards.

Three points must be nonnegotiable as we design assessment systems. First, there must be an unwavering commitment to inclusion of all students in a fair manner. Second, tests cannot be valid if they do not permit all students to "show what they know." Too often, issues of accessibility are treated as an afterthought when in fact they threaten one of the most basic requirements of test design and use. Third, as this document illustrates, the assessment of academic standards must inevitably and repeatedly circle back to issues of opportunity to learn.


## CONCLUSION

During the past two decades, the process of assessment design I described in Philadelphia has occurred in the nation as a whole. Ambiguous standards have become sharper. Standards are far more parsimonious today than they were a decade ago. Even where they are not, officials recognize the desirability to move in that direction. Few states or cities rely exclusively on multiple choice tests and most recognize the value of criterion-referenced data. National policy as reflected in the No Child Left Behind Act endorses criterion-referenced tests and disaggregated data. The iterative process that will yield better practice has been underway in the nation as a whole in a way that is impossible in any given district. District decisions should make sure that they take advantage of state-of-the-art practice at any moment in time and set in motion a process to reevaluate practice as the state of the art improves over time.

## NOTES

1. For example, Achieve was established in 1996 by the nation's governors and many of the nation's corporate leaders to catalyze the standards movement by helping states develop standards, assess the quality of those developed independently, and otherwise work with states to facilitate the implementation of standards-based reform.

2. One of the problems of NCLB is that it expects each state to have already created such a test; thus, the problems of the differing content and performance standards of the various states are compounded by variation in test quality.

3. Other assessment-related criticisms came from several members of the school board who also had an ax to grind not unrelated to their relationship to the union. Their criticisms related primarily to the use of the tests, not to the tests themselves. I will leave discussion of those issues for the next section on accountability.

4. If a test is being used by other districts with whom comparison is desirable, the comparisons can be made in a criterion-referenced, rather than norm-referenced, fashion. The comparison will be with the proportion of its students, either in the aggregated or disaggregated form, who perform at certain criterion levels with the proportion in the other districts who do the same.

5. A group that is usually left out of the discussion of test inclusiveness is the poor rural white population, who are also likely to lack some of the background knowledge and experience assumed by test developers.

# 8

# Accountability

The ancient Romans had a tradition: whenever one of their engineers constructed an arch, as the capstone was hoisted into place, the engineer assumed accountability for his work in the most profound way possible: he stood under the arch.

Michael Armstrong

He that is good for making excuses is seldom good for anything else.

Benjamin Franklin

Accountability must be a reciprocal process. For every increment of performance I demand from you, I have an equal responsibility to provide you with the capacity to meet that expectation. Likewise, for every investment you make in my skill and knowledge, I have a reciprocal responsibility to demonstrate some new increment in performance.

Richard Elmore

Accountability is one of the three most controversial components of our proposals, along with providing the necessary resources to meet the opportunity to learn standards, and the requirement that all of the components be adopted simultaneously even though implementation will need to be phased. Whatever controversy it may create, an accountability system is the third essential leg of the standards-assessment-accountability stool. We provide here a framework of general criteria for standards-based accountability systems, and describe the specific accountability system put in place in Philadelphia and the challenges we faced in doing so.

An accountability system makes standards real. Without assessment and accountability, most academic standards will be no more than aspirational statements gathering dust in district and school closets. Accountability systems must apply not only to achieving academic standards, but to meeting the opportunity to learn standards as well.

Dick Riley's Education Improvement Act in 1984 was one of the earliest and best efforts to embrace such a comprehensive vision. It built standards, it provided annual comprehensive assessment, and it created one of the first accountability offices in the nation. Recognizing that supports were also important, Riley provided the leadership for a large resource increase through a penny sales-tax increase, sold by linking it to economic development.

Accountability must exist at many levels: the classroom, the school, the cluster,[1] the district, and the state. And, if we are serious about our national goal that virtually all students achieve at high levels, accountability for both academic and opportunity to learn standards should also exist at the national level.

Much as this society gives lip service to accountability, it is controversial in any setting. Human beings in general are nervous about being held responsible for the product of their work. This is true not only in education but also in business, where, for example, the media report on many CEOs whose contracts are written to ensure that they get huge salary increases and bonuses even when their companies perform poorly. Discomfort with accountability exists at every level— with administrators and teachers when accountability is applied to them, rather than just to students; with parents and students, when promotion and graduation criteria are at issue; and with politicians, business and civic leaders, and other taxpayers when we press them to make opportunity to learn standards real and hold them accountable for doing so. Superintendents tend to be held highly accountable, which is why the average term of the urban superintendent is so low, but that accountability is too often tied to political, rather than educational, accomplishments. And even superintendents tend to end up landing in another district, much like baseball managers.

There should be three parts to any educational accountability system: educator accountability (including school, regional, and central office staff), student accountability, and citizen accountability. The common thread that runs among and between them is that each is built on a system of rewards and penalties rooted in student performance. In addition, each part depends on coordinated implementation of the other two, but strategic sequencing of their development and implementation is crucial to their effectiveness.

## CRITERIA FOR ACCOUNTABILITY SYSTEMS

In Philadelphia we based our accountability system on the criteria shown below.

### Overall

1. Educational accountability systems must include reciprocal responsibilities[2] for the educators, the students, and the citizens. They should be based on the academic and opportunity to learn standards and their performance indicators.
2. Educator accountability should be implemented first, to build confidence in the teachers and the administration.
3. As educators demonstrate their accountability, the first phase of citizen accountability should be implemented by the infusion of critical resources.
4. The phasing in of student accountability should begin for each cohort only when those students have experienced improved instruction (demonstrated by student success) and opportunity to learn standards have been met.
5. Expectations for all three types of accountability should increase over time until adequate resources, high-quality instruction, and achievement by all students are in place.
6. Educator and student accountability consequences should be suspended if the citizenry does not meet the commitment to opportunity to learn standards.
7. The accountability systems should be phased in gradually, with each cohort of students expected to reach the final academic target at the point when it has experienced adequate resources and proficient instruction from preschool through grade 12.

This last criterion was one we arrived at in the course of implementation.

### Educator Accountability

#### Central and Regional Staff

1. The first year in office, the superintendent and cabinet should be held accountable for a set of program implementation goals.

2. Once a baseline of student achievement has been created, the superintendent, cabinet, and other central staff should be held accountable, with associated rewards, assistance, and penalties, for specific student academic progress goals as well as appropriate program implementation goals. Student progress goals can be defined on the same basis as they are at the school level, using the whole district (or subregions of the district) as the unit of measurement.

## School Staff

Expectations of school performance must be rigorous, not only for average students but for the groups with whom we have historically failed.

1. Schools should be provided with adequate and equitable resources and with the authority necessary to achieve the results for which they are held accountable.
2. Schools or small learning communities in larger schools, not the individual teacher, should be the unit of measurement.
3. Rewards, assistance, and penalties must be determined based on the increasing (or decreasing) proportion of successful students within a school. All students, including those with disabilities, should participate fully so that the entire system and its component parts have strong incentives to increase the success of every student.
4. School success should be defined in terms of student achievement of the high learning goals and performance objectives as measured by reliable and authentic assessment strategies.
5. Appropriate nonacademic factors such as graduation rates, attendance rates, dropout rates, retention, expulsions, suspensions, and participation in extracurricular activities and service should also be used to measure school success.
6. Progress measures should capture growth along the whole continuum of improvement—not just increased proficiency. Achievement thresholds set for each school for each measurement period should reflect an increase in the proportion of satisfactorily performing students and a decrease in the proportion of lowest performing students to ensure that achievement gains include those students with whom we historically fail (another way of approaching this criterion is the NCLB approach of disaggregating data by demographic characteristics).

7. Appropriate baseline data should be collected to permit valid measurement of gains or losses. Though assessment can be frequent for a variety of purposes, assessments for accountability purposes, with accompanying rewards and penalties, should occur at no less than two-year intervals since major changes in school practice do not occur overnight.[3]

8. Schools should not be compared with one another; rather each should be compared with its own previous performance.

9. The accountability system should be designed in such a way that all schools, not just a certain percentage, have the opportunity to perform at the level required to receive rewards.

10. The accountability system should be designed so that academic standards apply not only to small learning communities and schools, but also to all levels of governance (state, district, and any intermediate levels in larger districts). Opportunity to learn standards should apply at the federal, state, and local levels.

11. Rewards should include the possibility of significant financial bonuses to schools, to be spent at the discretion of school staff. Rewards should be commensurate with the degree to which a school surpasses its target of required performance growth.

12. If assessments indicate that a school is failing to achieve performance standards, the school should be eligible to receive substantial assistance in meeting its performance thresholds (for example, technical support, hands-on help, extra professional development, and eligibility for grants commensurate with need).

13. The consequences for persistent or dramatic failure to succeed with students should include a spectrum of penalties that makes clear at all levels of the system that we must succeed with all students. This accountability system must also have a sufficiently hard edge to warrant major investment of new resources in a district from the state or federal level. Legislators must be clear that significant new expenditures will result either in high achievement or further significant changes in practices and people (*Children Achieving Action Design*, 1995).

## Citizen Accountability

1. Citizen accountability should be based on opportunity to learn standards that define the learning conditions and necessary resources that will ensure that all students achieve the

proficiency standards for which schools and students are held accountable.[4]

2. These opportunity to learn standards should be specifically described and costed out, and a timeline for their delivery established that is correlated with student and educator accountability standards.

## Student Accountability

1. Students should not experience high-stakes accountability (denial of promotion or graduation) before educators and citizens are demonstrably fulfilling their responsibilities.
2. Students are entitled to assessments that allow them to demonstrate their full knowledge, unimpeded by such issues as language, learning differences, handicaps, or cultural and experiential background.
3. No high-stakes decision about an individual student should be based on a single measure.
4. Students are entitled to effective systems that diagnose and address obstacles to learning. We must establish the student accountability system so that they are not penalized (nonpromoted, nongraduated) before educators demonstrate they have the skills, capacity, and knowledge to succeed with the full range of students.

One approach to such a student accountability system could be to have new higher promotion and graduation requirements as a target of aspiration but not withhold promotion or graduation from students until the educators in a given school succeed with a certain percentage of the students (for example 65 percent for each demographic group disaggregated by language, income, disability, and ethnicity). When the educators in a school achieve the prescribed level of success with the students in a school, demonstrating they have the skills, capacity, and knowledge to succeed with all of the students, then the student accountability system becomes operative and new, higher promotion and graduation requirements become effective.

## PHILADELPHIA ACCOUNTABILITY

### Moving toward Accountability

Development and implementation of an accountability system in Philadelphia occurred in the context of low achievement in a school district with a majority of minority students and a high poverty rate. Expectations of the public schools were low, the city funds were overstretched given the tax base, the state government saw the Philadelphia school district as a poor investment, and the unions were unusually oppositional even for a big city system.[5]

## Central and Regional Office Accountability

As indicated in the criteria above, both fairness and effective leadership required that before any others were held responsible, district leadership had to be accountable for measurable goals, with both rewards and sanctions. I insisted on an accountability provision in my contract. It specified that I was eligible for a bonus based on year-to-year outcomes established by the board and me each year.

That process worked well in the first year. We established goals; I met them; I received a bonus and contributed it to a charity (wanting to blunt criticism of my receiving a bonus but wanting to establish the principle). In year two, we established goals for me, and, based on them, I established goals for my cabinet. At the end of the year the board had become so split politically they refused to vote on whether the goals had been met, defaulting on the whole process.

For year three, board leadership deteriorated further as they could not even agree on goals. After waiting for weeks for the board to meet its responsibility, the cabinet and I moved on. Determined to remain focused on outcomes and committed to transparency, we established our own goals, assessing and announcing at the end of the year where we met them and where we did not.

Developing goals for the cabinet, including the creation of an ongoing monitoring system, was an important learning process. First, it was made clear that every cabinet member was to be accountable for districtwide student performance goals. This included those with responsibility for facilities, finance, school security, and maintenance. The message was that even noninstructional staff had direct connections to whether students achieved academically.

Each cabinet officer also developed a small set of goals related to her organization. Again, all cabinet members were held accountable for meeting all of these goals—not just their own. The message was, "we're a team, and if you fail, so do we all." This led to much less blaming across the organization, and much more willingness to, for example, lend staff time to another office that was struggling to accomplish a key task.

The monitoring system toward these goals was a progress report by each cabinet member three times each year, and requests for group help as needed. Discussion of midpoint progress was also an opportunity for cabinet members to let the group know if another office was letting them down. This led to further discussion, follow-up, and a report back to the superintendent. It also provided the opportunity for one office to step forward and offer support to another that was struggling. We worked very hard at breaking down the traditional bureaucratic structures. We used the accountability system as a significant tool.

## School Staff Accountability

### The Philadelphia Federation of Teachers (PFT)

When I was interviewed prior to my selection as superintendent in Philadelphia, Ted Kirsch, the president of the local chapter of the American Federation of Teachers, was among those who interviewed me. When it was my turn to ask questions, I asked how he felt about accountability. He asked what I meant. I referred him to an article written by Al Shanker, then president of the American Federation of Teachers (Shanker, 1990), thinking that might carry some weight with him. The Shanker piece was a very good one that laid out a plan of accountability that I certainly could have lived with. Ted's response was, "Al and I disagree about a number of things." I should have known then that accountability was going to emerge as one of the biggest barriers to working productively with the local union leadership.

The response was consistent with a conversation I'd had with Shanker a few weeks earlier, when it had just become public that I might be interested in Philadelphia. When Shanker asked me about it, I told him I was interested and asked whether he and I would be able to work together with the local leadership to create in Philadelphia a partnership that would include accountability. He said, "David, if you become superintendent anywhere in the United States where we (the AFT) represent the teachers, we can work together—except in Philadelphia."

## First Steps toward Accountability—Reconstitution

During my tenure, we negotiated three contracts with the union: one that was completed fifteen days after I took office in 1994, another two years later in 1996, and finally the one begun on my watch but completed in October of 2000, two months after I officially stepped down in August. Each negotiation included significant and unsuccessful attempts to include accountability in the contract. In the 1994 contract, we secured the right to reconstitute[6] schools that were academically distressed. This was one of the few reconstitution provisions that was ever negotiated into a contract, as opposed to being forced on a district and union by a court decision or by legislation.

While my intention was to put into place an overall accountability system that gave schools time to improve before imposing a drastic sanction like reconstitution, it was apparent on my arrival that there were schools in the district that had been performing so badly for so long that to wait for drastic action was little short of criminal. It was also important to send a signal about how seriously we took accountability. We established a planning group to develop implementation processes, timelines, and selection criteria consistent with the new contract. The union leadership was asked to designate participants; they refused to do so, indicating that they could not afford to appear to be part of such a process, even though they had agreed to it.

Several high schools were at the bottom of the group of low-achieving schools. In 1996, about a year and a half after negotiating the reconstitution provision, we decided to move ahead and reconstitute Audenried High School and Olney High School. On multiple measures, including test scores, graduation rates, and long-term achievement trends, both schools' performance put them at the bottom of the list for that year—and the pattern of very low achievement had persisted across many years.

Furthermore, unlike some other low-achieving schools, there was no evidence that the staff were making a serious, collaborative effort to turn the schools around. Many attempts had been made to provide special programs and support at each site, but none had succeeded. We decided that enough was enough—that it was wrong to permit this continuing travesty of justice.

Each school had a unique history. Audenried, a very small school, was the highest-poverty high school in the city, and was virtually 100 percent African American. It had been carved out in the 1980s to deal with interracial gang and turf problems that were leading to violence at South Philadelphia High School and threatening the safety of black students on their way to school. Much had been promised to the community, but few promises were kept, and the outcomes had been dismal. At Audenried, the proportion of students who started grade 9 in 1992 and graduated on time four years later was 21.9 percent. The proportion of students who in 1994–1995 earned enough credits to be considered "on time" toward graduation was 38.3 percent—and for the ninth graders it was only 29.1 percent (School District of Philadelphia,

1993/1994–1995/1996). A large proportion of the students in the attendance area transferred to other high schools.[7]

Olney was large and diverse and had generations earlier been one of the schools of which the city was especially proud. It was not among the poorest schools in the city; however, other schools with higher poverty than Olney's were outperforming Olney's students. The four-year graduation rate, 1992–1996, was 31.6 percent. The proportion of students who earned enough credits to be considered on time to graduate in the 1994–1995 school year was 51.3 percent and for grade 9 the on-time-to-graduate rate was 39.7 percent (School District of Philadelphia, 1996).

In September 1994 we had appointed a new principal at Olney. Renee Yampolsky was a veteran who had turned a middle school and an elementary school around at other points in her career. She inspired confidence in the students, she was an expert on curriculum and instruction, and her behavior defined energy. We asked her to take on Olney.

When she received virtually no cooperation from the faculty, her record of successful experiences in other schools suggested that the problem did not rest with her. We became convinced that while some of the faculty leaders were obstacles to change, the real problem was what might be characterized as a "sick building" syndrome. The culture of the school was such that the radical change in behavior that was required could not occur with the current mixture of staff.

We announced the reconstitution of the two schools in late January of 1995, meeting the contractual deadline of February 15 of a given year. Since reconstitution under the contract made up to 75 percent of the staff eligible for involuntary transfer, it was not surprising that the staff reacted negatively.

The faculty were quick to blame the students and their parents, commenting that "they don't come to school and, if they do, they act out; they roam the halls and don't behave." The faculty also blamed the middle schools and elementary schools from which the kids came. Fingers were pointed at everyone but themselves. This was especially true at Olney, which was, ironically, a hotbed of right-wing opposition to the union leadership (itself, hardly progressive).

However, we were surprised to find that many students reacted equally negatively, especially at Olney. This was, in part, because teachers were urging students at Olney to walk out of school (which they did for the first several days). However, many were genuinely hurt by our action. They felt that it was a direct reflection on them rather than on the way they were being served. Many of them were receiving decent grades and were being told they were performing well.

However, the tests told us that the vast majority of the students had reading, mathematics, and/or science skills and knowledge at a middle school or, in many cases, an elementary school level. Yet they had been told, and had bought into the proposition, that they were doing well just because they were doing better than many in their neighborhoods. We in the system, from the state legislature to the board and superintendent to the teachers, had failed them miserably.

There was some pushback from Audenried students, but their reaction was relatively mild. Perhaps they understood better than the Olney students that their school was not serving them well. On the other hand, their life experience in this high-poverty neighborhood may simply have led them to believe that protest would be futile. Perhaps both were true.

The second group whose reaction surprised us was the parents and others in the two communities. For the most part, they reacted passively. Many expressed the view that the schools were "doing the best they could with what they had to work with." Part of what they meant was that the schools had inadequate resources. But they were also expressing their own low expectations of the students. It was not unusual to have a community member say something like "well, these kids are poor," or "many of them don't speak English," or "their home life is a mess."

We had meeting after meeting with community and students in an attempt to communicate our purpose and our message, but I can't say that many who turned out were persuaded. They had internalized the low expectations of the very society that was letting—or keeping—them down.

We began the reconstitution process, including taking steps to reassign the teachers, recruit new teachers, and develop new plans and programs for the two schools. However, the union submitted a grievance attacking our interpretation of the reconstitution provisions in the contract. They set forth an interpretation that was, in our opinion, ridiculous on its face. It would have permitted the union to stop the process cold at each of a number of implementation stages. They also claimed that there had not been sufficient consultation, despite the fact that the union had refused to participate in the committees set up to plan the process.

The labor arbitrator ruled that the administration was correct in its interpretation of the reconstitution clause in the contract, but supported the union's claim about inadequate participation, thereby ending the possibility of reconstitution at Olney and Audenried in that year. In other words, like many arbitrators, he "split the baby."

At that point, shortly before the opening of school, we did manage enough collaboration with the union to permit teachers who wanted to leave either school to do so without penalty, thus creating space for some of the new recruits, and to bring in some new programs and resources. However, little fundamental change was accomplished. Nevertheless, the process had been upheld, and the very attempt to reconstitute sent a signal throughout the district and the city that we were serious about accountability.

### The Attempt to Negotiate a Comprehensive Accountability System

After the 1994 contract was signed, we made a number of attempts to discuss accountability with the PFT in informal settings or through third parties. We sent management and union representatives together to a national conference on the subject, brought in Allan Odden for an informal discussion, and made several other attempts to provoke a conversation prior to the pressures of formal negotiations for the 1996 contract, but to no avail.

The major effort to negotiate a comprehensive accountability system was made during the 1996 negotiations. We first simply put the topic on the table as a major issue to work on together, hoping that the PFT might take some initiative on the particulars so that they would actually have a voice in developing the system. They did not offer any suggestions or even say no. There was—literally—no response. We then offered principles for a comprehensive accountability system similar to those laid out above. We asked that we craft together a system that conformed to those principles; again, there was no response.

As negotiations continued, with no willingness whatsoever from the union to discuss accountability, we proposed a comprehensive system which would have included contractual changes; the silence persisted. Finally, we developed the system set forth below, which required no contractual changes. We informed the union that it would be implemented as management prerogative unless we could jointly negotiate a system as part of negotiations. They responded that we could not implement it unilaterally. They were, of course, wrong.

In the end, we did manage to negotiate one small additional piece of accountability into the 1996 contract. That provision stated that any teacher who was rated unsatisfactory (a rare occurrence) would not be eligible for a salary increase in the following year. Two consecutive unsatisfactory ratings were required in order to dismiss a teacher; thus, up until that provision was agreed to any teacher declared unsatisfactory had received a raise in the following year just like anyone else.

While the change was very modest, it was the first time in the collective bargaining era of Philadelphia schools that any connection had been achieved between a teacher's performance and a teacher's pay. We considered that an important breakthrough, albeit a ridiculously small one.

The leadership of the PFT trumpeted the "victory" that the contract did not have the word accountability in it. Sadly, that was true. They simply refused to accept the responsibility for the product of their work. Indeed, it was at the end of that negotiations that Deborah Willig, the longtime counsel for the PFT made a statement to the effect that there is no connection between teacher performance and student achievement, an attitude of the union leadership that explains why it proved impossible to negotiate a reasonable accountability system.

### Implementing Philadelphia's Educator Accountability System

Following the settlement of the contract, we proceeded to implement the accountability system that we had described late in negotiations that was based entirely on management prerogative. To avoid appearing to take a confrontational stance against the union, we agreed to substitute the term "Professional Responsibility System" for "accountability." The system included a Performance Index, long-term and short-term achievement goals, and a system of rewards, supports, and, ultimately, sanctions; it was premised on interlocking implementation of both citizen and student accountability.

Building on experience in Kentucky and other states, we designed a performance index to track student achievement over a twelve-year period of time (one student generation). Our purpose was to develop a measure that would indicate when a school, cluster, or the district as a whole had reached the high standard of performance we sought; provide us with baseline data and annual progress reports; and allow us to set achievement targets.

Consistent with the principles laid out above, the Performance Index consisted of test scores (with reading, math, and science each accounting for 20 percent of the total index), graduation rates for high school and promotion rates for schools with grades K–8 (20 percent), and student and staff attendance (10 percent each). Each was measured, and then these scores were combined into a single number for a given school in a given year. The baseline year was 1996, and the target score for the final year (2008) was 95, which would be achieved when, on average, 95 percent of all students and schools performed at the proficient level on all measures.

### The Test Scores

Relying largely on the judgment of the expert panels that had been convened by Harcourt Brace, we decided that a SAT-9 score that met their criterion for proficient constituted the level of performance we wanted 95 percent of all students to achieve. (We could have made other choices; the state of California, for example, used the SAT-9, but lowered the cut-off score for proficiency).

The SAT-9's traditional scoring rubric included four levels: Advanced, Proficient, Basic, and Below Basic. Given the fact that the vast majority of our students were scoring in the Below Basic category, we were concerned that, at least in the early years, there could well be significant growth across the wide range of scores that Below Basic included without this progress registering on the four-point Harcourt scale.

Therefore, we asked Harcourt Brace to subdivide this level into three categories: Below Basic III (nearest Basic), Below Basic II, and Below Basic I. Subdividing the bottom category permitted us to make the progress of our lowest-achieving students visible and thereby encourage staff, parents, and students to keep trying.

### The Untested

We also had to decide how to deal with the reality that in our baseline year, a large proportion of the students had not received a test score. The untested included students who did not take the test at all, due to absence or to administrative decisions to exclude them; students who put their name on the paper but did not actually respond to the questions; and students who responded to so few questions that they did not meet the Harcourt Brace criteria for a valid score.

The vast majority of these students were those most likely to have low scores—those with poor attendance or poor achievement, English-language learners, and students with disabilities. The fact that this problem existed across the nation in poor districts did not make addressing it any less urgent.

We were determined that all of our students would be included in the testing system, so that the low achievement of these students would no longer be hidden. We decided to include 100 percent of our students in all of our reporting by adding the category of "untested" students, thus creating a seventh level of performance reporting (in addition to Advanced, Proficient, Basic, and Below Basic III, II, and I). The schools then received a weighted score for each performance level (see table 8.1).

It was crucial that any school that succeeded in including more students in taking the test not be penalized by receiving a lower score. This system was designed so that moving any student from the untested category to any other level would improve the school's score in that performance cycle, no matter how poorly the student scored. Thus, the incentive was to include students. In subsequent cycles, however, in order for the school's score to improve, these students would have to show actual achievement progress. This created an incentive to teach even the lowest performing students successfully.

**Table 8.1.   Weighting for Performance Index (PI), a Hypothetical Distribution of Students, and Calculation of Total PI Score.**

| Level | % of Students | Weight | Score |
|---|---|---|---|
| Advanced | 10 | 1.2 | 12 |
| Proficient | 10 | 1.0 | 10 |
| Basic | 30 | 0.8 | 24 |
| Below Basic III | 10 | 0.6 | 6 |
| Below Basic II | 10 | 0.4 | 4 |
| Below Basic I | 10 | 0.2 | 2 |
| Untested | 20 | 0 | 0 |
| Total | 100 | | 58 |

### Other Indicators

The district also developed performance levels for other measures. At the high school level, we measured persistence to graduation (the proportion of students entering the ninth grade, minus those who transferred out of the school district, who graduated "on time" four years later). A 95 percent persistence rate was rated proficient; above 95 percent was advanced, 91–94 percent was basic, and so on (use of a four-year persistence measure was very unusual at that time, but NCLB now requires it).

For schools that included grades K–8, we used the proportion of students promoted each year. These made up another 20 percent of the school score. The final 20 percent of the total Performance Index score was divided evenly between student attendance and staff attendance, since the district had serious problems with both. We referred to the attendance indicators as "enabling" criteria.

For all of these measures, a 95 percent rate equaled proficiency; other levels were given common-sense definitions, based on what we would consider appropriate in a school where our own children might attend.

### Setting Targets

The Performance Index (PI) provided a framework for determining a school's progress toward having 95 percent of its population at the proficient level of performance in reading, math, science, persistence to graduation or promotion, and student and staff attendance within twelve years. The highest possible score was 120, which would be earned if all students performed at the advanced level. Reaching the goal of 95 percent proficiency would produce the PI score of 95.

### Criticism of the PI and Targets

Not surprisingly, there were many criticisms of the Performance Index. Some of these criticisms were simply challenges to the basic idea of accountability based on measured outcomes; others focused on the elements and assumptions of the PI itself. Among the controversial elements was the inclusion of student attendance, which some felt was beyond the schools' ability to influence, and therefore not their responsibility. Pointing out that schools with comparable demographics and locations sometimes had wide differences in attendance, we disagreed.

Another was the inclusion of staff attendance (which had been suggested by the principals), particularly since the index simply counted the percent present each day, without regard to the reason for the absence. Teachers saw this as communicating that their absences were illegitimate.

Our response was that there was no judgment intended with regard to individual teachers—there were already contractual provisions for dealing with abuses of sick days and personal leave—we simply wanted to make clear that the absence rate was an important indicator of the quantity and quality of instruction students were receiving. Whether a teacher missed a day for illness, a religious holiday, jury duty, or a frivolous reason, the class was without its teacher.

Principals too often took no steps when excessive absences occurred (districtwide we had a teacher absenteeism rate of about 10 percent). The culture among many teachers suggested that they were entitled to take sick days regularly for their "mental health." Including teacher absence in the index was a signal that these practices needed serious reexamination at the school level.

Another criticism came from schools that were at the top, or the bottom, in terms of performance. Those already scoring close to the goal of 95 felt that the system was unfairly hard on them, because there was "so little room for progress." Those at the bottom felt that their huge biennial improvement targets (as big as ten points over two years) were completely unrealistic, and set them up to fail.

In fact, over the first cycle the proportion of schools meeting their targets did not differ significantly by where the school had started or by the poverty rates of the schools. By the end of the second cycle, however, as the resources needed from the state were not increasing, the low-baseline schools did indeed have less success in meeting their targets. However, the large majority of these schools were high schools, which were handicapped by the problem described below.

In terms of the mathematical assumptions of the index, the criticism that was most valid was that the secondary schools and the elementary schools were all given the same twelve years to meet the targets, despite the fact that students were significantly farther behind when they entered grade 9 than upon entering grade 1. It was politically impossible to address this issue in 1996. It was one that we would have had to address had I remained in Philadelphia. It is also one that will have to be addressed in the NCLB accountability system.

The sensible solution needs to take a longitudinal as well as cross-sectional approach. This means taking into account that while the secondary schools can and must make significant improvement with the students they currently have, they will not be able to ensure proficiency for virtually all students until substantial improvements have occurred in the skill levels of the students who enter them.

It could also have been argued—but seldom was—that the standards themselves, especially at the high school level, were simply too high, even if the timeline had been significantly extended. They were certainly higher than most state standards. As a society, we can and should debate the appropriate level of academic difficulty that

American children need for life success. However, we felt that any lowering of the SAT-9 standards would be perceived as admitting to low expectations for urban students, and/or as an attempt to "look good." We chose to stay "on message," maintaining the high expectations.

There were two other criticisms that we did not consider legitimate. The first was the argument against the inclusion of students with disabilities and English-language learners in the assessment system. Our view is that leaving these children out of our assessments is a statement of low expectations that leads to a reduced sense of urgency about their achievement. Previous experience indicated that once these populations are included, instruction becomes more ambitious and focused, and performance gradually improves. This proved to be the case.

The criticism that we considered least legitimate of all involved our inclusion of the untested students in the scoring system. For reasons described above, schools could get small increments of additional points for one year by testing categories of students who had not previously participated, no matter how low these students actually scored. Critics argued that this was a deliberate attempt to create a false impression of progress.

Our response was (1) that it was genuine progress to include students previously excluded, (2) that we were also making public the changes in scores based only on the "tested" students, so that the public could measure our progress in both ways, and (3) that we could not argue that All Means All and simultaneously implement a system that created an incentive for schools to exclude the students most likely to have low scores rather than including them. Schools got "credit" in their PI only once for reaching out to include previously untested students; once they moved out of the Untested and into Below Basic, it took continuing achievement increases to keep scores rising.

Over time, after a panel of national experts reviewed our accountability system and warmly endorsed this provision, these criticisms became less strident.


### Rewards, Supports, and Sanctions

Based on aggregated performance on the several indicators, each school was deemed to have:

- Met or exceeded its target,
- Improved from its baseline, while not reaching its target,

- Shown no improvement from its baseline, or
- Missed its performance target two performance cycles in a row.

These data were made public annually, to provide opportunities for course corrections; however, rewards and sanctions were implemented only at the end of each two-year cycle.

### Rewards

Schools that met or exceeded both Part I (overall improvement) and Part II (succeeded in reducing the proportion of students Below Basic by at least ten points) of their target received public recognition and a sum of money equaling $1,500 for each certified staff member and $500 for each noncertified staff member. The funds were to be spent on school improvement activities.

I had advocated that an allowable expenditure, if the staff decided that was what they wanted to do, should have been for the money to be paid out, in whole or in part, to the staff themselves as bonuses. However, since compensation was subject to negotiations, I could not unilaterally make that decision. Since the union would not even talk about accountability, this was not an option.

### School Support Process

Our plan was for schools that improved but failed to meet the target to be given assistance at the cluster level. Those that showed no improvement were to receive assistance from cross-cluster school support teams and were subject to closer scrutiny of teacher and administrator performance through the district rating process.

However, in the first round, we selected the schools that performed the very most poorly—those who not only did not meet their target, but had in fact declined in their performance as reflected in their overall performance and in the proportion of students who were performing at the Below Basic level. Even though there were many more schools that needed the help, we were not able to provide assistance beyond these thirteen schools since we did not have the resources to work with more.

A school support team, consisting of ten to fifteen carefully selected district staff and led by members of our senior staff, conducted an in-depth analysis of each school's strengths and weaknesses, including data analysis, extensive interviewing, and classroom visits, and made recommendations for changes. Recommendations were made not only to the school, but also to the cluster office and to the central office, and all levels were held accountable for follow-up.

The team was then available for follow-up, and a committee including district staff and representatives of the PFT, the administrators union, and the Home and School Association met quarterly to review progress and make further recommendations, site by site. Schools that made it at least halfway to their new two-year target "achieved out" at the end of that school year; the others remained in the process.

The process was successful. At the end of the next two-year cycle, all schools with support teams improved and seven of the thirteen actually improved so much that they exceeded their goals and achieved reward status. At this point, the standard for inclusion in the process was raised. No schools were now going backward on the PI scores, so the six that had made the least improvement were designated for the next cycle, along with the six of the original thirteen that had not "achieved out."

Another important phenomenon emerged from the first cycle of accountability results. Given that all schools had targets to reach—not just those at the bottom—any school in the district might be identified for school support if it did not improve. One of the schools that declined in both overall performance and the proportion of students performing at the Below Basic and Untested categories was the Greenfield School.

Greenfield had been perceived as one of the top elementary schools in the city; it had a small number of slots available each year as part of our desegregation choice plan, and the waiting list was enormous.

The announcement that it was one of the thirteen schools in the "needs assistance" category was met by disbelief and outrage on the part of its parents, staff, and those who were more generally critical of the accountability system.[8] However, its high average performance had declined; more importantly, the average had been pulled down primarily by declines in the scores of its lowest achievers.

In fact, Greenfield represented a problem that exists in many communities across the country. In schools with excellent to decent performance by the majority of their students, there is often an invisible cadre of students constituting an unsuccessful underclass. The average performance of students is satisfactory when the children of the more educated and affluent parents are performing at an acceptable level. Children from lower socioeconomic levels, minority children, and English-language learners are not expected to perform at high levels. Thus, if these children are behaving, they are generally promoted regardless of their knowledge or skill level. We were committed to putting a stop to that practice.

One of the very positive aspects of No Child Left Behind is the requirement that each subgroup of students must meet the standard for a school to be deemed successful. The happy end of the story for Greenfield was that, after much gnashing of teeth, they went through the review process, developed sound strategies to meet the needs of their children and, at the end of the next cycle, emerged eligible for reward status. The system worked as it was designed. The historically ill-served children were the beneficiaries.

### *Sanctions*

Schools that did not emerge from the process after two or three years[9] were subjected to increasing levels of scrutiny—including reviews of school leadership—and, after three years of not meeting their goals, some received additional resources targeted to particular problems. The most serious sanction was reserved for schools that missed their performance targets two accountability cycles (four years) in a row; they would be candidates for reconstitution. My departure in August of 2000 prevented us from facing the decision of whether to use that option, since the accountability system was suspended at that point by the administration that replaced me.

### Citizen Accountability

Before turning to the accountability of citizens in general, a few comments about "Parent Accountability" are in order. In discussions of the failures of urban schools, the three groups most likely to be blamed are the educators, the students, and the parents. In Philadelphia, one of the cries from the union was that we couldn't hold teachers accountable until we found a meaningful way to hold parents accountable.

Clearly, when parents have the economic and social capital to provide youngsters with a stable, literate environment including good nutrition and health support, high-quality child care (inside or outside the child's home), and lots of exposure to early reading and math experiences, the job of the school is easier.

Ensuring good attendance, positive attitudes toward school, help with homework and other school projects, and ongoing learning experiences—activities that many middle-class families take for granted—are also very helpful. However, these are not behaviors that a school is in a position to "enforce"—nor should schools write off children whose parents, for whatever reason, cannot or do not provide them.

We did develop a system of parent-school contracts, which encouraged these behaviors in parents while also making it clear that schools should be providing parents with information about their child's progress and appropriate supports when a child was struggling. However, our bottom-line position was that it is redundant to "penalize" a parent for not being supportive of a child who was not making progress in school, since the child's failure is already a huge penalty for a parent. Similarly, a child's success is a huge reward for the parents.

However, we were very clear that, while both educators and students can and should be held accountable, citizens have a role in the accountability scheme as well. Too often, there is sentiment that educators are simply slackers who are not working hard enough, that there are plenty of resources and they need to work harder and/or smarter. But educators cannot be expected to succeed with all children without the fundamental tools. Many of these cost money.

It is clear that money alone does not guarantee success. After the Abbott decision was handed down in New Jersey in 1985, declaring the state's system of financing public education unconstitutional, for example, the so-called Abbott districts had in excess of $12,000 per pupil to spend. From the perspective of Philadelphia, spending at that time between $6,000 and $7,000, it would not be hard to conclude that something besides inadequate resources is at issue in places like Camden and Newark where performance remains very low.

However, the fact that adequate resources alone are not sufficient to guarantee success does not mean that they are not necessary. In Philadelphia, we were in a situation in which the spending gap in average yearly expenditures per pupil between the city and the surrounding sixty-one suburban school districts ranged from $1,500 to $2,000 depending on the year. Calculated another way, it equaled $37,500 to $50,000 for every classroom of twenty-five students every year.

In addition, the building stock in Philadelphia was extremely old; the average building was more than sixty years old, and several buildings were more than one hundred years old. This was particularly problematic since we also did not have the funds to provide proper maintenance. We had many classes in 1994 in which secondary students could not take books home for homework because there was only one full classroom set. Many students had a lab science course without the lab or, if they had a lab, it could easily be one that had no running water.

Many schools had no art teacher, music teacher, or librarian. Book budgets for the school library were around $7 per child, not even enough to buy one book per child per year to replenish libraries that had been neglected for decades. There was no summer school, much less after-school tutoring by qualified teachers. Class size in the secondary schools was capped at thirty-three under the contract; at the elementary level, it was capped at thirty. It was routine for a kindergarten class to have a teacher-student ratio of 1:30.

Worst of all, teachers were in seriously short supply, in terms of both quantity and quality. Teaching conditions certainly contributed to the difficulty in attracting and keeping teachers, but salaries were also woefully inadequate. The average new teacher in 1994 was paid $3,000 less than her counterpart in the suburbs. For those with fifteen years of experience, the salary gap had grown to $15,000.

We were asking our teachers (and recruiting new ones) to produce world-class results while dealing with larger classes, students with more challenging learning barriers, outdated and sometimes nonexistent supplies and little extra help for students in the way of counselors or other support staff, while paying them increasingly less than their suburban counterparts. And the situation was even worse with school administrators. As soon as a principal had proved her mettle, a suburban district would begin to try to lure her away with increases in salary of $25,000 or more. While many said no, thank you, many also said yes, and we would lose some of our best and brightest.

Within the three-part framework of accountability encompassing educators, students, and citizens, we decided that educator accountability needed to be put in place first. We believed that students should not be held accountable until they were being provided with consistently good instruction, and that citizens would not step up to their responsibilities until they saw educators both holding themselves accountable and producing better outcomes.

We implemented the educator accountability system described above, built on baseline data, in 1996. However, we made clear from the beginning that by 2000 we would need to begin to implement citizen accountability by phasing in significant new resources. In 1998, when we identified the new student accountability measures in the form of graduation and promotion requirements, we also became quite specific about the opportunity to learn standards that would be required if student and teachers were expected to continue to improve achievement in a major way.

The opportunity to learn standards were as follows (School District of Philadelphia, 1998).

**Table 8.2.   Opportunity to Learn Standards**

| Domain | Performance Standards |
| --- | --- |
| • Increased instructional time for at-risk students | For students not succeeding:<br>• Three hours/week of extra time<br>• Summer school<br>• Time for teachers to meet to address student needs |
| • Reduced class size | • Class size limits for grades K–3 of 17:1<br>• Part-time assistants in kindergarten |
| • Early childhood instruction | • Prekindergarten for all three- and four-year-olds. |
| • Intensified supports for grades 4 and 8 students who are several years behind | • Reduced class size<br>• Year-round school<br>• Professional development for teachers<br>• Social workers to connect students to necessary services |
| • School-to-career | • Paid work experiences for high school seniors<br>• Identification and supervision of paid and unpaid work experiences.<br>• Identification and supervision of opportunities for student learning |
| • Technology/library enrichment | • 6:1 student-computer ratio<br>• Printers, modems, software<br>• Network compatibility, electrical upgrades<br>• Staff for training and help<br>• Full-time library services for all schools |
| • Services to English-language learners | • Expansion of English instruction (ESOL) and bilingual programs (teaching content areas in the native language) to include all eligible students |
| • World language elementary | • Three class sessions each week with a native speaker, overseen by the classroom teacher |
| • Alternative school calendars | • Changing the school calendar to distribute instructional time over more calendar months, and/or avoid the need to construct additional buildings; longer days to support student learning. |
| • Providing alternatives for disruptive students | • Provision of learning settings for students with behavioral problems that will address their special needs and reduce classroom disruptions |
| • Enhancing teacher and principal effectiveness | • Time and training to allow all teachers to continually upgrade both content knowledge and instructional methods<br>• Extra support for the schools making the least progress in student achievement |
| • Assessment/testing | • Development of citywide finals and elementary literacy and math assessments<br>• Test administration and scoring<br>• Training staff in new measurement methods |
| • Parental/family engagement | • Printing and translation costs for outreach efforts<br>• Communications outreach<br>• School council training |

| Domain | Performance Standards |
|---|---|
| • Attendance, safety, health | • Full-time nurses in all schools |
| | • Additional psychological and social services |
| | • After-school programs |
| | • Safe corridor programs |
| | • Anti-drug, anti-violence programs |
| | • Increased security |
| | • Attendance outreach |
| | • Technological supports for attendance and health monitoring services |
| • Transportation tokens | • Funding to allow the city to provide free transportation to income-eligible students who live over one mile from school |
| • Improvements in existing buildings | • Funding for facility renovations to prevent ongoing erosion in the value and utility of school buildings |

Source: *Reaching Higher (1995), School District of Philadelphia.*

These opportunity to learn standards were widely distributed throughout the community and became the basis of our program and budget planning. They were designed to be incorporated in a manner that supported the promotion and graduation requirements laid out below. There were implementation details and costs identified for each.

One opportunity to learn standard that we did not explicitly include was competitive pay. We knew the cost of such an initiative was beyond our means to even contemplate at that time. We did include substantial funding for increased time for teachers for professional development and for planning meetings, which we used as a resource for pay increases in return for a longer school day in the 2000 negotiations. However, we did not include as much funding for teacher pay as we believed necessary. This was a failure of our nerve.

At the time, we felt that we were having such difficulty convincing the powers that be of the most rudimentary needs of students, that it would be absolutely foolhardy to suggest that we pay the teachers substantially more. This was especially true in light of the union's resolute opposition to any semblance of accountability. If we had done what we should have done we would have mounted an aggressive campaign to make the public assertion of the need for substantially higher teacher salaries, in return for increased accountability, prior to the 2000 negotiations. At the same time, we should have altered radically the nature of the compensation system.

In developing the opportunity to learn standards, we promised that we would not enforce the educator accountability standards or the student accountability standards in 2000 and beyond if citizens did not meet their accountability standards. In fact, when higher fourth- and eighth-grade promotion standards were slated to go into effect for school year 2000–2001, we had insufficient funds to meet the obligations to the students we had pledged in 1998. I took the position that we had to follow through and suspend the promotion requirements.

The first and second impulse of the board was to maintain the requirements despite the absence of the necessary supports. We spent hours in closed-door sessions arguing strenuously. The board, of course, was sensitive to the inevitable charge that we were lowering standards by not enforcing them for promotion. We understood this concern but to focus on it was to be blind to the fact that to do otherwise would be to wholly absolve the citizens of Pennsylvania and Philadelphia of their responsibility or accountability. We adults were again prepared to impose high stakes on children—they are not organized and they don't vote—but we were not prepared to hold our fellow adults to high standards.

In the end, the board kept faith with its original policy. It agreed to commit resources adequate to enforce the fourth-grade promotion standards for June 2000, but suspended the eighth-grade standards for lack of support. Had the lack of support continued, the policy would have also required the suspension of educator responsibility. The central point is that the connections between student, educator, and citizen accountability must be explicit and coherent.

## Student Accountability

Student accountability is the third leg of the accountability stool. Historically, in most districts it has been the only operational leg. There is no hesitation to impose rewards and penalties on students in the form of tests, grades, promotion, graduation, and a host of other positive and negative incentives. In the first grade, we give smiley faces and stars; later, participation in sports and other extracurricular activities is dependent on a student's behavior and academic performance.

Most educators, whether teachers, school administrators, or central office, believe that high stakes for students is not only the way it is but the way it should be, arguing that if rewards and punishment are not tied to behavior and academic performance, there is far less likelihood that students will work as hard, focused, and smart as they otherwise would. We educators have ignored the irony in insisting on accountability for our students while resisting it for ourselves.

In Philadelphia, while we felt that educator accountability must be the first branch of accountability to be implemented, and that citizen accountability should accompany student accountability, we also believed that students should rise to the challenge of accountability, too.

We announced an eight-year phase-in of the student accountability system; it would commence in the fourth year of the educator accountability system (2000) and be fully implemented in year twelve (2008). The requirements, which applied for admission to grades 5 and 9, and for graduation, included three categories: grades, projects, and test scores. A student had to satisfy all three requirements. Grades were included to recognize the importance of ongoing classroom work and of teacher judgment. Projects were included to ensure that more project-based instruction would take place, and to recognize kinds of learning not often assessed in public schools. Test scores were included to ensure that consistent high standards would be met.

The board initially adopted requirements in 1998 effective for June 2000, remaining at the same levels for June 2001, and rising for June 2002. The plan was that these would continue to rise in 2004, 2006, and 2008, as more supports were put into place and as the student cohorts who had had the supports from the early grades moved through the grades. Thus, the student accountability requirements would increase parallel to the increasing supports (citizen accountability) and the rising performance index targets (educator accountability).[10]

### Test Score Alternatives

It is important to note that while each student had to receive an acceptable score on a test, we were not satisfied with a single score on a single test on a given day. When the stakes are this high for individual students, it is critical that there be multiple opportunities to pass, and that tests not be limited to the formats that are currently available for standardized assessments. For these reasons, and in order to have city-wide assessments that were more sensitive to ongoing instruction than the standardized tests could be, we set about developing two additional sets of tests.

### Second Chance Tests

For the elementary students, we developed "second chance tests" in reading and math. The purpose of these tests was to identify students who, despite not meeting the standard on the SAT-9, could demonstrate that they knew the material at the required performance level. For reading, we developed a holistic test that was administered individually, and consisted of reading passages and responding verbally to comprehension questions. The math assessment was administered in small groups, and included use of manipulative materials and other approaches designed to address alternative learning styles. Both the reading and math alternative tests were given to students who, despite their low scores on the SAT-9, were performing at a C level or better in the classroom. Professional staff from outside the school who were trained in administering and scoring administered them. These resulted in substantial increases in the numbers of students meeting the standards.

### Citywide Finals

For the upper grades and for graduation, we began developing a set of citywide finals for grades 8–12, beginning with reading, math, and science. These closely tracked the standards and the curriculum frameworks. They heavily emphasized constructed response items. The test results were required to count as a percentage of the teacher grade, to begin the movement toward more consistent grades. Students who performed satisfactorily on them could substitute these scores for the standardized test score requirements.

## CONCLUSION

In Philadelphia, we began to implement new graduation and promotion standards four years after we began implementation of the educator responsibility system, and simultaneously with the citizen accountability system as measured by the opportunity to learn standards. I now believe that we did not go far enough toward ensuring that the system was prepared to teach all students successfully before we imposed significantly higher stakes on the students. Even with our delay of student high stakes, it was still quite possible for high stakes to apply to students before educators had made the changes in program and attitude that would be required to have students be successful.

The argument supporting our actions was that if a school staff were not successful, the educator accountability system of sanctions would begin to change the school's practice and, in the extreme circumstances, the school staff, until they began to get it right. However, while this several-year process was underway, a lot of students in any given school would be failed, left back, pushed out, dropped out, and/or not graduated. As noted earlier, in retrospect, I now believe that the implementation of high stakes for students should be delayed until each school or small learning community has demonstrated that it can be successful with its students.

There are clearly other accountability models. There are those who believe that simply establishing a punitive system in which teachers and principals in particular are punished if they do not produce desirable results will whip them into shape and get better results. Others believe that publishing test scores will sufficiently embarrass school staffs that they will improve their performance. Still others focus exclusively on what they refer to as "professional accountability." This relies on the idea that the intrinsic value system of a professional is such that if the person has sufficient training, time to think and plan, the opportunity to work with colleagues of a like mind, strong support from administrators and the system, and the authority to make decisions, that a sufficient sense of accountability will be at work in each person that there is no need for a system of extrinsic incentives, positive or negative.

A common mistake is the tendency to think that only one or two of these accountability systems need to be in place. Some only want to impose accountability on the educator, others think that sanctions on students are sufficient, and others embrace the view that if citizens produce enough money, all will automatically fall into place.

The point we wish to emphasize is that all three accountability systems are necessary. This idea is different from the oft-heard proposition that "everyone is accountable." The proposition that everyone is accountable is almost never accompanied by standards, rewards, sanctions, or other consequences attached to student performance. An accountability system does not exist unless there is some sort of positive and negative consequence attached to achieving or not achieving the desired end result.

A discussion of accountability sharpens the idea that all the component parts discussed in this book are necessary to effect the radical changes required for all students to perform at world-class levels. We need well-designed accountability systems that are interconnected for educators, students, and citizens. We need those accountability systems built on standards, assessments, curricula, and tools of the classrooms that are aligned. We need students coming to school ready to learn from families that are respected by the school system, and we need systems of organization and structure, including collective bargaining agreements to be such that the best of teacher professionalism is emphasized.

Accountability is simply one lens through which one can arrange or design the other necessary parts of the system. Indeed, a main message of the theory of action behind this book is that one can begin the analysis of the school system through any of its component parts, and be led inevitably to all of the others. That is the way that one should think about what components are nonnegotiable parts of a school system that is designed to be successful with all students.

A final point. In Philadelphia, a common charge against us was that making all these changes simultaneously was unrealistic. It was unrealistic to expect that much new money; it was unrealistic to think that educators could learn all of what is implied in these very large areas of change; it was unrealistic to think that the business community or the political power structure or the teachers union would come together to support that much change.

What is really unrealistic is to think that children, all children, can learn to high levels unless all of these things do come together. The critics were right. We did not get the money; many stakeholders had trouble embracing all the components at once; the business, political, and labor communities remained split. And while there was a huge improvement in student performance during the six years I was superintendent because we were able to get many of the interconnected factors contributing to student achievement all moving in a synergistic manner, in the end, the fact that we were unable to sustain this change ensured that all students did not move to a level of performance that I would find satisfactory for my grandchildren. Unfortunately, we were right also. The cycle of failure arising from these self-fulfilling prophecies continues.

## NOTES

1. This term is the one used in Philadelphia during my administration to describe a K–12 feeder pattern of schools. The terms *subdistrict* and *region* are other comparable terms.

2. The term was coined by Richard Elmore, and supported by the Cross-City Campaign for Urban School Reform, an organization that enables reform leaders from inside and outside school systems to share information, mount collective efforts, and create a national voice for public schools.

3. I recognize that No Child Left Behind as originally enacted effectively provides that there will be one-year accountability cycles. My hope is that as Congress and the president propose changes in the law based on experience, they will learn that annual cycles are too frequent.

4. A serious flaw of the NCLB accountability system is that it provides no significant expectations or sanctions beyond the district level. The feds set the standards and are not required to help; states identify districts and schools that are not measuring up but there is not way that state departments of education, chief state school officers, legislators, or governors are held accountable if a proportion of schools or districts do not meet annual yearly progress goals even though heads can roll at the district and, especially, the school level. These are the facts even though every state is the responsible party for producing education for its children and the federal government has assumed responsibility by passing an act like the NCLB.

5. It should be noted that the teacher's union officials were referred to by their national as "dinosaurs," and the principals had voted, based on differences with an earlier administration, to become the only Teamsters Union principals bargaining unit in the nation.

6. This term is used to describe a process in which students continue to attend school at the same building, but most or all of the staff are changed, and new educational programs are implemented.

7. The district had a high school choice program in effect before I arrived, as a result both of desegregation programs and special admission schools. While about half of the students districtwide attended their neighborhood high school, at Audenried, the proportion was far smaller.

8. As we write in 2008, the New York City School System, which has included in its accountability system the same premise that even relatively high scoring schools are expected to make progress, is experiencing the same controversy that we did—and, like us, is holding firm.

9. Bear in mind that while schools were only eligible for rewards or for identification for the process at the end of each two-year cycle, schools in the process could emerge from it in the interim years if they went at least halfway to their two-year target.

10. The reader will find the details of graduation and promotion requirements at www.childrenachieving.com.

# 9

# Quality Teachers

The difference between a good and a bad teacher can be a full
level of achievement in a single year.

Eric Hanushek

One-half of the achievement gap between black and white
students would disappear if poor and minority children had
the same quality teachers as other children.

Ron Ferguson

My granddaughter Holly entered kindergarten in the Philadelphia public schools in 2001. Her kindergarten experience was not a good one,
because the class had to endure five different teachers. As soon as a relationship between Holly, her parents, and her teacher began to
emerge, the teacher was gone, and new relationships had to be built.
As the teachers changed, so did the behavioral expectations. The
rhythm of the school day and the dynamics of the classroom community changed five times. Each new teacher had to take time to learn
the strengths and needs of the class as a whole, and of each student.
All of this was imposed on a group of children who were experiencing
"real" school for the first time.

Despite their strong commitment to public education, my son and
daughter-in-law, unwilling to tolerate a rerun, seriously considered
sending her to a private school for the first grade. Then they found out
that the public school class to which Holly was assigned was taught
by someone whom "everyone" considered an outstanding teacher.
They decided to stay and were delighted with the result. I tell this
story to underline the fact that for generations parents have known

there are good teachers and worse or bad teachers, and they have fought to give their children the advantage of the good ones. Parents know teachers are not fungible. And they know that providing quality teachers to all students is an essential learning condition if all are to learn to high standards.

## THE IMPORTANCE OF HIGH-QUALITY TEACHERS

In the last decade, educational research has caught up with what parents have always known. Eric Hanushek, for example, concludes that "the difference between a good and a bad teacher can be a full level of achievement in a single year" (quoted in Haycock, 1998, p. 3). Ron Ferguson has determined that "one-half of the achievement gap between black and white students would disappear if poor and minority children had the same quality teachers as other children" (quoted in Haycock, 1998, p. 3). William Sanders, the pioneer of value-added testing in Tennessee, has shown that elementary grade children taught math by the best teachers improve their performance far more than children taught by the worst teachers (Sanders & Rivers, 1996).

The impact of high-quality teachers persists over time. The gains in achievement from one highly effective teacher are still present in student test scores two years later. In one metropolitan district, William Sanders and June Rivers found that students taught by very effective math teachers for three straight years performed on average at the 83rd percentile level, while those with the least effective teachers were on average at the 29th percentile level (Sanders & Rivers, 1996, p. 12). Furthermore, struggling students benefit the most from effective teachers. The students in the district who had been lowest-performing at the beginning of the study gained an average of forty-six points after three years of highly-effective teaching. The second-lowest group gained thirty-three points, the second-highest group gained fifteen, and the highest-scoring group at the beginning of the period gained fifteen points (Sanders & Rivers, 2006, p. 9).

The importance of having good teachers cannot be overstated. The gains in performance that result from high-quality teachers can make the difference between students being assigned to remedial classes and students being identified as gifted. Kati Haycock has observed that the teachers we assign to our students can determine whether a student goes to a four-year college or flips hamburgers for a living (Haycock, 1998, pp. 4–6). If the importance of having quality teachers is indisputable, the issue becomes how to produce the necessary numbers of effective teachers, how to retain them, and how to increase the odds that the best teachers are teaching the students most in need.

What constitutes the essential elements of teaching knowledge? Or put it another way, what qualities would you like your child's teacher to possess? The National Commission on Teaching and America's Future says,

> when we speak of "highly qualified beginning teachers," we mean teachers who:
>
> - Possess a deep understanding of the subjects they teach;
> - Evidence a firm understanding of how students learn;
> - Demonstrate the teaching skills necessary to help all students achieve high standards;
> - Create a positive learning environment;
> - Use a variety of assessment strategies to diagnose and respond to individual learning needs;
> - Demonstrate and integrate modern technology into the school curriculum to support student learning;
> - Collaborate with colleagues, parents and community members, and other educators to improve student learning;
> - Reflect on their practice to improve future teaching and student achievement;
> - Pursue professional growth in both content and pedagogy; and
> - Instill a passion for learning in their students. (2003, p. 5)

## CREATING HIGH-QUALITY TEACHERS: PRE-SERVICE

How are such qualities developed? Where do we recruit, train, grow, and identify people with the qualities of a good teacher? We examine here certification, alternative routes to teaching, and professional development.

### Certification: Teacher Training Institutions and the Role of the States

Teacher training institutions are much maligned, often with good reason. A university's school of education is its least highly regarded division, tolerated because it generates more cash than it spends and is therefore a net income producer for the institution. Much of this income comes from part-time students who are pursuing credits and degrees in order to qualify for higher rungs on district pay ladders. Teacher candidates are rarely among the best-prepared students coming to the campus measured by their SAT scores.

The states seldom contribute in significant ways to ensuring that all students have good teachers. While certification standards established by the states are slowly beginning to require true competence in subject matter and in pedagogy, there remain many questions about the rigor of state standards for teacher training institutions. For example, forty-eight of the fifty states require only fifteen weeks or fewer of student teaching, and twenty-nine require ten weeks or fewer. Thirty-six states claim to identify low-performing teacher training institutions, but only fifty-seven such programs were identified in 2001–2002. Forty-six of these were concentrated in five states. The National Council for the Accreditation of Teacher Education is the premier accreditation body in the country. Nevertheless, only 67 percent of the teacher education graduates in 2001 graduated from NCATE accredited programs (*Education Week*, 2003, p. 92). Only five states hold teacher training institutions accountable for the performance of their graduates.

States have done little to make sure that all teachers are qualified to do their job. Some would argue that certification requirements are worse than useless when they create the illusion that graduates have the qualities of a quality teacher.[1]

### Alternative Paths to Teaching

According to *Education Week*, as of 2003, twenty-four states and the District of Columbia had established alternative routes to teacher certification. Although all twenty-four states require that these alternatively certified teachers have bachelor's degrees, and all provide training before and mentoring during the first year, other aspects of these programs vary. Only thirteen of these programs include classroom experience as part of the training. Eighteen require entrance exams of their candidates, but just ten require candidates to exhibit mastery of their subject through standardized tests. Eleven states seek teachers for subjects, like math and science, with shortages of teachers, but only three—Massachusetts, Missouri, and Texas—have programs "designed specifically to place teachers in high-needs schools" (*Education Week*, 2003, p. 58).

### Teach for America

Teach for America is one of the most well-known alternative routes to teaching. Founded by Princeton graduate Wendy Kopp, TFA recruits from the graduating classes of the most competitive colleges and universities in the country and places new teachers only in urban and rural school districts where there are concentrations of students who are particularly challenging. In 1999, 86 percent of the corps members were leaders in college. They had an average GPA of 3.4, and average SAT scores of 1248—about three hundred points higher than the national average. In addition, 36 percent of TFA members were people of color (Kopp, 2000, p. 51).

Still, some studies have found that students of Teach for America teachers perform no better than the students of other "underqualified" teachers, and that the students of neither perform as well as the students of qualified teachers (Laczko-Kerr & Berliner, 2002). Other studies have found that while Teach for America teachers are not "magic bullets" under whose direction student achievement soars, their students perform at least as well as the students of other new teachers hired by the school district in the same year (Raymond et al., 2001).

In 2007, over 90 percent of principals surveyed said that the Teach for America members were at least as effective as other new teachers and made a positive contribution to their schools and that they would hire them in the future (Policy Studies Associates, 2007). All else being equal, I would much prefer to hire teachers with the strong college records of TFA members, who *also* had strong pedagogical training, several months of student teaching, and knowledge of child and human development. But given the severe shortage of teachers for high-needs schools we cannot always have what we want and need. During the last three years of my tenure in Philadelphia I began each school year with two to three hundred classrooms with no teachers. I would have been happy to fill all those spots with TFA members.

A final word on Teach for America. Of the five thousand members who participated in the first decade of TFA, 60 percent remained in education, and 37 percent of those in teaching. Of the 40 percent who left education, many found themselves in leadership positions elsewhere in society. It is my experience that, to create effective citizenship, there is no substitute for first-hand experience with the strength and struggles of the poor. These thousands of TFA members who do not stay in education carry with them for a lifetime an insight that is valuable to their role as citizens and will benefit public education through the generations.

## In-Service Professional Development

Our beliefs about education must frame the way we look at professional development.

Teachers must believe that there is a positive connection between teaching and student performance if they are to be successful.

When I first went to Philadelphia I said that we must believe that the children we teach can in fact learn what we teach them. After a brief period, I changed my language saying that we "must believe or act like we believe." I did that for three reasons. First, we would all be dead and buried before everyone's actual belief system changed, so we could hardly frame that as the starting point. Second, I concluded that in many parts of our lives, our beliefs arise out of what we do, what we experience, not out of what we profess. Third, it is quite possible "to live as though," "to act like," to "behave as if." Acting or behaving like we believed that all children could learn to high standards became the basis of policy development for us.

Accountability systems can be built "as if" all students can learn to high levels; standards can be set, assessment systems adopted, and curricula chosen on the principle that minorities, English-language learners, and poor children have the capacity to learn what we teach them. Teachers and principals can learn to exhibit high expectations behaviors. If we are only "acting like," the immediate result will probably not be as good as actually "believing," but the longer and more deeply we act, the fuzzier the line becomes between acting like and believing; and one day, each of us makes the crossover, as our new experiences with children increasingly become self-fulfilling prophecies, creating a new reality.

If a student fails, however, our operating assumption must be that some aspect of the student's education must have been lacking. Educators should then acknowledge that they need help, and administrators and central office staff should acknowledge that they need to provide teachers and principals with the support, professional development, and tools they need to succeed with that child, class, or school. We need to create a radical openness to quality professional development. Historically, professional development has been seriously underused, and is often one of the first programs cut in times of financial austerity. Skeptics of professional development argue that teachers learn all they need to know in college or on the job. This incorrect view is reinforced by the frequently shoddy programs that pass for professional development. Often, the little time that is devoted to professional development occurs after long days of teaching and is taken up with announcements and other business not related to instruction that is better suited to faculty meetings or e-mails. Instruction is the heart of the profession. It is what we should develop.

## WHAT GOOD PROFESSIONAL DEVELOPMENT
## SHOULD LOOK LIKE

In "Professional Development: The Consensus View," Richard Elmore says that good professional development:

- Focuses on a well-articulated mission or purpose anchored in student learning of core disciplines and skills.
- Derives from analysis of student learning of specific content in a specific setting.
- Focuses on specific issues of curriculum and pedagogy.
- Derives from research and exemplary practice.
- Connects with specific issues of instruction and student learning of academic disciplines and skills in the context of actual classrooms.
- Embodies a clearly articulated theory or model of adult learning.
- Develops, reinforces, and sustains group work.
- Requires collaborative practice within schools.
- Networks across schools.
- Involves active participation of school leaders and staff.
- Sustains focus over time—continuous improvement.
- Uses models of effective practice.
- Occurs in schools and classrooms.
- Keeps practice consistent with message.
- Uses assessment and evaluation.
- Involves active monitoring of student learning.
- Includes feedback on teacher learning and practice. (Elmore, 2002, p. 7)

### Implementing Good Professional Development

Since we know what good professional development looks like, the next step is figuring out what it takes to make high-quality professional development the norm in all schools. Superintendents, school boards, school administrators, and legislative bodies must use professional development to provide reasons for teachers to believe that the failure of certain students need not be permanent. Schools and districts should ask themselves several questions. Is there a vision and a coherent mission for the school or district? Are there clear standards? Does the assessment system measure the standards? Is the curriculum aligned to the standards and the assessment? What has the administration done to demonstrate they know that instruction is central to the mission? Is there time for teachers to learn through quality professional development, and is this time prioritized, and not just squeezed in around other things?

Is professional development connected to instruction? Are compensation and other incentives built around quality instruction? Does the administration help teachers solve the daily challenges to providing high-quality instruction? Is there competent school staff dedicated to facilitating teacher learning, offering suggestions, teaching model lessons, observing classes, and giving constructive feedback? Are schedules arranged so that teams of teachers have the opportunity to integrate, scaffold, and build on the skills on the team? Having set the framework for good professional development, let me address more directly several of the major issues that arise around this topic.

What counts as professional development? Real professional development is designed to improve learning outcomes for the children with whom a teacher is presently working or expects to work in the near future. It is not career development, although it may contribute to career development incidentally. It is not personal development or a morale booster, although good professional development may contribute to both. Professional development is directly related to whether one's students know what they are expected to know and can do what they are expected to do, as measured by the rigorous standards that define expectations for the student and the teacher.

Given those criteria, who should determine the content of the professional development that is offered? This depends largely on the capacity at the school level.

In a school that is making the achievement progress expected of it, the key decision-making about professional development for teachers can be made by the school itself. Generic professional development is less useful than professional development directed at the concrete needs of a faculty in a particular school. Professional development for a school faculty should be grounded in specific needs, and shaped by the strengths and weaknesses of specific people in specific schools working with specific students. In schools that have demonstrated the capacity to make independent progress, these decisions are best made by the principal and teachers within the school itself.

However, in order to make good decisions, the teachers and principals need to be able to identify the strengths and weaknesses of their students through observation and data analysis. They must know each other well enough to perceive and describe strengths and weaknesses in the faculty, creating a supportive atmosphere in which teachers can be developed without feeling judged. And they must have the resources and connections to be able to find those who can help provide them with the professional development they feel they need.

Teacher input in the content of professional development is important, but the decision should not always be left up to the teachers. In the case of a school where children fail over time to make sufficient progress, professional development should be designed under the guidance of people outside the school, who have knowledge of the school's needs and expertise in designing training. As noted in the section on school-based decision-making (chapter 12), freedom to make decisions does not in itself lead to improved performance. If a faculty does not know how to improve its own effectiveness and its children are not succeeding, giving them the authority to make independent choices runs the risk of perpetuating failure.

Neither school faculty nor school administration always has enough knowledge to make these decisions. Across the country, the culture of most schools does not encourage the development of these capacities. Many school districts veer to an extreme, either dictating all professional development in a top-down way, or letting the schools make all their own choices with no oversight or guidance. Ideally, faculty should work in concert with administration for these decisions. There needs to be a web of support.

The self-knowledge necessary to make professional development decisions is itself something that can be improved through professional development. Increasing evidence suggests that the single best professional development investment a school district can make is to bring in an outside facilitator, coach, or school-based professional developer who can help a faculty identify its professional needs, and then deliver the needed development activities.

**Implementation Models**

My first experience with these outside professionals helping at the school level was as part of the Kentucky Education Reform Act in 1990, which provided that the state commissioner of education would be able to place "Distinguished Educators" in schools that were persistently failing with their students. These educators were to be the "best of the best," identified and chosen each year through a rigorous process. Each distinguished educator continued to teach in his or her home school unless assigned to a school or district in need and, if assigned, spent between six months to a few years giving direction to improve student achievement in the particular school or district. "Giving direction" was not barking orders; it meant leading by example and developing capacity. Though already regarded as experts, the class of

"Distinguished Educators" went through a rigorous, multiweek training process to further develop their capacity.

One of the first commitments I made during my tenure in Philadelphia was to provide "instructional facilitators" to assist with every school. The action design called for one facilitator for every three small learning communities. Every school would have at least one facilitator, and many schools would have several. We began to build a Teaching and Learning Network (TLN)[2] in every cluster, each with about fifteen facilitators. The facilitators would have different strengths, content expertise, and pedagogical strength. Each facilitator would work primarily with small learning communities in a single school, providing professional development, classroom demonstrations and observation, and support in the identification of instructional best practices. They would rely on the others in the network for additional strength and capacity.

We were unable to build the network we envisioned. We did not have the funds for the number of facilitators we projected. We could only provide one facilitator for every three or four schools, except for the largest cluster, for which we obtained a $13 million grant from the William Penn Foundation for more. We assigned sixteen facilitators to this cluster, which had sixteen schools and between thirty and forty small learning communities—a slightly higher ratio than called for by the action design but close. Although the cluster's performance was disappointing during the first year, in each of the three subsequent years, it came in either first or second in student performance among the twenty-two clusters. I would ascribe an important part of that performance to the facilitators.[3]

There are several final points that need to be made about professional development. Time for professional learning must be built into the school year, and it must be ample. Policy-makers should accomplish this by adding paid workdays to the teachers' year. Absent adequate time to learn and hone one's craft, instructional time will be far less productive. To underline the point, I believe that it is better, if necessary, for the students for teachers to have ten days of high-quality professional development time and the students to have 170 days of classroom instruction than for the students to have 180 days of instruction while the teachers have no high-quality professional development time. That forced choice ought not be necessary, but since budget exigencies exist, I make the point to be clear how important high-quality professional development is to student learning.[4]

Professional development must focus on both pedagogy and content. Expertise in a subject does not mean that one knows how to create the conditions that result in student learning. At the same time, one cannot teach what one does not know, no matter what pedagogical skills one has. Year after year, a huge proportion of classes—especially science and math classes, and especially in districts with students with whom we have historically failed—are taught by teachers who have not mastered the content of their subject matter.

Effective professional development must be an iterative process. It starts when a teacher learns about a particular strategy or content area, ideally by seeing it practiced in the classroom of an expert. Next, the teacher tries the strategy out. This is most productive if an expert is there giving feedback, providing coaching, and occasionally demonstrating the practice. The teacher repeatedly practices to build the new skill for normative classroom work, to learn how to adapt the strategy for a range of students with different learning styles and challenges, and to understand how to combine it with other instructional strategies. All of this takes time and support as these stages of effective professional development are repeated.

The on-going analysis of student work is a particularly powerful tool in professional development. We have to be familiar with the range of advanced, proficient, basic, and unsatisfactory student work to be able to recognize it when our students exhibit it. An indispensable strategy of good professional development is the analytical and reflective review and evaluation of student work. In this process, teachers study the characteristics of "anchor papers" or "anchor work" that have been graded by experts and that exemplify various levels of proficiency.

Teachers then sort the work of their students based on what they have learned, and someone skilled in the analysis critiques this sorting. Groups of teachers then periodically sort and analyze their students' work to help them understand what instructional strategies they employ that result in the most success with their students. This process is an example of a student-centered instructional activity that aligns standards, assessment, accountability, curriculum, and instructional strategies.

Professional development is not a series of discrete experiences. It is continuous. What follows should be connected to what occurred before. Content must be connected to pedagogy and vice versa.

Finally, it is useful to point out that the most successful professional development system is one in which groups of teachers grow into a continuous learning community, when learning and application of new skills becomes routine, when formal professional developments are seen as vehicles for the staff to use a new lens or framework to think about their continual learning process, and where every teaching experience is also a learning experience that the faculty member can share with his or her colleagues.

## COMPENSATION AND PROFESSIONAL DEVELOPMENT

Nationwide, our biggest professional development investment is in the higher salaries we pay to teachers as they accumulate additional credits and degrees. Many districts across the country also pay for teachers to get these credits and degrees. However, the degrees and credits have little if any demonstrable relationship to improved instruction and student outcomes. The funds dedicated to paying those with the additional course work could be far more productively spent on sustained, intensive professional development activities that are directly related to the assignment of the teacher involved.

To that end, Philadelphia began to move toward a system of compensation based on the work of Allan Odden, a professor at the University of Wisconsin–Madison. My first contact with him was in Kentucky, where the legislature adopted a compensation system based on his work. Schools became the unit of measurement, and teachers could receive bonuses of as much as $1,500 based on the performance of the students in their school. It was not individual merit pay; rather, it was additional pay that everyone on a school team could receive based on the improved performance of students in the whole school. This pay-for-performance system was part of a larger systemic change strategy that included a large new emphasis on professional development.

In late 1999 and early 2000, as part of our preparation for renegotiating the collective bargaining agreement with the Federation of Teachers, I asked Odden, in consultation with our director of human resources, Marj Adler, and a team of district and union representatives, to design a plan for Philadelphia that would address four issues. First, we wanted a system that paid teachers based on their skills, knowledge, and ability to create student achievement—not for the degrees that they held or the number of years they've worked. Second, the pay scale had to create incentives for continuous learning and improvement of knowledge and skills. Third, the system needed to fit with our accountability system and other incentive strategies we wanted to develop. Fourth, we needed to increase teacher salaries substantially. Our salary schedule was noncompetitive with the schedules in the surrounding sixty-one school districts that constituted our recruitment market area, impeding our ability to attract and keep the most talented teachers. We knew we needed to spend more on teacher salaries, and we wanted to spend this money as effectively as possible by basing salaries on the performance criteria above.

The plan Odden proposed met these criteria, and in the ensuing contract negotiations was used as a backdrop to the creation of an "enhanced compensation system." Details for implementing the system were left largely undefined, subject to continuing conversation after the contract was signed. After my departure, much hard work was done on designing and piloting the system, but the new leadership in Philadelphia eventually let it drop, due to ongoing union opposition.

## INSTRUCTION-BASED COMPENSATION

It is clear that the four compensation-related issues laid out above require a solution if every child is to have a quality teacher. We developed an approach that can work. While it is different in some of its details from the proposal Odden made to the district, it draws very heavily on that model.

The new compensation system is framed by six basic categories of knowledge and skill that build on one another. They begin with the Apprentice level, which is at the entry level with an initial professional license, satisfactory performance on a basic content and professional knowledge test, and subject to peer assistance, mentoring, and induction. A teacher then progresses through the categories of Novice, Teacher, Career Teacher I and II, and Accomplished Teacher.

The standards for each successive level are more and more rigorous. If designed correctly, most teachers will spend a career at the Career Teacher I or II level. Teachers at the Career Teacher II and Accomplished levels can earn more than many administrators in a district, thereby permitting the teacher to remain in the classroom and enjoy relatively high compensation. This system would ensure high levels of pedagogical and content skill related to student performance.[5]

## OTHER TEACHER CONTRACT ISSUES

### Teacher Assignment

If a state's certification system is based on the knowledge and skills necessary to create teaching and learning conditions in which students meet the requisite standards of academic achievement, if there is adequate and appropriate professional development, and if the compensation system creates incentives for continuous teacher knowledge and skill development, a district will have improved substantially the likelihood that every student will have a highly qualified teacher. Indeed, the teachers that would emerge would be at a higher threshold of excellence than is common today.

However, in the short run, we are still challenged by the fact that the most highly qualified teachers tend to teach the privileged and advanced students who are least in need of their talent, and the least qualified teachers tend to have responsibility for the most challenging students. Districts must take steps to ensure that the students in greatest need have the most highly qualified teachers. That will require a combination of the following[6]:

- Substantially higher pay for teachers who, through choice or assignment, teach the students most in need of their abilities.
- Better working conditions in schools with great need. This includes smaller class size, professional working space and support, more time to plan with colleagues, and extra assistance in dealing with the family and community challenges their students face.
- The elimination of seniority as a determinative factor in the placement of teachers.
- The ability to adjust teacher placement based on student need.
- An accountability system that rewards rather than penalizes teachers who teach in the most difficult schools.

## CONCLUSION

The quality of teachers will determine the quality of education students receive. One can have good books, facilities, and technology, high standards, sound assessment instruments, good mental health service, and the other tools of education, but without a teacher who knows the subject matter and knows how to teach, a student is unlikely to be well educated. Nothing sums up the opportunities and responsibilities of teaching and the imperative that citizens ensure it better than the famous quote of Christy McAuliffe, the astronaut who died in the Challenger, "I touch the future . . . I teach." Teaching will make the difference for the individual, the family, the community and all that flows from them.

## NOTES

1. A report from the Baltimore-based Abell Foundation stated, "Maryland's requirement that individuals must complete a prescribed body of coursework before teaching in a public school is deeply misguided. This process . . . is neither an efficient nor an effective means by which to ensure a competent teaching force. Worse, it is often counterproductive."

2. The TLN was part of our Office of Schools, which served both line and staff functions in relation to the schools.

3. See *Evaluation Report: Children Achieving* (William Penn Foundation, 2001). This report is based on evaluations done by Econsult Corp and Teachers College of Columbia University.

4. I have two comments to add. First, I have referred to time or its resource equivalent. The point is that a school or district does not need to mete out professional development time in a straight line, so many days for each teacher, one size fits all. To refer to time or its resource equivalent is simply a budgeting device. Second, many successful industrialized nations provide much more time than we do in the United States for teachers to learn and to engage with one another. In Japan, for example, it is not unusual for Japanese teachers to have student class-based contact time that is as little as half of the time they are on the job. The other half of their work life is spent learning, planning, and relating to parents and the wider community. It is understood that the teacher is still "on the job"; indeed, teaching and learning cannot occur as productively without these support activities.

5. The reader can review a description of the compensation system at www.childrenachieving.com in a model collective bargaining contract.

6. The No Child Left Behind Act provides a much faster timetable than my comments anticipate for having a highly qualified teacher for every child. I predict that either the types of supports I suggest here will be required or the definition of highly qualified will erode or the federal government will overlook noncompliance as it has overlooked the fact that many states use Title I to make up part of their own failure to adequately and equitably fund schools, not for genuinely compensatory education. When race, language, and income are at play, the federal government is not often much better than the state and local offenders in protecting the affected children other than to issue edicts without support.

# 10

# Quality School Leadership

Management is doing things right; leadership is doing the right things.

Peter F. Drucker

John Merrow, PBS's veteran and insightful education observer, followed *Children Achieving* closely for its six-year history. This led to several national productions focusing on our education reform efforts in Philadelphia. The last one, reflecting on the role of the superintendent, was titled "The Toughest Job in America" (Merrow Report, 2000b). Merrow, for all his skill as a journalist, was wrong about this point. As hard as a superintendent's job is, the positions of teacher and principal, especially in high-poverty settings, are tougher.

The commitment, the energy, dedication, compassion, intelligence, and sense of humor of many of the principals I worked with in Philadelphia were inspiring. In recent years, my understanding of and sensitivity to the challenges and pressures of the position has been further enriched through the experiences of my two sons, both of whom are school principals in urban Baltimore.[1] There is no profession to which society owes more respect and gratitude than that of school principal, especially in urban areas.

The principalship is particularly demanding and complex at this time in our history. A principal is faced with the opportunities and the pressures of outcome-based systems, in which accountability for increased student achievement rests at the school level, and therefore with the principal. This is particularly challenging because in many cases, the principal has relatively little power. Short on power but faced with high expectations, the principal is on the proverbial hot seat. Furthermore, increased diversity of students and staff creates new challenges, from increased cultural awareness to understanding of instructional responses to language and learning differences. Meanwhile, the principal must adapt the educational program to deal with the profound effects, both positive and negative, that technology is having on the learning process.

There are many reasons that finding, retaining, and supporting good principals is difficult. In addition to the challenges of meeting achievement and accountability goals, principal compensation is often little more than what is paid to teachers and, in the eyes of many, is not enough to compensate for the stresses and responsibilities of the job. Principals frequently put in twelve- to fifteen-hour days, and work weekends and during the summer (often despite not being paid for those days). An inordinate amount of a principal's time is dedicated to essential yet frustrating tasks, from dealing with plumbing that doesn't work to tracking down supplies that have not arrived. The pressures from the community can be staggering. And if the principal is unlucky enough to be in a school where he and the union representative do not see eye to eye, the ongoing task of building a school team can be daunting. However, if all children are to meet high standards, high-quality school leadership is an essential learning condition.

## PERSONAL QUALITIES

Effective principals must possess several key personal qualities in order to perform their job effectively.

### Vision and Passion

The principal's job requires a vision of what the school needs to accomplish and how to achieve it. This requires a passion that creates a sense of urgency and generates energy.

### Communication and Listening Skills

A principal who cannot listen with respect and a genuine attempt to understand is in the wrong job. While not needing to be an eloquent toastmaster, a principal needs to be articulate and to have the presence to hold an audience of staff, students, or community members.

### Resilience

A principal has to be able to see the good in staff, students, and parents. Principals must overcome frustrations, thrive on small wins, and bounce back from repeated defeats without losing hope.

### Grit

Grit is a mixture of perseverance, intensity, courage, and heart. It is needed to endure the day-to-day work that must occur if vision and passion are to be translated into reality. A measure called *GRIT* developed at the University of Pennsylvania has been shown in preliminary studies to be a better predictor of occupational success in a variety of fields than measures like tested intelligence, talent, or grades (Duckworth et al., 2007).

## ORGANIZING THEMES AND ROLES

Principals play an enormous number of roles, emphasizing different ones depending on their personal strengths and the needs of the school. These roles are not played in an orderly or independent manner. Some overlap, while others compete; some can be planned for, and many become necessary on the fly. Their relative importance can be dramatically changed by unanticipated events, from sudden imposition of new district policies to a violent incident in or near the school. A principal must be skillful in balancing all these demands.

Nevertheless, there are themes that can be used to provide a loose framework for thinking about how an effective principal operates, and which can be used to inform programs intended to develop and support their effectiveness and professional growth. Useful organizing themes are (1) providing an instructional vision, inspiration, and goals; (2) ensuring the primacy of instruction; (3) improving staff productivity and growth; (4) increasing resources; and (5) monitoring and managing.

All of the themes and roles described below must be carried out in order for a school to succeed. However, that does not mean that a principal must personally carry out each of them. Rather, it is the responsibility of the principal to see that all staff understand the values and mission of the school, and then to orchestrate effective implementation. Many of the themes are impossible to carry out successfully without cooperation from and delegation to staff. Shared leadership increases the effectiveness of the principal by drawing on the strengths of multiple staff members. It improves the quality of decisions and staff investment in them, and creates time for the principal to focus on areas of special strength.

The examples provided below are drawn from Philadelphia and from other urban areas facing similar challenges.

## Providing an Instructional Vision, Inspiration, and Goals

A principal needs to understand the big picture and be able to energize the staff to work together toward shared goals. The principal may derive authority from statute and the school board, and gain technical knowledge from training and experience, but the principal derives leadership standing and shapes school culture from the ability to passionately communicate a vision based on a sense of what is right and just.

### Inspirational Leader

There are several ways a principal can provide inspiration. The principal is pivotal in determining the belief system and vision of the school. If the principal acts on the belief that all children can and must learn to high standards, that belief will orient the moral compass of the school toward the intertwined values of excellence and equity. These values dictate that teachers' assignments take into account student need, that curriculum is based on high expectations, that professional development enhances the skills necessary to succeed with all students, and that the principal protects the teacher who has done something unconventional in the reasonable belief that the action was necessary on behalf of students.

Passion differentiates the principals who merely do their job from the principals who feel a sense of mission and purpose. Does the principal model hopefulness daily? Serve as an example of "going the extra mile"? Act with high expectations of students, staff, and self on a daily basis? If the principal feels and communicates the vision passionately, that feeling will spread throughout the school.

I worked with many Philadelphia principals who were passionate in their belief that all children can learn to high standards, and understood how to connect their vision to the district's standards, assessments, and accountability system. Rather than complaining about accountability, they expressed confidence in the capacity of their students and staff, and used the accountability framework to concretize the vision and create a sense of urgency around it.

A principal also reflects values in the way students, staff, and community members are treated. Is the school a place of tolerance and respect for those who may be different from the majority? Are destructive gestures such as offensive bathroom graffiti quickly removed? Do parents feel welcomed into the building? Does the principal know each child by name? Do teachers feel that their needs are understood? The visionary, passionate principal will see the child as the center of a picture that requires a synergy among parts to make the result productive.

## Ensuring the Primacy of Instruction

A principal must treat instruction as the first priority, devoting to it all possible resources, attention, and protection.

### *Instructional Leader*

The best principal will usually be an instructional expert. She must be able to demonstrate and identify good teaching, must be able to organize a sound professional development program for the school's staff, must know what works and what doesn't in her particular school, and must have a repertoire of strategies so that she can engage meaningfully in problem-solving efforts with faculty around individual children. Principals need not be catalogs of every possible instructional strategy, but they do need to be comfortable with and conversant in the pursuit of the very best instruction for the children in their school. Instructional leadership can be shared with other faculty members, but the best principals will almost always play a strong role.

Unfortunately it is the norm for principals to spend many days in a week doing almost nothing that is directly related to improving classroom instruction. Even a principal with a strong orientation toward instructional leadership can go to work intent on observing and coaching teachers, meeting with faculty about student progress and staff development, but find himself delaying those tasks to deal with a fight that happened on the bus, an angry parent, or a lack of substitutes to cover the day's teacher absences. It is also easy for planning to relate more to the logistics of running a building, having the garbage picked up, or assigning lunchroom duty than about promoting the instructional growth of staff. Ensuring the primacy of instruction requires understanding and prioritizing other activities of the school so that everything serves instruction.

### Strategic Leader

The role of the strategic leader is integrally related to that of the instructional leader. A principal must strategize and set priorities to determine how all the efforts of a school synergistically fit together to emphasize that the school is a learning community and to focus on classroom instruction. Many observe that the best leaders are able to "see around the corner," just as the best teachers can "see what goes on behind their backs." For example, the principal needs to foresee the consequences of different sets of faculty, student, grade, and schedule assignments. These decisions must be "strategic" to optimize results.

Strategic leadership demands maintaining focus. There are many wonderful initiatives and activities that could indirectly contribute to student learning or school climate, to community contact, or valuable changes. However, time and energy are finite. A grant to support an activity that was not part of the school's vision and plan might feel like an additional resource, but unless it can be adapted to align completely with school priorities, it will in fact be a resource-wasting distraction. The opportunity to attend a conference may contribute to professional growth, but an effective principal makes sure that what he is likely to gain is more important than what he will miss while he is gone.

In Philadelphia, one of our best high school principals made it his business to model the strategic interconnection between instruction and the budget, and to involve others in the annual budgeting process. He displayed the budget prominently in the faculty lounge, including an analysis of total dollars going into a number of functions. Faculty members were struck at how many school resources were allocated for security, and were willing to see some of those funds redirected to instruction, even being willing to take on some additional duties related to security such as hallway or lunchroom responsibilities in a manner that was contrary to strict interpretation of the contract.

Strategic leadership is employed in decisions about the use of space. What room assignments improve student movement? How do we resolve competing needs for space for particular student activities versus needs for locations where staff can meet together? How can we ensure that space assignment represents student and faculty need—not staff seniority or habit?

Strategic leadership involves knowing when to fight and when to fold. There is a principal with a strong instructional background who faced a dilemma during the summer following his first year as principal. In a marked improvement from its recent performance, the school had met its annual progress goals under the No Child Left Behind Act. In addition, for the first time in several years no teacher asked to be transferred because as one of them commented, "this is the first time in years that I felt hope."

However, the principal then learned that because of the previous years of failure in the school, it was on a list of schools mandated to use a different instructional model. At the time, the school had been using the Direct Instruction method, which the young principal might not have chosen but to which the staff had dedicated much time and energy to learning. The principal, recognizing the investment faculty had made in the model fought against the change in a reasoned but assertive way on behalf of the staff and children. As a consequence, the school was permitted to continue its successful practice, good instruction was preserved, and the leadership role of the principal in the eyes of his staff was enhanced. For this and other reasons that school has met its annual achievement goals every year since.

### Data Expert

Part of instruction leadership is the design, collection, and interpretation of data on student progress. This role has become increasingly important in the past ten to fifteen years, both because we know more about the importance of measuring ongoing progress, and because of the growing prevalence of high-stakes accountability. The principal must ensure that the measures used on a daily basis capture the most important features of student learning, and that there is ample opportunity for staff to review these data together and use them to generate instructional strategies.

She must also understand the meaning of the tests used as accountability measures. Judgment becomes critical, as priorities must be negotiated between the achievement of short-term and long-term goals. Results must be presented to the community in a logical way. Balance must be struck between noting weaknesses to spur improvement and heralding strengths to encourage hopefulness.

### Change Agent

Change does not occur easily or automatically. Many people resist change, but even those who desire it may not be able to provoke it if the culture in a school is committed to the status quo. The principal has the chance to create the expectation of continuous improvement, built on the idea that there is no such thing as "good enough." That means change and improvement must be constant. Ronald Heifetz (1994) compares this process to using a pressure cooker: The principal has to turn up the heat but needs to monitor it to keep it from blowing.

The principal must make a series of difficult decisions to set the right temperature for change. He must understand that change does not occur in a vacuum. If one attempts to provoke change without also being moral leader, instructional leader, good manager, and team builder, success as a driver of change will be much more difficult.

### Scheduler

In Philadelphia high schools where there were as many as three thousand students and over one hundred teachers, there were hundreds of classes to roster. Indeed, every high school had a staff person dedicated to this task. But in all schools the scheduling buck finally stops with the principal, since a successful schedule is crucial to a successful school. The schedule determines how and when faculty and staff are deployed, which students are assigned to which teachers, how smoothly and safely lunch and passage time can occur, and how coordination with cleaning and transportation crews is arranged.

The principal must ensure that the schedule is created to provide the best possible instruction, and not for the convenience of the staff with the most seniority. This includes making sure that there are not large numbers of class periods where teachers are diverted to roles such as discipline or ordering supplies, thus raising the size of classes taught by others.

### Disciplinarian

When we were children, the principal's role as disciplinarian was burned into our brains with the image of being sent to the principal's office. Dealing with bad behavior certainly is part of the principal's job. But a principal's responsibility to ensure good behavior begins with setting the tone for conduct in the school and the culture within which discipline is meted out. Is the environment constructive? Consistent? Respectful? Fair? The culture around discipline will be a significant factor in determining the nature of classroom management, the community's perception of the school, the moral and citizenship lessons children learn, and the satisfaction with which staff come to school everyday. Discipline is thus tied to classroom learning.

A favorite story from Philadelphia concerns a principal in a high-poverty school that regularly outperformed the level its demographics predicted. He had a large chart in his office that graphed each student's progress in relation to reading on grade level. When a student was sent to his office for misbehavior, he would begin by asking them to find their place on the chart. Those who were below grade level were immediately told that they had no time for fooling around—they had lots of catching up to do.

## Improving Staff Productivity and Growth

The sine qua non of effective instruction is a quality staff. Helping teachers to continuously improve their teaching skills and enlisting the full talents and energies of all staff are essential to effective school leadership.

### Team Builder

Schools are successful when the faculty adopts the attitude that they are a team, and that their responsibilities do not stop at their classroom doors. The success of a third-period teacher hinges, in part, on what happened during second period. The success of the fifth-grade teacher is determined in part by the success of the fourth-grade teacher. School climate is determined by how the faculty and staff work together to manage hallways and lunch periods. The longevity and success of new teachers flow in part from the mentoring and guidance they get from the veterans.

There are many ways to build a team. Vision and passion go a long way toward inspiring teamwork in support of shared goals. Staff social gatherings and team-building exercises can be helpful. In the end, though, the principal, through the respect and involvement accorded faculty and staff, will set the tone. Team building requires listening, consistency, patience, clarity, firmness, and a set of operational standards. In a personal interview with Christopher Mark Gaither, one of my two sons who are principals, he commented that it is important for the faculty to unify around positive attitudes, not common enemies like unreasonable parents or the central office of the district.

### Buffer

When the central office makes a decision that impacts the school negatively, a member of the community wants to do something detrimental to the school, a parent makes unreasonable demands of a teacher, or a teacher's attitude negatively affects the school team, the principal must step in and take the lead in sorting through the dilemma to the best end result possible, allowing the teachers to keep their attention focused on instruction.

## Counselor

Staff and community rely on the principal to be a counselor, sensitive to personal circumstances ranging from abuse to disease to crime. The challenges in this regard are endless. The principal is also likely to play the role of mediator in school-related disputes, and must have the skills to reduce conflict and develop a reputation for fairness.

## Supervisor and Rating Authority

However much a principal builds shared leadership, establishes a sense of team, and provides personal guidance, in the end she is also the rating authority for the staff. This authority, if exercised with fairness, instructional emphasis, and courage, can make an enormous difference in improving staff productivity and growth. A key task for a principal is to help struggling teachers develop the knowledge and skills they are missing, and if this fails, to deliver an unsatisfactory rating.

For the large majority of staff who range from competent to excellent, the observations required by most school districts can be an important tool for growth. The evaluation form itself needs to reflect the values of the system—less about straight rows and silent children than about evidence of engaging instruction, student work, and instruction tailored to student need. Evaluations can include a section that reflects evidence of student progress, thus promoting an opportunity to connect instruction to outcomes. The process should be a tool for keeping both the principal and the teachers focused on instruction.

## Increasing Resources

Maintaining the best possible stewardship of the budget provided by the school district is critical when looking to increase resources. Inspiring the best efforts of everyone on staff in the service of student learning is also crucial. However, there are also ways to reach beyond the school building for important forms of support.

### School Spokesperson

The principal is the face of the school. He represents the school to the media, to the central office, and in meetings with the local police officials and social service officials. The principal takes responsibility for the newsletter and other communications that are sent from the school to the parents and wider community. The principal conveys the personality of the school, and can make or break its reputation as a successful place, a friendly place, and a place that is seen as an asset in the community.

### Community Liaison

Schools have to find ways to succeed with all students, even when parents choose not to be involved—but every educator knows that it is much easier to succeed with involved parents than without.

There are multiple ways of filling this role with parents. The times when parents have the opportunity to meet with teachers must be varied—some during the day, some during the evening, some specially arranged at a time mutually convenient to principal or teacher and parent. Communication, verbal and written, needs to be in a language understood by the parents.

Fund-raising can also be a way of building links with the local community. One of our principals, who quickly became a cluster leader, was a whiz at this. For example, for one fund-raising effort she set a high goal, and told the Home and School organization that if it were met, she would throw a party in the gym for the parents, and dance on the table. It was—and she did, complete with fishnet stockings.

While parents are the first community to which a principal must pay attention, good relationships with the wider community are also important. Schools are important community institutions. Indeed, the local school is often the place around which communities are built. Children are well served by living in communities where the residents share a sense of responsibility for the common good. Faith communities can be wonderful sources of volunteers, and many do or will run free after-school programs. Local businesses can not only shoo students out the door at school opening time, but also make contributions—in-kind or financial—to address school needs.

The principal of one inner-city majority Latino school holds daily "morning meetings" for parents, students, and staff. Not surprisingly, there is a strong sense of community cohesiveness around the school. That same school holds festivals and other community events, making the school a center of community activity. It generates significant volunteer support from the community including people without children in the school. The principal ends up spending many weekend days at the school working alongside the parent community volunteers. Another school has an extraordinary newsletter that, in addition to typical newsletter fare, celebrates student and faculty accomplishments and meets a variety of community interests by including recipes, restaurant ratings, and movie reviews. A school in a low-income neighborhood has built an upscale playground through a special partnership with a local home improvement business. The only limitation to community outreach is a staff's and principal's imagination.

### District Meeting-Goer

This role can be important as the principal needs to be aware of district requirements. It can also be a vehicle for collegial learning and support. Nonetheless, it is a source of irritation for many principals. Part of the resentment arises because the content of meetings is sometimes irrelevant to what the principal needs. A second reason is that so much of what passes for principals' professional development is of poor quality. And third, this poor-quality development takes up time that could be better spent on pressing responsibilities at the school. If I ever again assume the role of superintendent, a major priority will be to reduce circumstances that take a principal out of her building during school hours to an absolute minimum.

### Political Schmoozer

This is an often unpleasant, but necessary role. For the principal, key officials are the state senator and representative, a city councilperson, school board members, and sometimes a congressperson. The relationship between schools and elected officials is complex. Elected officials often desire the good will of those connected to the school, since they make up a large group of constituents. The elected official will want to be seen as helpful to education in general, and the constituent school in particular. On the other hand, schools often have to curry favor with particular politicians to get the resources they need when they need them. This relationship is most constructive when ways are found for the officials to visit the school, to become invested in its success and well-being, and to create the circumstances in which the elected officials know the school personally. This can lead to a long-term increase in resources and constructive intervention when problems arise.

### Student Advocate

A school must be an advocate for students who need help from the community's health, social, and mental health services. This requires that someone establish a network of connections with various agencies, refer and then fight for their students, and monitor whether needs are being met. A strong counselor or social worker will ideally fill this role, but the principal must also be involved in establishing and nurturing the network, and being a "big gun" when there is need for it.

### School Advocate

The principal is an advocate for the school itself in dealings with the district's central office. Especially in large districts with inadequate resources, a principal must often be a "squeaky wheel" to deal with urgent and persistent managerial problems. She may also need to find ways to resist district directives that do not meet the needs of her students, or otherwise divert energy from more important activities.

An example is provided by a new principal who, when he arrived during the summer, was confronted with the prospect of losing several teachers based on projections of declining enrollment in the school. He was confident that the projections were wrong, but his budget had been based on the lower projections. When he approached central office, he was told that if the projections were inaccurate he would have the number of teachers restored—but they would not be the same teachers whom he had lost. So, the principal refused to turn in his budget until the school year began, so that in proving the projections wrong he could keep the same high-quality, experienced teachers who had become important parts of school culture. Courageously, he sat on the budget until he was proved right.

I realize many superintendents would view such behavior as insubordinate. But I would argue that when confronted with a situation like this, a superintendent should look at the situation from the perspective of the principal, and loosen up requirements if the principal is acting as strong leader and advocate for her school. We need to give our principals the space to be leaders.

## Monitoring and Managing

When vision has been developed and communicated, strategic decisions have made instruction the priority, processes for staff growth have been established, and resources have been secured, a principal still must engage in the ongoing tasks of management and monitoring. In this, resilience may be the strongest necessary attribute.

### *Manager*

The principal is responsible for the effective use of millions of dollars and scores of people. She manages custodial, security, transportation, food, community, and social services. Even in a relatively small school, a principal will supervise a few dozen employees, a budget of $2 million, and a facility that must be cleaned, heated, cooled, and kept secure. This managerial role often relates only indirectly to the principal's central role in focusing on instruction, but it needs to be mentioned prominently because it takes up so much of a principal's time and attention. If the boiler breaks, the roof leaks, the special education student's cab breaks down, or there is a suspected case of child abuse that must be reported to social services, the urgency of the situation tends to preempt whatever classroom evaluation, demonstration lesson, or instructional leadership meeting might have been scheduled.

Many principals' chief complaint is that they don't have enough time in the classroom when, in fact, they consider classroom supervision to be their most important job. And it is also often these managerial tasks that keep principals working late at night or on the weekends. An important part of the solution is a central office that solves school-identified problems promptly, reducing the number of times a principal has to identify a problem or issue. That will become highly productive and, likely, less expensive.

### *Default Decision-Maker*

The buck stops with the principal. Even when a decision should be in the purview of someone else in central office or in the school, when those decisions fail to get made, they fall to the principal by default. These decisions a principal ends up making are almost never pleasant—

if they were, someone else would have already made them. But the decisions are necessary. Is the mark on a child a sign of abuse that should result in social services being called? Should a child be suspended or sent back to class? Which staff will be assigned to cafeteria duty? Who is going to talk to the parent about the child's behavior? These decisions often fall to the principal, no matter whose technical responsibility they are.

### Monitor

A staggering number of balls must be juggled to keep a school going. A principal needs to know what has to get accomplished by when, and what progress has been made. She also needs to make sure that delegated responsibilities are taken seriously, and that plans are actually implemented. Sometimes this necessitates a major change in the culture of a school.

Monitoring may also require setting new priorities and course corrections. Extra support services may need to be moved from one class to another, depending on where progress is slipping. Some activities may have to be dropped because others have become urgent, and there is not time and/or money for both. These are tough and sometimes lonely decisions.

### Synergy, Authority, and Leadership

However well the principal performs these roles, the school will be effective only if she is a good "orchestra leader," knowing when, where, and to what degree each role needs to be emphasized. The synergy among roles determines the success of a school.

The success cannot arise from a principal's effectiveness in only one or two roles. The successful principal develops the school through leadership rather than authority, a distinction articulated by Ronald Heifetz (1994, p. 2). One cannot create an effective school team and positive climate by ordering that it be done. It may be expedient to be the authoritative manager rather than the leader, but at best it produces short-term results. The energy and momentum in a school must become self-actualizing, greater than the sum of its parts. This occurs when competent faculty and staff feel empowered in a climate of trust with a commitment to common goals and outcomes.

Richard Neustadt points out that "'leadership' for Heifetz is distinct from the positions of authority which usually are thought to be its starting point" (quoted in Heifetz, 1994, p. xi). A principalship is a position of authority in which one can also exercise leadership within the school, with peers within the school's external community, and even with those in the hierarchy at authority levels normally considered to be the principal's superiors. Heifetz's rules apply to anyone who wants to get something done in the company of others (Heifetz, 1994, p. xi).

> Leadership doesn't necessarily have all of the answers. Leadership may, rather, be a call to address tough problems, change attitudes/behaviors and values. As in music, dissonance is an integral part of harmony . . . leadership is not a position [of authority]. It is an activity that results in others wanting to accomplish things for the common good. It may even involve challenging authority. Leadership is a moral concept, arising from one's values. (Heifetz, 1994, pp. 1–9)

Success in a school arises from the degree to which the school leader, driven by her values, creates synergy among all the actors to bring powerful coherence among the parts in a timely manner. The principal is both engineer and artist. The challenge is to create a culture in which moving parts are aligned and coherent.

Heifetz also makes the useful distinction between providing technical direction and leading adaptive behavior. Technical behavior deals with the routine. It gets one through the day with a minimum of disasters. But adaptive behavior is the product of leadership. It is reading the situation well. It requires imagination; it involves seeing around the next corner. But it also requires a high degree of accuracy. "To produce adaptive work, a vision must track the contours of reality" (Heifetz, 1994, p. 24).

*Children Achieving* was built on the premise that educators must "act like we believe that children can learn to high levels," expecting that such a belief would become a self-fulfilling prophecy, thus changing the culture of expectations in the district. The culture needed to change, but authority could not mandate such a change. Instead, it required leadership from many people at many levels.

Heifetz's thinking also leads to the conclusion that real leadership may arise from or even require conflict or disequilibrium in contrast to always pressing for traditional or technical solutions to problems, especially long-standing ones. Sometimes people don't even know there is a problem. The first step of leadership may be to surface the problem, which inevitably will create unease if not conflict. It follows that if one is struggling with a problem and suddenly everyone feels good, the problem has likely been swept under the proverbial rug with symptoms, not causes, dealt with (Heifetz, 1994, pp. 43ff). The single biggest example of our attempt to deal with such an issue in Philadelphia was the effort to raise conversation around race to a conscious level and address its broad and deep impact on many aspects of the district's work.

Generally, race is too painful a subject to address directly in most of our society. Yet in the context of our commitment to all children (80 percent of ours were minority children) and our underlying value of equity, we believed it important to discuss race, beginning with the top leadership. To that end, with help from a terrific facilitator, Linda Powell, we made race a centerpiece of our annual summer multiday learning retreat of the cabinet that consisted of the thirty-five most senior administrators in the district. We then made sure that we returned to the issue on an ongoing basis in our monthly cabinet meetings throughout the year. We pursued this pattern over a several-year period.

We discussed everything from curriculum and assessment bias to staffing patterns to relative results of cluster leaders' evaluations of principals. We reviewed together many kinds of disaggregated data, including not only achievement results but also patterns related to admission to and dismissal from special programs, suspension and expulsions, and access to adequate facilities and instructional materials. We had these discussions in the group as a whole, in race-alike small groups, and in small groups that were racially diverse.

There were tears and anger and hugs. It was difficult; it was not always constructive in the short run; it was very important to do. People learned things about themselves as well as the group dynamics of such discussion. We began to get at deeper issues that each of us lived with in our schools and communities on a daily basis. We were determined to grow as a community, to place ourselves in a position in which we were better educators and better leaders. I think most of us emerged from the several-year conversation feeling more responsible in our effort to deal with what is the most difficult issue in America.

The preceding example involved central office leadership, but the principle is equally important at the school level. The distinctions between authority and leadership, and between technical fixes and adaptation, get at the core of a principal's job. Some actions, some of the time, in some roles, necessitate a principal exerting authority to mandate technical fixes. But real change occurs when leadership helps the whole learning community identify and focus on the needed changes in culture and practice, and work together toward those changes. When that happens, students learn. A principal I know describes these moments as "when the future looks brighter; when it works; when it's coming together; when it's working for faculty and children alike . . . it's not just the numbers; if it's just the numbers you know it won't be sustained; it's when one knows the culture has shifted; that's when you are grateful you became a principal."

## SCHOOL LEADER PREPARATION

I believe that it is possible to be a successful superintendent with no regular classroom experience. I was such a superintendent, and though I believe it is much more desirable to have classroom experiences, a superintendent's job can be accomplished without them. On the other hand, it is difficult, if not impossible, to be a successful principal without successful classroom teaching experience. The role of instructional leader requires a principal to have practiced the art of teaching first-hand. Of course, not all high-quality teachers make good principals; the roles are different. When looking for principals, school districts should hold out for successful teachers who understand why they were good educators, and have the talent and skill necessary to perform the other roles demanded of the principal.

Training programs leading to state certification for principals are often bad. As with too many masters programs for teaching, a large proportion of those enrolled take evening or summer classes and base their schedule on convenient class times and light workloads rather than on the skills that they need. State departments of education set course requirements with little basis in research that would establish a connection between the courses and successfully running a school. As Mark Tucker and Judy Codding observe, our certification system meets the needs of everyone but students. The institutions of higher education have their cash cows, the principal candidates get certification and higher salaries with little effort, and the school districts have a ready supply of people who meet certification requirements, arbitrary as they may be. Too often, this route to leadership fails to produce people who are able to create the conditions and culture within which learning takes place (Tucker & Codding, 2002, pp.1ff).

In contrast, a number of excellent principal and leadership development programs have arisen in the past three decades. The Principals' Center at Harvard and that of the Gheens Professional Development Academy in Kentucky were both established in the 1980s. In the early 1970s, when I was serving as executive deputy secretary of the Pennsylvania Department of Education, we established the Executive's Academy with Secretary of Education John Pittenger's leadership. When I became state superintendent in Maryland in 1976, I asked Herman Behling to design and build a Maryland version, but limited to principals. There are now more quality programs such as these.

Another excellent program was the Aspiring Principals Program in Providence, Rhode Island. A collaboration between the Providence School District and the University of Rhode Island, it was a two-year, competitive selection program with three tracks. In the formal academic track, the sixteen students in the cohort participated in a weekly class with university, district, and guest faculty. The cohort was expected to attend other district professional activities, such as sessions with the Institute of Learning at the University of Pittsburg. In the second track, the cohort focused on in-depth, hands-on mentoring opportunities. Each member of the cohort with which I am familiar had the opportunity to work full-time for a semester with each of two mentor principals. The student principals were thus exposed to two skilled and experienced principals, to observe different leadership approaches and styles.

The third track, which many of the sixteen found most valuable, consisted of a variety of formal and informal settings for the student principals to work together. Each member of the cohort had been chosen for the program because they were quality educators and most had some sort of successful administrative experience. Thus, they brought a wealth of insight to share to each other.

## PHILADELPHIA'S EXPERIENCE

A program for a different level of leader was developed out of necessity in Philadelphia. At the start, sixteen of the twenty-two cluster leaders we appointed did not have a superintendent's certificate, which meant that by law they could not evaluate principals. We did not envision the cluster leaders evaluating the principals in their clusters even though, for some purposes, we did envision the cluster leader to have line responsibility for the work of the principal. We thought the relationship that we wanted to create between the cluster leader and the principal might be thwarted if the principals saw the cluster leader as an authority figure charged with determining whether they received a raise or not at the end of each year.

After about a year, we realized that we did need to vest evaluative authority in the cluster leaders. Since most of the cluster leaders did not have the superintendent's credential required under Pennsylvania law to evaluate principals, we went to Acadia University, which had an approved Superintendent's Certificate program from the State Department of Education. We asked them to design a special program that would meet the state standards, but in an accelerated time frame and with content that reflected the Philadelphia context. They helped us deliver a quality tailored program that allowed all of the cluster leaders to obtain the requisite certificate within six months.

We also built a homegrown principal development program. We believed we had to create our own "farm team" because the routine principal prep programs in the colleges and universities did not do an adequate job for us. Marilyn Moller, who had run a program for aspiring principals before I came to Philadelphia, codesigned our new program with Chris McGinley, who had moved from his job as cluster leader to support principal development from the central office. *Children Achieving*, with its emphasis on school-level decision-making and increased accountability, made principals more important than ever before. It was out of that redefinition of the nature of the principalship and school leadership that the Leadership in Education Apprentice Design (LEAD) program was born.

LEAD provided growth opportunities in nine areas:

- Organizational Development and Climate
- Assessment of Instructional Programs
- Supporting Teacher Growth and Success
- Addressing Issues of Equity
- Coordination and Design of Services for Children and Families
- Planning and Governance
- Communications and Community Relations
- Evaluation, Problem-Solving, and Resource Management
- Leading and Managing Personnel

The LEAD program provided constant evaluation and feedback to the candidates. The program began with an entry assessment, and concluded a year later with the candidate's presentation of her portfolio to a review committee. The portfolio included biweekly evaluations done by two mentor principals, as well as site-visit reports from each apprentice assignment. The review conference always included the program director, LEAD staff, and both of the mentor principals.

The program also used the Interstate School Leaders Licensure Consortium standards as one reference point for the design of the program. Participants read extensively and attended weekly seminars conducted primarily by district staff that anchored many of the other experiences the apprentice was having in district policy and practice.[2]

Apprentice principals who demonstrated strength and expertise through the LEAD program joined a pool of people eligible to be appointed to be principals and assistant principals. Those who fell short were eligible for additional experiences through an individualized personal development program. When they achieved the requisite qualities they could join the eligible pool.

Many successful LEAD candidates came from the ranks of teachers who had served at the regional and then cluster level in positions variously called facilitators, instructional support teachers, and so forth. They linked schools to districtwide instructional and equity goals. In addition to organizing and providing staff development, they worked closely with principals and school leadership teams in data interpretation, school improvement planning and execution, and the design of school-based professional growth activities. This experience led many to become highly effective principals.


## SELECTION OF SCHOOL LEADERS

Selection is always a challenge. Homegrown candidates have the advantage that they know the culture, and their superiors know them and have observed their performance. But additional steps can be helpful. In Maryland, we established a partnership with the National Association of Secondary School Principals (NASSP), using the NASSP Assessment Center model they had launched in 1975 with the assistance of industrial psychologists and the American Psychological Association. In this model, an assessment director trained by NASSP leads teams of six assessors, who evaluate twelve aspiring principals in an intensive process. Candidates are asked to role-play in a variety of challenging situations. Based on their performance, using an NASSP scoring rubric, the evaluators issue both a numeric score and a narrative evaluation (Tucker & Codding, 2002, p. 366ff). This extremely rigorous evaluation became a required component of school administrator certification.

We used the Assessment Center process as part of LEAD in Philadelphia, not as a determinative factor in the selection of leaders, but to inform our judgments about the suitability of people for particular jobs. We also used the results to design particular continuing professional development opportunities and to place candidates in the position to design their own training/development opportunities in an informed manner.

## DISTRICT SUPPORT OF SCHOOL LEADERS

There are several important tenets that guide the provision of support to principals:

- Select leaders with care. Careful choices prevent setting someone up for failure.
- Provide on-going professional development that includes instruction and mentoring support for all of the roles expected of the principal.
- Provide a mentor for new principals, as well as continued support for experienced principals. Every principal needs a relationship with someone who deeply understands the multiple roles and the stresses of the job, and whose first instinct is to support the principal.
- Back the principal up. Too often, central office will acquiesce to the demands of politicians, parents, and other outsiders, who often make unreasonable demands of the principal or seek personal favors.
- Give the principal significant authority in making the decisions that will determine whether his school is successful in educating its children.
- Make sure that the priority in the use of the principal's time is for the principal to be in her school.
- For a new principal, it is helpful to provide a manual of the most frequently asked questions, with advice and suggestions from other principals.
- Employ a governance model that protects the school.

### Philadelphia

One of the single most important initiatives we took to support principals in Philadelphia was to abandon the old district organization, which had an average of thirty-six elementary, middle, and K–8 schools within each of six regions plus a separate region that contained all forty-two high schools. The new district organization was a cluster system, with an average of twelve schools in each. Each cluster had six to eight elementary schools, two or three that included the middle grades (including K–8), one comprehensive high school into which students would feed (unless they applied to go somewhere else), and one all-city competitive admission school.

That number and configuration of schools, representing a feeder pattern of students in grades K–12, allowed all the principals to gather regularly at the same table and become a brainstorming group of colleagues, a support group, a learning community. Most of the principals developed a commitment of accountability and support among one another and with the cluster leader and a sense of loyalty and joint responsibility that marks small communities of any kind that have a common mission. These twelve or fourteen leaders in a cluster met often. The meetings were informational, but they were, more importantly, designed to be instructive and helpful directly and emotionally around all of the roles that the principals had to play.

They mapped out clusterwide strategies and plans of professional development for themselves (and for the teachers and other staff in the cluster). For example, the University City cluster, under the leadership of Janet Samuels, participated in a two-year professional development program, designed by Lauren Resnick at the Institute of Learning; the Kensington cluster, led by Nilsa Gonzalez, conducted intensive studies of cluster and school data, as well as creating a course on thinking skills and brain research in which the schools in her cluster participated.

Cluster meetings were also the setting in which principals thrashed out clusterwide approaches to the central office about common facility or commodity and materials purchases or staff development needs. In some instances, a cluster would present a strong challenge to a central office practice. These were sometimes fairly strident instances of advocacy; however, despite the discomfort they could cause for us at the central office, they were an important part of our commitment to giving the schools more voice, and making the central office "client-friendly."

The small number of principals in each cluster was crucial in the cluster leaders' capacity to support the effectiveness and growth of the principals. In the previous regions of thirty-five and more schools, the leadership could do little more than "drive-by" supervision. By contrast, cluster leaders, with twelve or fourteen sites, knew each school well, provided personalized coaching, mentoring, and support to both new and experienced school leaders, and conducted an evaluation process that was formative as well as summative. Nearly all of the cluster leaders had been principals prior to being asked to assume the leader's role.

There were other, smaller ways in which we supported principals in their work. A fun and instructive moment was the Principals Convocation that started off each year. There was always a great buzz at the Convention Center over coffee as the day began. I would give a state of the schools address that emphasized the priorities for the year. That was followed by an address by an educational luminary. In most of the years we gave each principal a copy of a book that the speaker had written. Then the principals broke up into clusters, and the balance of the day was spent with the cluster leader and her principals beginning the year's collaboration.

Unfortunately, we were unable to support our principals by extending their contracts from ten-months to full-time. To have been able to make them full-time would have contributed significantly to opportunities for professional growth, school readiness, and relationships to the communities, parents, and students they served, but we could not afford to do so. However, we took major steps to increase school and principal control over their school's budget, a process that had begun under my predecessor.

Beyond the basic teacher allotment, which was assigned based on school population, we stopped assigning positions (e.g., one secretary, two nonteaching assistants, one reading specialist), and instead provided equivalent dollars. This meant that the school could make its own trade-offs, eliminating positions that were not serving the students as well as other positions and/or programs could. This practice made it possible for a principal to lead the school in focusing their budget on the instructional priorities that grew out of their achievement data and the other needs of the students, and also provided an incentive for staff to make their activities as useful as possible to the students.

Equally important was a policy change in the determination of the teacher allotment for each school year. Every district struggles annually with the number of teachers it will need in each school at each grade. In most districts across the country, this number is determined in the spring, so that teachers and principals are clear on who will be where in the fall. However, large urban districts often have to deal with considerable student mobility, as well as contractually determined teacher transfer rights, which combine to create a large and ongoing churn in the teaching staff of those schools that teach the students in most need.

This churn starts in the spring, when many teachers receive layoff notices due to uncertain state funds, and continues through the summer as those who are called back have to apply for existing vacancies, which may or may not be at the school they were in. However, even worse is the fact that, on my arrival, I learned that in Philadelphia the process was not completed by the opening of school. Rather, in the interest of ensuring that no school had more teachers than the minimum required by the union contract (thus minimizing costs), the numbers of teachers at each site was not finalized until the end of October or even the first part of November.

This would result in another round of dislocation in which teachers were forced to leave their own building, and transfer to the vacancies in the sites that were gaining staff. Thus, large numbers of classes had to be reorganized, to adjust to the new number of teachers in the school, and many students had different teachers two months into the school year.

At the beginning of my second year, I simply decreed that this "leveling" process would take place at the end of the second week (even that is a dumb way to run a school district—it's just better than doing it twelve weeks into the year). That, of course, cost about $5 million since it meant that there were many schools with an "overallocation" of teachers due to the uneven enrollment that naturally occurs. But the move was hugely supportive of students, teachers, and quality instruction, and helped principals immensely.

A second illustration of the way we tried to support principals was to change the manner in which work orders from schools were handled. In my initial round of twenty-two meetings with the cluster leaders and principals in each cluster, the single most often heard complaint involved maintenance, routine and major, from broken toilets to leaking roofs. Principals were justifiably frustrated and angry at the time they had to take away from their instructional roles to fight for the basic adequacy of their buildings.

The process in place was that principals filed paper work orders, which were to be dealt with in the order they were received, except in cases of urgency. There were a number of problems with the system. The paper-based work orders were often lost. In addition, neither the cluster leaders nor the principals had a way to track their orders. There were orders that were several years old; in some instances this had resulted in costly deferred maintenance.

Another serious problem with the work order system was the favoritism that resulted from the intervention of politicians, board members, or senior central office personnel. The best way to move to the head of the line was to get someone in power to call the facilities office.

We improved the facilities situation by automating the work order system, making it transparent and setting up schedules that fixed reasonable expectations for problem resolution. We also went a long way toward eliminating the political fix by setting a procedure of review that the facilities office was required to follow for approval of any special request coming from a senior administration official, a politician, or a board member. The result was a systemic improvement that permitted principals to spend less time on such things as well as getting things done faster and with greater quality.

## CONCLUSION

Success as a principal requires technical knowledge. It requires understanding the rules and regulations of the system, and how to work with human resources, stay within the bounds of the union contract, formulate the budget, meet the minimum standards of community involvement, construct a professional development day, put out a newsletter, and articulate the component parts of an evidence-based instructional strategy. But as Terry Deal and Lee Bolman observe, "the heart of leadership lies in the hearts of leaders" (Bolman & Deal, 1995, p. 6). That's where the extra mile, the next ounce of energy, patience, and courage lies. It's the heart that makes the difference.

## NOTES

1. Matthew is in his sixth year as principal of Hampstead Hill Academy, a pre-K–8 school (he added the middle years), where he has improved achievement and made the school such a center of community pride that it has a waiting list to enter. Mark now in his fourth year at Wolfe Street Academy, also pre-K–8, the only majority Latino school in Baltimore (Mark is Wolfe's first Spanish-speaking principal), achieved Adequate Yearly Progress every year (the school was on the federal watch list when he arrived). Both schools are Title I schools; 85 percent of Wolfe's students are eligible for free and reduced meals, and Hampstead Hill is at 82 percent. Both are conversion charters that consider themselves very much part of the Baltimore City Public Schools, with strong instruction programs and outreach to the community.

2. Additional information on the LEAD program can be found at www .childrenachieving.com.

# ⬤⬤

# Promising School Strategies— Part I: Instructional

> The definition of insanity is doing the same thing over and over and expecting a different result.
>
> Anonymous

Decisions about instruction; class, school, and district organization; amount of and use of time; curriculum, technology, and facilities; child health and social supports; and what we do in and around schools related to student achievement should be guided first by practices for which there is evidence of effectiveness or, in the absence of such evidence, by well-reasoned thinking, and, if available, a research base. Too often, we use the same failed strategies and practices year after year despite substantial evidence that they are repeatedly unsuccessful. To create the learning conditions that will lead to all children learning to high standards, we must be willing to make changes, guided by evidence. In this chapter, we highlight practices that relate to instruction; in the next, to practices that contribute to student achievement but more indirectly.

It's also worth noting that using programs that are effective if faithfully implemented, or based on high-quality research on learning, will often be no more costly than ineffective programs. In the long run, the most costly program is the one that is ineffective.

The following are specific policy strategies related to instruction based on research, evidence, and/or good sense that if faithfully implemented will result in significant improvement in student achievement.

## EARLY CHILDHOOD EDUCATION FOR EVERY THREE- AND FOUR-YEAR-OLD

### Long-Term Effects of Interventions

A number of programs have demonstrated the lasting and substantial effect of quality preschool experiences on IQ and other learning outcomes. In 1962, the High/Scope Perry Preschool Project began in Ypsilanti, Michigan. This project involved a longitudinal study of 123 African American three- and four-year-olds. All the participants were from high-poverty families, and had IQ scores between seventy and eighty-five, with no organic impairment. The participants were divided into an experimental group of fifty-eight children, who received a preschool program, and a control group of sixty-five children who did not. The groups were matched by a number of factors including IQ, age, gender, and socioeconomic status.

The preschool program experienced by the experimental groups consisted of two years of a two-and-a-half-hour program of very high quality five days a week, plus weekly home visits for each family and monthly parent meetings. Both groups of children were followed up yearly between ages four and eleven, with further data collected at ages fourteen, fifteen, nineteen, and twenty-seven.

The long-term effects of this part-time program for three- and four-year-olds are profound. The program group scored 29 percent higher on standardized tests at age fourteen, and had significantly higher literacy scores at age nineteen. Only 15 percent of the program group members were recommended for special education, compared to 34 percent of students in the control group.

The students who had half-days of preschool when they were three and four had higher high school GPAs than those who did not. Of the students in the program group, 71 percent graduated from high school, compared to only 54 percent of students in the control group.

The relative socioeconomic success of participants was also extraordinary: public assistance—15 percent versus 32 percent; monthly earnings of $2,000 or more—29 percent versus 7 percent; home ownership—36 percent versus 13 percent; car ownership—30 percent versus 13 percent.

The impact on social responsibility was significant with program participants having fewer police contacts, less serious misconduct, less fighting and violent behavior, and less engaging in property damage.

Obviously all these good things made life better for the participants themselves as they grew up and for their families, neighbors, and community. In addition, there were extraordinary implications for costs and taxes associated with the participants' good outcomes. There was an estimated savings to the public of $7.16 for every dollar spent on the program (savings in welfare, special education, criminal justice system, crime victims, and more tax revenue from higher income) (Parks, 2000). Some might comment that these outcomes are still not up to the level usually achieved by middle-class suburban white students. However, we need to bear in mind that the study involved a high-poverty group of children, and that the special support of this program was a tiny intervention—part-time for two years. If an intervention this small can have effects this great, it seems clear that, if provided with ongoing support of the kind most suburban children receive, these students would have been capable of similar outcomes.

Our recommendation is a simple one. We must ensure that every three- and four-year-old has access to a quality, developmentally appropriate early childhood program. The evidence is that the rhetorical commitment to succeed with all children is a pipe dream for the majority of students who are poor or otherwise face significant barriers to learning, as long as they continue to start school two or three years behind their wealthier fellow students who also come from homes where the education level of their parents is higher and most of whom have had quality early learning opportunities.

We need courageous, pioneer, and prescient work of political leaders like South Carolina's Governor Richard Riley, who initiated that state's support of a strong early childhood program as early as 1984, and Governor James Hunt, who initiated the acclaimed Smart Start program in North Carolina in 1993. Given what we know, politicians today who profess fealty to "leaving no child behind" in school are disingenuous when they do not throw their full weight behind 100 percent funding for Head Start or an equivalent state initiative for all three- and four-year-olds, as well as to the other supports necessary throughout the K–12 experience.

Anyone who spends time with young children observes the tremendous growth that occurs every day as they learn from their experiences. Children who have a rich variety of experiences and lots of support learn more. Those with less learn less. Children's verbal skills increase when adults talk to them and with them. Absent serious brain damage, every child learns the rudiments of survival, but the quantity and quality of their early experiences will greatly affect the richness of their success in school and in life.

If we want an ample, well-qualified workforce, lower crime and higher employment rates, fewer special education students, more high school graduates, fewer expulsions and less disruptive behavior, higher grades, and fairness of opportunity among and between all children, then quality, developmentally appropriate preschool programs for all students beginning by age three or earlier are essential.

The changing nature of the family also makes early childhood opportunity more imperative. In 1950, 33 percent of women were in the workforce; in 2000, 60 percent were, including 72 percent of those with children between the ages of three and five and 61 percent of those with children under age five. For children from families with the financial means, these opportunities are within reach. But for children poor enough to be eligible for Head Start barely half have a slot when they are four years old and less than 5 percent when they are three years old.

We know the kind of experiences that young children need to be well prepared to learn, and we know that many children have little access to such experiences at home. We know that preschool can provide many of these experiences, and what a quality program needs to look like. We also know that the children who would most benefit from the quality preschool experience are the ones least likely to be receiving it, not because their parents don't want them in preschool, but because such programs are not available to them for financial and geographic reasons. Thus, if we want all students to achieve to high standards, it is necessary to see that all students have access to quality, developmentally appropriate preschool programs. The fact that we have not done so is a choice, and a failure, on the part of each and all of us.

Quality early childhood programs have long-term benefits not just for the students who participate in them, but also for the whole community. More than a generation of solid research reinforces this message. Despite the widespread perception that achievement gains from programs like Head Start were not sustained as the children entered middle and high school, we now know that a quality preschool program has long-term positive impact. The three most cited and respected longitudinal studies of the effect of quality, developmentally appropriate preschool are the High Scope/Perry Preschool Project in Michigan, the Abecediarian Educational Child Care program in North Carolina, and the Chicago Child Parent Center program. Each followed children at least until their early twenties. The High Scope Project has been underway even longer; they were still tracking 95 percent of the original participants at age twenty-seven.

The results are powerful. These projects determined that quality preschool programs have the following results decades later:

- Higher cognitive test scores.
- Higher academic achievement.
- More years of school completed.
- Superior school adjustment.
- Lower cumulative rate of grade retention.
- Lower incidence of special education.
- Fewer juvenile arrests.
- Greater commitment to marriage.
- Lower incidence of participants receiving welfare.
- Lower teen unemployment.

In addition:

- Participants were older when their first child was born.
- Mothers of participants ended up with more education.

As the imperative for all children to achieve at higher levels grows, a crucial learning condition is that all children come to kindergarten and the first grade ready to learn, not ready to catch up. Being read to, having one's curiosity stimulated, learning to interact with others constructively, knowing one's colors, numbers, and letters, developing the confidence of problem-solving, beginning to understand connections and interactions, and appreciating and creating music and art all must be routine experiences for children long before they turn five.

### Availability of Quality Preschool

As this is written, there are only eight states that seek to guarantee the availability of prekindergarten programs for four-year-old children. Not even those eight actually provide pre-K to even 70 percent of their four-year-olds. And the quality in all of them is mixed. There are no states that guarantee the availability of quality pre-K programs for three-year-old children. Until recently, Pennsylvania has had one of the worst records of support for early childhood education.[1] The absence of quality early childhood programs for millions of American children demonstrates better than any single other example a key premise of *Choosing Excellence in Public Schools*: that we know what to do to succeed with children—we simply choose not to do it.

Our neglect falls, again, disproportionately, on the poor. According to the Committee for Economic Development, in 2002 only 44 percent of parents of young children with incomes below $10,000 had their children in early childhood centers, while 71 percent of those with incomes in excess of $75,000 did. These numbers have persisted over time, being almost identical to those reported by Ernest Boyer in 1991 from his analysis of National Center for Education statistics (Boyer, 1991, p. 51).

## Designing Effective Preschool Programs

The National Association for the Education of Young Children criteria for accreditation are useful in helping to evaluate the quality of a preschool program. Their criteria consider ten factors:

- Interactions among Teachers and Children
- Curriculum
- Relationships among Teachers and Families
- Staff Qualifications and Professional Development
- Administration
- Staffing
- Physical Environment
- Health and Safety
- Nutrition and Food Services
- Evaluation[2]

These criteria make it clear that, as with successful programs for K–12 education, a comprehensive and systemic set of strategies is necessary for effective preschool programs.

There are a number of factors that states and districts prepared to commit to early education must consider.

### Delivery System

Districts should be open to using a delivery system that is broader than the one that is the norm. Preschool programs do not have to be in school buildings; they can be in churches, neighborhood centers, and other community buildings. They do not have to be run by the school district; the employees do not have to be school district staff. We need to focus on the quality of the programs and staff, not on bureaucracy and governance.

Barriers to universal early childhood programs include the arguments that develop between the day-care community and the school community about money and power. Children often lose out in the turf wars. A government entity should insist that programs are of high quality and are developmentally appropriate, not just baby-sitting operations. Government should provide the money and should have ultimate authority and responsibility for the outcomes achieved by the children. But school districts need not "run" the programs.

### Staff Quality

We must pay particular attention to the quality of the staff. The staff in many child-care settings are poorly trained and ill-equipped. Forty percent have only a high school diploma or less and often are paid an amount comparable to the minimum wage. Understanding the developmental characteristics of young children, knowing how to talk with them, what language to use, what behavior is appropriate for their age, knowing the stages of language development, understanding something of how the brain develops, realizing that two children the same age may be very, very different—an early education provider needs to have in-depth knowledge of all these topics and more to ensure that he or she is able to serve children well. Four years of college should be a minimum expectation for responsibility during these crucial developmental years.

### Access for Poor Children

Poor children need to have access to quality developmentally appropriate preschool for free. The fees for quality private programs are far too high for many parents. Even where some access does exist for poor children, it is not unusual for families to pay 15–20 percent of their income on child care or preschool, often of poor quality. If a district is offering a public, quality preschool program, many parents who can presently afford to pay for early childhood programs would be willing to pay for a district-provided program if it were of high quality. It is appropriate for districts to consider reducing some of the costs in that manner.

While public school districts should accept responsibility for providing a quality preschool program to all its children (if for no other reason than to fulfill its obligation to provide a quality K–12 education that results in high achievement for all its students), the district need not treat the operation of the preschool effort in the same way except to make sure that the programs are of high quality, are run by quality staff, and are realistically available to every child.

*Children and Family Authority*

Universal quality early childhood programs for all of America's three- and four-year-olds would represent a tremendous breakthrough. However, the real answer to child need goes beyond such an effort. What I propose may appear impossible. In fact, versions of it are routine in several European countries.

## PHILADELPHIA

We tried to move forward with a comprehensive program for young children prenatal through age five in Philadelphia. When we were designing the *Children Achieving* program, I proposed that we establish a Children and Family Authority to serve young children in a manner such that by age five they would arrive at school ready to learn.

### Program Design

As we stated in the *Children Achieving Action Design,*

> Philadelphia statistics portray a grim situation regarding our youngest children:
>
> > About 4,000 babies are born every year whose mothers have had inadequate or no prenatal care;
> >
> > More than half of the pregnant teenagers in this city do not receive early prenatal care; Between 25 and 30 percent of eligible women and young children do not participate in the Women, Infants, and Children program (WIC), a federally funded nutrition program;
> >
> > More than half of the city's two year olds are not fully immunized; in some sections of the city, the percentage of unimmunized toddlers is much higher;
> >
> > Approximately 15,000 children who are eligible for Head Start cannot be accommodated by any of the providers in the city;
> >
> > The gap between available slots and demand for subsidized and licensed day care for children age five and younger is over 70,000;
> >
> > Two thirds of the 14,500 children enrolled in kindergarten are in half-day programs, 3,500 kindergarten-aged children are receiving no educational services. (*Children Achieving Action Design,* 1995, p. V-1)

Such facts are hardly unusual in a large American city. During my tenure, we solved the last problem. By 1996, although not required by

Pennsylvania law, all of our elementary schools offered full-day kindergarten to all students. However, with the notable exception of immunization, on which dramatic progress was made, the city made little progress on any of the other problems outlined above. Still there was no systematic or coordinated response to the needs of young children. The majority of our children were still coming to kindergarten vastly under-prepared.

### Existing Delivery Problems

There were many problems with Philadelphia's nonsystem that serves young children. They include the following: (1) funding streams were fragmented; (2) the nonsystem was operated on an input, not a results basis; and (3) children were served based on their deficits, not based on the affirmative obligation to establish and preserve their well-being. A child can receive services in early intervention programs at age one or two or three, but there is not a systematic way to provide his or her mother with prenatal care to prevent low-weight birth, retardation, or brain damage in the first place.

Personnel operated in silos unconnected to one another and, thus, unconnected to others whose success with a child is important to their success with that child. A system of outcomes, assessment, and accountability is difficult if not impossible to establish since the subsystems do not relate in a logical way to the whole. Each piece of the service bureaucracy has the luxury of saying they did their best but since they don't control what some other piece of the bureaucracy does, they cannot be responsible for the overall outcomes with the children needing more than their narrow service.

### Proposed New System

To address these issues, I proposed that the school system, health department, and the human services department create a new agency, the Children and Family Authority (CFA), and turn over to it all of their respective programs, funds, personnel, and responsibility related to children and families up to age eight. The overarching goal of the new institution would be to attend to the well-being of all young children beginning with prenatal care for the mother and to deliver each child to the schoolhouse door healthy, socially and emotionally fit, and academically ready to enter the fourth grade.

The CFA was to be designed to create a seamless web of services to provide necessary support to young children and their families.

According to our analysis at that time, we served children through a deficit model of services. We identify a category of need, appropriate some money for addressing it, and then serve as many children as we could for as long as we could before the money ran out.

This is radically different from at least the philosophy if not the reality of K–12 education. We operate our schools on the premise that every child is entitled to an education. We don't begin to serve all students well but the system is at least thought of philosophically as one of entitlement, not of privilege. We give a single system the responsibility for delivering education, providing us at least the possibility to create an accountability system. In general, the child health and social service system is so fragmented and driven by available money that it is not possible to create even a theoretical system of accountability. Its operating premise is serving the child as a result of largesse not right.

The current system of K–12 education underserves poor children, but the ragtag, fragmented nature of the rest of the child service system is worse. The Children and Family Authority was intended to respond to this crisis, not because health and social services were the business of the school directly, but because the school cannot succeed in its business until children come to school prepared to learn. The CFA would help accomplish that.

The CFA was envisioned to follow the same organizational tenets that are necessary in education:

- The targeted audience would be all children—not just some.
- Desired outcomes would be established. They would include a reduction in the number of low-weight births, an increase in the proportion of immunized two-year-olds, a reduction in the number of untreated hearing and seeing defects on entry into school, an increase in the proportion of five-year-olds who know their alphabet, can count to ten, and identify colors accurately, and an increase in the number of students who, at the end of third grade, are able to perform at grade-level proficiency. (National Center on Educational Outcomes, 1993)[3]
- Measurement instruments would be designed to evaluate the established outcomes.
- An accountability system, made feasible by the CFA's new organizational structure built on the system's affirmative responsibility for all children, would be established based on the identified outcomes.
- Decisions about individual children would be made at the neighborhood level through a decision-making structure that

would be a counterpart to the site-based council in the school framework.

- Personnel would be reorganized and would perform different functions, at least insofar as they relate to other professionals. Thus, significant emphasis would need to be placed on staff training.
- The CFA would have a major role in coordinating the work of all private human service agencies in a given neighborhood. All public agencies serving children ages 0–8 would be already subsumed within the authority of the CFA.
- Certain resources would be required for the agency to be successful, such as sufficient staff to ensure a reasonable case load of children for a team of professionals, and specialized personnel such as psychologists and well-trained early childhood educators.

Finally, all in the CFA would need to understand the importance of all of these pieces working together comprehensively and simultaneously.

We could better serve young children by organically folding together all of the employees, money, and goals of relevant public agencies. Early childhood educators, primary school teachers, health workers, social service workers, and the various employees of some of the smaller agencies working with young children would become employees of the new Authority. They would shed old titles and organizational structures. There could be a team of former school district employees, social service workers, and health workers responsible for delivering a group of three to five hundred students to the fourth grade who are healthy, secure, and academically achieving at a level necessary to progress satisfactorily through the rest of their school experience.

Rather than cubbyhole the staff in departments, they might be characterized as Child Workers I, II, or III. We need to break the patterns of the failed system and initiate a new one to serve the new positive entitlements of all children. The whole team would bear this responsibility. Accountability incentives would be created and tied to the achievement of outcomes at appropriate points. The system would be designed so that teams and subteams would be deemed to have succeeded—or not— based on the well-being of children 0–8.

No longer would it be possible for teachers to blame a child's poor academic performance on unhealthiness, or for social workers to say that because the school district or the health department are not doing their job, they cannot do theirs. The team succeeds and fails together; the team has the power to determine strategy; the team has the responsibility to be advocates. Moreover, a citizen accountability system would be necessary to ensure an adequate level of resources to produce the identified results just as we have argued is required for schools.

## REALITIES

A terrific district Task Force on School Readiness chaired by Christine James Brown, then a Philadelphia school board member and president of the United Way (now president of the International United Way), and Ruth W. Mayden, dean of the School of Social Work at Bryn Mawr College, fleshed out an operational process to work on the design of the Children and Family Authority. It became a recommendation of the *Children Achieving Action Design*. The proposal was subsequently seriously considered by the Mayor's Cabinet on Family and Children, which was comprised of all of the agency heads with any responsibility for children.

Unfortunately, in the end, fears arising from the city budget led the cabinet to back away. I should say parenthetically that the CFA would have changed personnel policies, shifted power, altered long bureaucratic practices, and set up new ways of thinking about children. Lurking in the background, in addition to financial concerns, was concern that the city's unions would oppose the effort. In addition, it was clear that some city agencies were not prepared to do things differently. Three people in the mayor's cabinet who were prepared to move forward were Mike DeBarardinis, now state secretary of the Department of Conservation and Natural Resources; Donna Cooper, now state secretary of Planning; and Estelle Richmond, now state secretary of Health.

The idea of the Authority made a brief comeback several years later. Chris James Brown remained interested in it, as did Shelly Yanoff, who had coordinated the work of all of the Task Forces that produced the *Children Achieving Action Design*, and Estelle Richmond. We decided that one of the reasons that the effort had failed the first time was the fact that the idea became public before we satisfactorily addressed such questions as how the Authority would actually work, how much it would cost, how we could tap into the various federal funding streams, how union contracts would have to be amended, and how large the teams would have to be. We had proposed a process that would have answered all of those questions, but opponents were afraid to let the process move forward for fear that its momentum would be too great to turn back later.

This second time we decided to approach the task very differently. We kept it outside of government though we included key government people in it. We decided to create a model authority with real people, real contracts and real funding streams in two neighborhoods in the city. We believed that some of the political roadblocks in the plan could be solved or at least amended in a manner that would secure enough support to earn the support of the powers that be.

I went to the Annenberg Foundation and the Carnegie Corporation for $450,000 in funds for about nine months work with the intention of securing the involvement of the best minds in America to do the work. Unfortunately, the effort lasted into the spring of 2000. I resigned that summer, and the work of the effort took on a decidedly different direction. It ended up once more focusing on coordination, collaboration, and cooperation, but not on meaningful structural changes.

That was doubly unfortunate since Estelle Richmond was selected by the new mayor, John Street, to head all children's programs. I have often thought that if we had been ready to go with an imaginative, powerful Authority plan, it might have met a different fate. But it did not. The product of the effort is basically gathering dust like so many others because the public will and political resolve did not exist to see it through.

## SUBSTANTIAL EXTRA AND/OR DIFFERENT USE OF TIME FOR BOTH STUDENTS AND TEACHERS

Learning in U.S. public schools is circumscribed by time, rather than by what students know and can do. The typical pattern is 180 days of school per year. Schools run from about 9 am to 3:30 pm (earlier in high schools—often due to the schedule and routes of buses, not student needs to learn). While some changes have occurred in the last decade or so, the six-hour day in secondary schools is divided into periods that are about fifty minutes. The school year almost always starts in late August or early September and is over sometime between May 15 and June 15. How much students learn is determined by how much they can learn between those prescribed times.

Roy Romer, former governor of Colorado and superintendent of schools in Los Angeles, often asked the rhetorical question, "Would you rather fly with a pilot who was licensed on the basis of having accumulated a prescribed amount of classroom hours or flying time or would you prefer to fly with one who had learned how to fly, however much or little time it took?" The answer is obvious. Time in American public education should be treated the same way. We must create the conditions in which teachers and students have the time they need that will result in students knowing and being able to do all they must to succeed. If we think of time as flexible and standards as fixed, it will result in our considering a large range of different approaches to the design of American public education.

Significant numbers of students must have much more time to meet the new and higher standards necessary to academic, career, and citizenship success.

In Kentucky in 1990, I recommended that the financial resources should be provided for at least one-third of "all students to attend school for as many as 240 days per year including time on the weekends, summers and longer school days" (Hornbeck, 1990, p. 62). In a Center for American Progress report for Massachusetts in January 2007, Hilary Pennington recommended a large pilot effort in which all students would have about 30 percent more time per year (Pennington, 2007). In terms of days that would translate into 234. Nearly every reform effort addresses time in some manner. Unfortunately, because adding time involves adding money, it is nearly always left on the cutting room floor.

### Time Must Be Used and Organized in Very Different Ways

If the only change were to do the same things longer, it would certainly help some, perhaps many, children who simply need more time to practice, to think about subject matter. However, more time used and organized differently, and recognizing different learning styles, would be far better. For example, some students, especially high school students, starting school later in the morning may bring them to school with a better attitude. In Philadelphia we had great success with some of our most challenging high school students by starting their school day in late afternoon and extending it into the evening. It accommodated jobs for some, different sleep patterns for others. It simply changed the perception of school for others, especially when coupled with smaller classes (which is itself a way to increase time, since the time a teacher has with an individual student increases).

Other ways in which time is used differently include block scheduling, tutoring for small groups of struggling students by trained teachers (Reading Recovery, Success for All), four-day weeks for students in the school building with a day a week engaged in community-based learning and/or service learning. We must abandon our fealty to the fifty-minute period. These different uses of time arise from asking one of or both of two questions. How much time is necessary to learn certain content of knowledge or develop certain skills? When, during the day, week, or year, is it best for a given student to have learning time?

### Time, for Example, That We Now Consider "Afterschool" Must Become Part of School

Time can thus be used to address academic, safety, enrichment, and mental health needs of children, especially children whose present alternative is simply hours "on the street."

### Time for Teachers Will Enhance Instruction for Students

Teachers will have time for team and individual planning. In many schools in Asia, for example, a teacher's actual instructional time with a class is only three or four hours per day. The rest of the day is spent with colleagues discussing instructional improvement and individual students, personal planning time, and working one-on-one with individual students. Additional time for teachers will permit them to engage in more authentic assessment of students. Additional days will create time for professional development without tacking it on to the end of the day after a teacher has taught all day and without sending the children home on a professional development day thereby reducing instructional time. Teachers can also make more time for parents.[4]

### The Age of Compulsory Schooling Must Be Extended

Today most states require students to attend school until age fourteen to sixteen. The original rationale was that was enough time for a child to acquire basic skills before entering the workforce on the farm or factory floor. That rationale is ridiculous in today's world. When coupled with the fact that the dropout rate skyrockets around the ninth grade when students reach that age, it should follow that we consider extending the compulsory schooling age to accommodate the higher necessary standards and the fact that students tend to stay in school for however long we say to them and their parents that they must.

### The Commitment to a Free and Appropriate Education Must Be Extended until a Student Achieves the Prescribed Standards

Limiting a guaranteed free education to age twenty-one makes no more sense than saying those 180 days or six hours a day shall be the school year or day. We should consider guaranteeing education opportunity until the standards are met so long as there is a certain amount of progress each year.

## EFFECTIVE INSTRUCTIONAL MODELS

In July 1991 with leadership from President George H. W. Bush, Governors Thomas Kean and Booth Gardner, philanthropist Walter Annenberg, Deputy Secretary of Education and former Xerox CEO David Kearns, Louis Gerstner (then CEO of IBM), and others, the New American Schools Development Corporation (NASDC) was launched. It invited anyone who was interested to submit ideas for breakthrough school designs that would result in greater effectiveness with students. The response was extraordinary with thousands of design proposals submitted. Ten were chosen. Within a year the number was down to seven. This effort was an important one in developing the idea of using effectiveness as a criterion for choosing whole school or whole district reform models.[5] I was part of NASDC's work and other efforts to use defined program effectiveness criteria in school reform. However, in this volume, we want to emphasize effectiveness analysis as a state of mind rather than try to sell a particular model.[6]

The most basic entry point of analysis from this perspective is how all students, and demographically disaggregated groups of students, are performing when measured against the standards we wish them to meet. Even the most cursory analysis of performance in most schools in the United States when analyzed in the context of graduation rates, achievement test data, rate of return of students to a second year of college, proportion of community college students in remedial courses, comparisons with students in other countries, must lead us to the conclusion that there is much room for improvement. If an overlay of poverty, race, language, or disability is placed on that same data, the emerging picture darkens considerably.

Nevertheless, there is probably no institution in America that conducts its business more like it did fifty years ago than public education. Even the superficial analysis suggested above makes it clear that we should stop doing much of what we do and conduct our business differently.

We do not advocate new initiatives for their own sake. Fortunately there are ways of thinking about what we do that will result in better performance, based first on some strategies for which there is a lot of evidence of effectiveness and, second, on strategies that simply make sense and, at least, don't have years of evidence of ineffectiveness.

How does a school or district choose what effective strategy to pursue? The following criteria are informed by but not identical to those used by the U.S. Department of Education during the Clinton and Bush administrations as they pursued the idea of comprehensive school reform models:

Goals and benchmarks: has measurable goals that fit district goals for student performance, and benchmarks for meeting those goals that when achieved will result in students having met the district's academic, career, and citizenship standards.

Supportive staff members: ensures that programs are selected and supported by school faculty, administrators, and staff before implementation.

Methods and strategies: based on evidence they are effective, can be replicated, and have reasonable promise of improving achievement.

External assistance: uses high-quality external technical support with experience or expertise in schoolwide reform and improvement.

Parental and community involvement: provides for the meaningful involvement of parents and the local community in planning and implementing school improvement activities.

Professional development: provides for high-quality and continuous teacher and staff professional development and training.

Coordination of resources: identifies how all resources available to the school will support and sustain the school reform effort. In particular, it should make efficient use of federal, state, local, and private financial and other resources to foster the school's improvement plan.

Annual evaluation: includes a plan for evaluating, annually, the implementation of the schoolwide reform and its impact on students' academic achievement.

Comprehensive approach: has a comprehensive design for effectiveness that includes instruction, assessment, classroom management, professional development, parental involvement, and school management, and that aligns the school's curriculum, technology, and professional development into a schoolwide reform.

If a school staff comes together using criteria like these, and chooses or builds a strategy, and if implementation is energetic and faithful, there will be a huge difference in student performance. I emphasize energy, faithfulness, joint decision-making, and the use of data and criteria, since even strategies like Direct Instruction and Success for All, which many claim to be effective, will work only if the adults in a school thoughtfully have their hearts and minds in it.

At the same time, strategies such as the Coalition For Essential Schools and Atlas Communities, for which there is little systematic evidence of improved student achievement, could be more effective than current practice in many schools if thoughtfully, energetically, and faithfully implemented. I say this because the strategies underlying these approaches are based on psychological and educational research that makes a great deal of sense, and addresses the current needs of students.

## SCHOOL-DEVELOPED STRATEGIES

A school staff can build its own strategy that works using the kind of criteria suggested above. In so doing it can draw on the work of multiple formal and informal comprehensive reform models including those for which there is little traditional control group evidence of effectiveness. If district and school goals include, for example, critical thinking and problem-solving, the "essential questions" that are at the heart of the Coalition and its emphasis on exhibitions of student work as an important assessment strategy would have to be considered. That sort of work can be combined with the standards-driven, more uniform, and more evidence-based approach of a model like America's Choice. I am not suggesting that a school can simply choose A and B from column 1 and D and F from column 2 and slap them together. I am suggesting that committed professionals who approach the work thoughtfully and aggressively, use data, engage in high-quality professional development on a sustained basis, and examine and share their work on a team basis can succeed.

## STATE AND DISTRICT ROLES

Finally a word on the state's and district's crucial role in enabling a school staff to successfully implement an effective instructional program. The state and district must ensure adequate resources. If a program like Success for All requires intense after-school academic support for small groups of students by qualified teachers and the funds do not exist to support the effort, choosing that program is worthless. Similarly, there are corollary supports that must be considered as well. Again, using the Success for All model, if students ride the bus, transportation must exist for students taking advantage of after-school instruction. School buildings must remain open and be climate-controlled. Other roles for the state and district include providing the technical support, as time is wasted, and the job is less well done if every school must do its own identification of the various effective programs.

The state and the district must be comprehensive resources. While much professional development can occur at the school level, much can be cost-effectively provided for multiple school staffs that have chosen the same effective strategy. The highest quality technical support cannot be available to large numbers of individual schools. The state and district will have to provide and coordinate these opportunities. And all of this is built on the basis of the state and/or district providing, in addition to high-quality opportunities to learn for all students, appropriate standards, rich assessments, and fair accountability systems, while monitoring and enforcing equitable practices among and within schools.

## EFFECTIVE SCHOOL ORGANIZATION FOR INSTRUCTION

In focusing on standards, assessment, and accountability, it is crucial that we avoid sucking human connections, imagination, and energy out of the pedagogical equation in a relentless drive to improve test scores. In education small and intimate is usually better. Bigger is less productive and, thus, in the long run more expensive. In Philadelphia, we pursued several strategies to reduce size and promote human interaction.

### Small Learning Communities

#### *High School Charters*

Philadelphia was a pioneer in the development of small learning communities (called charters at the time). In 1988, with support from the Pew Charitable Trusts, Superintendent Constance Clayton, Chief of Staff Ralph Smith, Michelle Fine and Jan Somerville launched the Philadelphia Schools Collaborative.

**Table 11.1.    Comparison of Underlying Principles of Small Learning Communities/Charters vs. Traditional Large Urban High Schools**

| Small Learning Communities/Charters | Regular High School |
|---|---|
| Small | Large |
| Same students for several years | Changing groups of students |
| Same teachers for several years | Changing teachers |
| Common academic themes | Do your own thing with your students |
| Common planning times for staff | Little or no staff interaction |
| Interaction among students and staff | Little or no interaction among students and staff |
| Charter driven decisions | Decisions made at headquarters |
| Contact with parents | Little contact with parents |
| A constructivist teaching environment | Often lectures or rote learning environment with little challenge. |
| Work collegially on instructional issues like assessment | Accept whatever is handed down |
| Peer-driven | System/Administrator-driven |
| Acceptance of multiple tasks by individual teachers | A different person for every job |
| Safer | Vulnerable |
| Collaborative | Everyone out for himself |
| Student-centered | More self- or institution-centered |

Source: Fine, M., and Somerville, J. (1991). Philadelphia School Collaborative, School District of Philadelphia.

More students in the charters were attending school on a regular basis, more took the SATS and the PSATS, more passed English, and more passed mathematics (NCREL, 1993).

Unfortunately, central office's support for the charters was short-lived. In 1990, Ralph Smith left the system due to personal conflicts with Superintendent Constance Clayton. Within eighteen months, Somerville and Fine were also gone. By the time I arrived in 1994, some charters still existed, but the energy around most of them had disappeared.

## Systemic Implementation of Small Learning Communities

### Philadelphia

Ralph Smith, one of my closest advisors during my first two years as superintendent, urged me to embrace small learning communities. We made them one of the systemwide organizing principles for all schools under *Children Achieving*.[7]

Nationwide, small learning communities had been most frequently established in high schools, but we decided that the principles that made small schools powerful for high school education would also bring benefits at the middle and elementary levels.

The transition to small schools in Philadelphia was not easy. We heard complaints that the Collaborative had been a failure, small learning communities were too expensive, and schedules could not be built with such small units. We experienced pushback from those at the middle and elementary levels who believed that small schools were "a high school thing." Because of the union's long-standing opposition to anything that required teachers to take on decision-making responsibility and accountability, increasing school-based decision-making became challenging.

Nevertheless, we persisted. We laid out a three-year timeline for all district schools to create small learning communities (SLCs) for all students. We judged whether a school was establishing small learning communities successfully based on the following characteristics[8]:

- Unity of Approach—Built around a unifying theme or instructional approaches.
- Solid Instructional Basis—Promotes the use of curriculum and instructional strategies that assist all students to reach high standards (standards-driven).
- Heterogeneity of Students—Includes all children, including low-income, racial and language minorities, students with disabilities. Reduces tracking.
- Multiyear Implementation—Structured to provide a close relationship among and between students, staff, families, and communities for more than one school year.
- Collaboration—Teachers have sufficient time to engage in ongoing, meaningful planning and professional development.
- Empowerment and Autonomy—Has the authority and resources to design its own standards-driven instructional program.
- Small Size—Population of two to four hundred students. The right number is one that allows everyone to know one another's names, lets the entire faculty and staff sit around a table and effectively problem-solve, facilitates communication with every single parent, and promotes student security by ensuring that the people in the halls know them and look out for them.
- Accountability—Responsible for improved student performance.

These characteristics emphasize that successful small learning communities are about more than just size. Being small is just the start.

## Looping

Looping is the concept that the same small group of teachers and students work together for several years at a time, again promoting human connections between and among teachers and students over time. Looping can occur either at the classroom level or across a grade level. In classroom-level looping an elementary teacher would stay with the same group of students as they moved through K–2, and then "loop" back to kindergarten for a new group of students when her classes are promoted to grade 3. In middle school, grade-level looping might be more appropriate. All 150 sixth graders in a particular school, for example, might be promoted to seventh grade with their whole team of teachers. This joint "promotion" of students and teachers could continue until the students moved on to high school, at which point their teachers would "loop" back to sixth grade and pick up a new cadre of students. An extension of this practice occurred in Philadelphia when a handful of eighth-grade teachers who had been with their students since the fifth or sixth grade decided to stay with their students through the ninth grade, perhaps the single most difficult year of transition in a student's schooling experience.

It was not easy to convince teachers to loop. Many had taught the same subject for years. They were experts on their grade level; they had their lesson plans in place that required minimal change. In my experience, however, once teachers made the shift to looping, they didn't look backward. They discovered that the relationships they built were as important to them as they were to the students, and that the payoffs in classroom management, in relationships with parents, and in their knowledge of what their students knew and did not know in the academic subject area for which they were responsible more than offset their new learning curve and the need, for a couple of years, to develop new lesson plans.

## Alternatives to Large Middle Schools

When I was in school in the 1950s, junior highs (generally seventh, eighth, and ninth grades) were the norm in early adolescent education. In the mid-1970s, the middle school (generally sixth, seventh, and eighth grades) movement swept the country. The logic was that ninth graders were more socially mature than seventh and eighth graders, and that it was better to have somewhat younger students together, with ninth graders being better matched in high schools.

I had the privilege of serving as chair of the Carnegie Task Force on the Education of Early Adolescents that produced the seminal report *Turning Points* in the late 1980s. One of our observations was that the developmental characteristics of students ages ten to fifteen are very powerful; as one person put it, "these kids have been mugged by their hormones." That led us to make recommendations that responded to the developmental characteristics of these children. These include understanding hormonal changes, the increased willingness of these student to make risky decisions that are health threatening, the intensely malleable nature of young teenagers, the influence of the peer group, the ambivalence of young adolescents toward their parents, and the very wide developmental spectrum and the uneven changes that take place among these children.

During Task Force deliberations, we considered the possibility of recommending that school districts reorganize themselves from configurations with elementary, middle/junior high, and high schools to configurations with K–8 and high schools. While I am certain that a majority of the Task Force would have favored such an approach, we were afraid that such a hard-edged recommendation might divert attention from the central point—whatever the grade configuration, certain principles arise out of the developmental/cognitive needs of young adolescents that need attention. Many districts would have been so constrained by the physical limitations of their buildings that they might have rejected all the other recommendations only because their facility restraints would not permit K–8 building assignments.

The idea of K–8 schools stayed with me. In going to Philadelphia, I discovered that many of the district's middle school age students were already served in K–8 settings rather than in middle schools. We analyzed achievement patterns and confirmed that middle school age students in K–8 schools achieved better. Because of all the other changes that were underway, we did not mandate a change in organizational structure, but we did encourage such a change. Several schools made the shift.[9] The idea was that in a K–8 school, it was possible to keep children "younger" longer. The school would remain elementary dominated and therefore more nurturing, discipline would be less of an issue, parents would continue participation in the parent/teacher organization longer, and teachers would be more open to working together and trying new things.

However, further analysis seems to demonstrate that the key to the success of these schools was probably not just 6–8 versus a K–8 grade configuration. Instead, performance evidence from Philadelphia indicates that the key is how *many students ages ten to fifteen* are in a given school. Sixth to eighth graders in a grades 6–8 middle school of only two hundred students do just as well as two hundred sixth to eighth graders in a K–8 school—additional evidence for the proposition that small is more effective.

## CONCLUSION

These effective practices underline the point that the challenge in ensuring that all children succeed lies not in simly inventing new approaches, but also in implementing those we already know, with careful attention to how they fit our standards, and the needs of the particular children we are teaching.

## NOTES

1. Until the election of Ed Rendell in 2003, Pennsylvania was one of nine states that appropriated no state funds to support preschool programs. Since his election, the investment of state dollars has grown to nearly $90 million.

2. These criteria are amplified in a number of NAEYC publications, including their website at www.NAEYC.org/accreditation/naeyc_accred/info_general -components.asp.

3. This publication suggests a framework of eight outcome domains for identifying measurable outcomes for young children: presence and participation, family involvement/accommodation and adaptation, physical health, responsibility and independence, contribution and citizenship, academic and functional literacy, personal and social adjustment, and satisfaction.

4. Interestingly, more time for teachers was the only recommendation I made to the Kentucky legislature that was not adopted. In a memo to David Karem on February 28, 1990, I sought to make the case based on: staff development, instructional planning time, participation in school-based decision-making, curriculum development, and time to work with the families and the community. The legislature provided for a huge increase in funding for the Kentucky School Reform Act but it did not include the extra teacher time.

5. I was part of the early years of NASDC as codirector (first with Mike Cohen, later with Warren Simmons) of the National Alliance for Restructuring Education. Our work, as a project of the National Center for Education and the Economy, became the comprehensive school reform model, America's Choice, that remains a prominent player in national reform efforts. Later I became a consultant to NASDC itself.

6. The reader will find links to the websites of a number of models for which effectiveness is claimed on www.childrenachieving.com.

7. In the years since our decision that small learning communities were the way to go, a large-scale research and experience base has begun to grow on this subject. The Annenberg grant in New York City was focused on the develop-

ment of small high schools. More than any other, the Bill and Melinda Gates Foundation made small high schools the centerpiece of their school philanthropic work for a number of years. The federal government has undertaken the Smaller Learning Community Initiative with the investment of $165 million in the creation and support of such communities. New York City with leadership from New Visions for Public Schools and funding from the Gates Foundation has implemented the idea of the small school more broadly than anywhere else in the nation. This work has reinforced the importance of small schools, but it has also made clear that it is not a silver bullet solution.

8. These criteria, developed under the leadership of the Office of Standards, Equity, and Accountability, were an example of a district-level opportunity to learn standard.

9. CEO Vallas made the decision after my departure to move all schools to a K–8 configuration.

# 12

# Promising School Strategies— Part II: Noninstructional

Learning from experience is a faculty seldom practiced.

Barbara Tuchman

Instructional strategies are, of course, pivotal in determining school success. We all know people who overcame incredible odds to succeed. However, we must move to a system of education that routinely succeeds with children who face the barriers of poverty, race, language, disability, poor health, the absence of social support, and the absence of parent and community help. While we celebrate children who "beat the odds," that they are the exception not the rule is an indictment of our nation. This must change through our aggressively pursuing promising noninstructional school strategies of serving children that complement sound instructional practice.[1]

## HEALTH AND SOCIAL SERVICE SUPPORT

Schools should not be asked to do the jobs of health, social service, and police agencies—the job of educating our children is work enough. However, schools cannot ensure that all children achieve high academic standards, progress through the grades, and graduate on time, unless all children are healthy, relatively safe and secure, and have sufficient food and housing, School systems cannot do this on their own, but what they *can* do is acknowledge the challenge that arises from poverty, and design responses that help connect students to the proper service providers in the community and help ensure that the students get the health, social service, safety, and security support they need.

## FAMILY RESOURCE AND YOUTH SERVICE CENTERS

Kentucky established an exemplary system to connect students with special needs to service providers. Their Family Resource and Youth Service Centers remain the broadest and deepest such program in the nation. It is one of the most successful components of the Kentucky Education Reform Act of 1990. Drawing on the experience of similar centers in Connecticut, developed by Sharon Lynn Kagan and Head Start founder Ed Ziegler, I recommended to the Kentucky legislature that they provide for a Family Resource Center "in or adjacent to each elementary school in the state in which 20 percent or more of the student body were poor." Similarly, based on the successful model in New Jersey, I recommended the establishment of a youth services center "in or adjacent to each school serving youth over twelve years of age for which 20 percent or more of the student body are poor" (Hornbeck, 1990, p. 59).

The legislature adopted the recommendations. In 2008, Kentucky had 420 Family Resource Centers, 268 Youth Services Centers, and 132 combined Family Resource and Youth Services Centers. These 820 centers serve students in 1,163 schools across the state. They serve 612,741 students, about 46 percent of whom are eligible for free school meals.[2]

Rather than providing services themselves, the centers serve more as "brokers" of services. The centers' small budgets pay the salaries of one or two staff members who are responsible for connecting students to relevant existing agencies and institutions, and for ensuring that the proper services are provided.

### Philadelphia

In Philadelphia, we adopted a different model to connect needy children and families to community service providers. We lacked the funds to properly staff them under the Kentucky model. Under the leadership of Gary Ledebur, we established a Family Resource Network (FRN).[3] Ledebur had crucial support from staff members Naomi Gubernick and Darryl Jackson, whose years of experience in the district, dedication, people skills, and doggedness made the Family Resource Network a reality.

They identified the existing staff at school, cluster, and central office levels whose responsibilities related to the nonacademic needs of students and families. At the school level, this included parent coordinators, counselors, school nurses, and a variety of other full- and part-time staff. Most schools had one to three such staff members; bigger schools had more. At the cluster and central office levels, large numbers of supervisors worked with the school staff on nonacademic issues.

Ledebur organized these staff by cluster into the Family Resource Network. Each cluster had between twenty and thirty staff members (two or three per school) in the resource network. One new position was created for a Family Resource Network coordinator in each cluster to support the work of school-based personnel. The new positions were funded by the elimination of other supervisory positions.

The members of the network connected other agencies and student/family need. As a network, working between schools, they were able to leverage services to a much greater degree. They developed clusterwide directories of services. When something was needed for a child in one school but unknown or not available, they were able to communicate with their colleagues across the cluster in an organized way increasing the likelihood of finding what the child, or children, needed.

The responsibility of the Family Resource Network was threefold. First, it was to connect the nonacademic needs of children and families to existing resources in the community to address whatever nonacademic problem might be impeding student learning. Second, if the necessary resource did not exist, the FRN was to take the lead in establishing the resource, most often in partnership with other institutions. And, third, if the resource did not exist and the FRN was unable to create the resource, it had the responsibility for assuming an advocacy posture with the superintendent, the school board, city council, another city agency, a church institution, or whatever body they thought could or should provide the necessary support.

### Truancy Courts

Attendance was one of the areas of focus for the Family Resource Network. Between 1996 and 2000, attendance improved for the groups whose attendance had been lowest in 1994. Historically, all students and parents hauled into Truancy Court went to a central location in downtown Philadelphia. That made it difficult not only for students and their parents but also for the school personnel who were expected to be present. It took a lot of time. Someone essential was often not present. Cases were postponed, or went forward despite missing someone important to the process.

We created neighborhood truancy courts to alleviate these problems. The neighborhood truancy court was closer to most parties, it was less time consuming, everyone could more easily be present, and even parking problems were reduced. Most importantly, this permitted earlier intervention. Previously, students were brought to truancy court after they had been absent fifty or more times. The efficiencies of the neighborhood truancy court were such that we were able to address the needs of students after twenty-five absences.

### Physical Health Support

Because many of our students were eligible for health service that their parents were unaware of, we established direct electronic access to the names of companies providing insurance to children on state public assistance. Access to these records was legal and appropriate, but had depended on a paper-based, labor-intensive, time-consuming process. This new process allowed school-based personnel, such as nurses and social workers, to immediately access the information.

It was critical to our effort to target eligible students whose families had not yet secured insurance. In 1999–2000, for example, we increased the percentage of students with documented health insurance from 52 percent to 66 percent—a 26 percent increase in one year.

### Mental Health Support

The Surgeon General has found that "Throughout the lifespan, mental health is the wellspring of thinking and communication skills, learning, resilience, and self-esteem" (Surgeon General, 1999, p. 4). However, minorities have less access to mental health services, and are less likely to receive such services. What services they do receive are more likely to be of poor quality. Minorities are also underrepresented in research efforts to improve mental health services (Surgeon General, 2001, p. 2). It is hardly surprising that in a city where more than 80 percent of the school population is both minority and poor, there was a notable absence of mental health services provided through the school system for Philadelphia's children.

In concert with the city's Health Department, the Family Resource Network established a behavioral health effort, which was piloted successfully in three clusters. The effort was designed to break through the red tape and bureaucracy that slowed children's access to mental health services. By 2000 the Family Resource Network established behavioral health collaborative agreements in fifty schools in eighteen clusters to provide on-site consultation with teachers and parents. Another nineteen schools obtained grants from the city-sponsored Community Behavioral Health initiative to provide on-site behavioral health prevention and early intervention services.

## PARENT AND COMMUNITY INVOLVEMENT

While it does not absolve school systems of the responsibility of succeeding with all children, it is extraordinarily easier if parents and the wider community are deeply engaged in helping. Over the years I have been struck by stories I have heard, particularly from African Americans such as Marian Wright Edelman, Otis Moss, Samuel DeWitt Proctor, and my first wonderful deputy superintendent in Philadelphia, Jeanette Brewer, about the strong sense of community in the neighborhoods in which they grew up. People took responsibility for one another's well-being. Adults looked out for all children, not just their own. Children knew that all the adults around them would support them in their successes, but also that they had to heed the watchful eyes of people sitting in windows, rocking on porches, and walking down the street, in addition to their own families. I never tire of hearing people tell these stories. They describe what I believe community should be like.

### Parents

Parent involvement and support gets students out of bed in the morning, and it reinforces positive student behavior. It provides support for teachers, helps ensure that homework gets done, and helps build relationships between home and school that strengthen the effect of education. Because the importance of parent involvement cannot be overstated, in Philadelphia we made special efforts to reach out to parents.

Many parents from low-income communities have failed in school themselves. It is imperative to create a welcoming atmosphere. Parents are often intimidated by the perception that the teachers and administrators are smarter than they are. Moreover, teachers are viewed as authority figures. I remember how much anxiety I felt during the first parent-teacher conferences for my children—and I had completed six years of graduate work, earned three post-graduate degrees, and was the state superintendent of schools. If I felt so intimidated, how much more intense must that feeling be for parents with little education or those for whom school was not a successful experience personally? We must make it clear that we value all parents, helping create a different image of the school.

Schools should schedule events to be convenient for all parents, whatever their work schedule—sometimes in the daytime, sometimes at night. The principal and teachers should be available (within reason) for one-on-one conferences of meaningful length at times other than scheduled parent-teacher nights. Principals and teachers should make it clear that they respect the community. One very effective way to do this is to call or visit the homes of their students. When Gloria Watts, a family friend, became principal of a school in Fresno, California, she visited the homes of every one of her five hundred students the summer before school started. Imagine the positive image that cast in the community.

The school and the district must be transparent about bureaucratic procedures, making it as easy as possible for parents to "negotiate the system." There are many ways to do this. Schools should make student performance clear, and explain expectations in language that parents understand. Teachers should ensure that parents know when and how they will learn how their children and the school are performing. Schools can provide parent training on questions to ask teachers. The budget, and how the budget reflects school values and priorities, should be clearly explained. These are just a few of the ways to send a message to parents and the wider community that the district wants them to be informed and involved.

## Philadelphia

Sheer availability was important. To that end, I personally had scores of public meetings every year throughout the city on both a cluster and school basis in which open-ended opportunities for questions were available. I preached in a different church once a month and stayed afterward for both formal and informal exchanges with members of the congregation. I sought out talk radio call-in invitations, including shows that were not particularly friendly.

We had a complex relationship with official parent groups, working closely with some and having more turbulent relationships with others. I met personally every month with representatives from these groups (about ten times more often every year than previous superintendents), but these meetings were not as productive as they could have been. In part, this was due to conflict between the groups. For a number of reasons, relationships with some groups were more constructive and with others less so.

Before I arrived there was a lengthy history of mistrust between the district/superintendent and parent groups. With some we were more successful than with others in establishing a new base of trust. The organizations that were more personality driven were more difficult to engage in problem-solving than those who engaged several of their leaders in dialogue with the district. Some were inclined to address issues from the beginning in the media; others would begin the process around any given issue with dialogue.

One of my goals was to establish an official policy of Parent and Family Responsibility, outlining the responsibilities that parents have to help their children in school. We wanted to provide a counterpart accountability process to the one embodied in promotion and graduation requirements for students and the professional responsibility system for teachers and other staff.

This effort never succeeded, in part because of resistance from official parent groups who had several problems with the plan. They were afraid it would embarrass parents who could not live up to the responsibilities. They thought it was unfair because the resources did not exist to help parents meet the responsibilities. They worried that the educators would not live up to their part of the responsibilities outlined. All of these concerns reflected a historical lack of trust between parents and schools. It was clearly not a problem created only by the parent side of the equation.

I must mention a strategy that did not work since so many districts use some version of it. There was time during each school board meeting when members of the public could make statements. In Philadelphia, individuals were given five minutes, representatives of organizations were given three minutes each, with a limit of five speakers per organization per meeting. Although a good idea in theory, these portions of the meeting usually deteriorated into "gripe sessions," with the same individuals often speaking week after week. Citizens with specific grievances or constructive ideas typically called or wrote the board or me, opening a more substantive conversation. The board entertained eliminating or reducing this generally unconstructive open mike period, but finally decided to maintain it to avoid the criticism that we didn't care about the public's view.

The time and energy spent in those sessions was largely a waste. It could have been better spent in scheduling personal meetings with the individuals who cared more about the schools than about the personal publicity often given them by Philadelphia's media.

**Volunteering and Direct Community Involvement**

We mounted several major initiatives to involve the wider public in direct ways through volunteering.

- Project 10,000—This strong effort to increase our numbers of volunteers had three components: persistent requests for help, the provision of meaningful roles for volunteers, and repeated thank-yous. Our original goal was to add ten thousand volunteers over five years. We succeeded in adding fifteen thousand over three years. We did this with one part-time central office person coordinating the work.
- Faith Partnerships—Long before President Bush began to promote his faith-based initiatives, Philadelphia was a leader in developing relationships between faith-based groups and public schools.

Other than schools, religious institutions are the most pervasive and stable institutions in a community. Public schools had too often developed an arms-length relationship to local congregations based on an unexamined assumption that the first amendment created a prohibition against any association. Having both a law degree and theology degrees, I strongly support and respect the lines drawn by the first amendment. However, that line easily permits extensive nonreligious relationships with religious institutions. Unfounded first amendment concerns were denying us tremendous amounts of important support.

To maintain compliance with the first amendment, religious institutions could not include any of their religious tenets in the programs, but we welcomed the presence of their moral values contributing to the overall culture of the school environment. While there were occasions when one or another of the institutions came too close to the proselytizing line, a conversation with the minister would usually put the school-church program back into its proper perspective.[4]

We reached out to faith communities in a number of ways. I often preached about children and youth issues in churches throughout the city. I built a strong relationship with the Black Clergy of Philadelphia and Vicinity, and the Metropolitan Council of Churches. For many years, churches throughout the city had partnered with schools in a variety of informal ways. We continued to encourage that, but by my third year, we specifically asked the principals to seek out such partnerships. By the fourth year we mandated a relationship with at least one faith-based organization in a school's attendance zone.

These partnerships produced after-school programs, volunteers, computer clubs, and, on occasion, space for overflow classes. In addition, the relationship often produced strong advocacy for the school. We also sponsored a national conference called Faith Communities and Public Schools: Building on Common Ground, that attracted over five hundred participants.[5] The meeting focused on ways in which congregations from all faith traditions could support public education through volunteering, advocacy, and other support.

## Business Partnerships

We forged many partnerships with the business community, which early in my tenure was a source of strong support. Representatives from the business community, including Rosemarie Greco of CoreStates Bank and Richard Mandel of Greater Philadelphia First's education partnership, were involved with and strongly supported my selection as superintendent, based in part on my focus on accountability and outcomes.

However, over time the support of most business leaders eroded, despite our implementation of the accountability agenda they had sought and our rising test scores. With leadership turnover, the replacement of locally owned businesses with national ones, and increasing business affiliation with the Catholic schools and the Republican voucher agenda, the business community fell well short of fulfilling their potential help.

Though they never delivered meaningful political support, the business community made some important on-the-ground contributions to our work. One of the most significant contributions was involvement in the district's innovative School to Career program, led by Mary Jane Clancy. In essence, at the ninth and tenth grade levels, students began to be introduced to various career options, in addition to meeting the district's high content standards. In the eleventh grade, students spent one day a week in mentored, on-site learning placements; in the twelfth grade, students spent two days a week in these placements. These placements, a form of apprenticeship, were with employers, large and small, throughout the city. Trained mentors, from a range of professions and vocations, worked one-on-one with students.[6]

Students participating in the School to Career program in high schools throughout the city had better attendance, lower dropout rates, higher grades, and were more likely to attend college than other comparable students. Our objective was to make the opportunity available to all Philadelphia students, which we were well on our way to doing when I resigned.

## SAFETY AND SECURITY

Despite the widespread perception that urban schools are violent places, the reality is that in any part of America, school is one of the safest places a child can be. Students spend more time at school than they do anywhere except for their homes, but schools are rarely where students get hurt (Dinkes et al., 2006, p. 1). Furthermore, over the past fifteen years school violence and theft were down, and the decreases were greater in urban settings than in suburban or rural ones (Dinkes et al., 2006, p. 73).

Even though schools are one of the safest places for our children to be, any crime at school is too much. Fear and anxiety of becoming a victim inhibits the ability of our teachers to educate and our students to learn. While any threat of serious violence contributes to such fear, another important cause is everyday misbehavior, such as bullying, disrespect, or teasing. For example, nationwide, 30 percent of students in grades 6–10 report being bullied or teased. Twenty-seven percent of the teachers report that student misbehavior keeps them from teaching a "fair amount" to a "great deal" of the time. Thus it is important to address both serious crime and common misbehavior in an aggressive manner.

Children and staff need to feel both physically and psychologically safe if they are to learn. Safety is a basic need that must be met before one can concentrate on English, math, and science, on thinking critically and solving problems. Issues of safety and security are central to schools meeting their mission.

It is not possible to overstate the importance of school success as the single most important strategy for reducing violence and student misbehavior. Any teacher or school principal will attest to the fact that the vast majority of behavior problems in school arise from students who are not performing well. There are occasional high performers, even more "gifted" (though often not high performers), who "act out." They are usually students who are dealing with mental health issues, who are not challenged in school, who fall into a "bullied" category (race, sexual orientation, physical characteristics, etc.), or who are facing challenging issues at home. But these students also generally will not be succeeding academically.

The point is that a quality early childhood education program at age three, or consistent quality teaching, or class size below seventeen up to the fourth grade, or extra time for learning will be far more effective in curbing violence and misbehavior than metal detectors and school police.

While it is critical to implement systemic changes like those mentioned above to permanently alter the culture of a school and district to address safety, security, health, and social service issues, it is also necessary to have tactical, short-term, safety intervention strategies to contain bad behavior, including violence, in the short term. In Philadelphia, we instituted many significant initiatives to reduce violence and bad behavior, as well as to reduce the public perception that such behavior was more widespread than it was.

## Philadelphia

Though I envisioned the long-term academic and nonacademic strategies as permanent solutions, I hoped that we would be able to abandon any or all of these short-term strategies after we implemented the rest of *Children Achieving* and students began to achieve (and behave well) at high levels (U.S. Department of Education, 1998).

### School Police

School police were already in place when I became superintendent. However, we undertook four major changes in the way they operated. First, we required all school police to wear uniforms. Second, we decided all school police should be sworn officers. Third, if our school police were to be sworn officers in uniform, they needed more training than they had previously received. To this end, school police officers began to attend the police academy. Fourth, we significantly increased the number of school police, from 246 at the beginning of my term, to about 500 before I left.

### Cameras

Nonteaching assistants, teachers, administrators, and other adults in buildings cannot patrol every hallway, every bathroom, or every room at every moment. Similarly, bus drivers can't constantly monitor what goes on behind them, as it is dangerous for them to constantly turn around or watch students in their rearview mirror. Therefore, we installed real cameras and dummy cameras in all middle schools and high schools, and in dozens of buses.

## Metal Detectors

One of the more unpleasant decisions we made was to install metal detectors in all of the high schools. It was the clearest physical indication of the fear that weapons might be brought into school. In the end, even though I think it altered school culture negatively, the existence of a fear of weapons led me to make the decision to install the detectors. We paid special attention to training those monitoring the machines so that students were respected and so that we could move thousands of student and faculty into the school relatively expeditiously.

## Identification and Swipe Cards

Even though the students had been divided into small learning communities, there were still large numbers of students in the buildings that previously housed the large comprehensive high schools. We concluded it was important to control access to the buildings. We began to mandate the use of picture identification cards. Toward the end of my tenure, we began to install the technology to permit use of swipe cards.

Many of these measures, including police presence, cameras, and ID cards, were accepted more readily than might have otherwise been the case because they were also being adopted at many office buildings, courthouses, airports, and other public venues. Such practices have become all too commonplace, but at least schools are not singled out; they simply find themselves, as in so many other ways, creatures of the towns and cities where they are located.

## Alternative Schools

Only in exceptional circumstances should a student be suspended or expelled, not only because of the negative consequences for the individual students but because it increases the likelihood of antisocial behaviors in the community. However, because of the negative impact some students can have on the school learning environment, and the special approaches they may need in order to change their behavior, some students need to be removed from their normal classroom assignments.

When I went to Philadelphia, the district had several "disciplinary schools." They were places where students were sent when the district didn't know what else to do with them. Most students who were sent to these schools ended up dropping out altogether. We implemented several alternatives to these disciplinary schools, including Twilight Schools, the TOPS (Transitional Opportunities Promoting Success) program, the Community Education Partners school, the Alternative Behavior and Learning Environment Center (ABLE Academies) and, in elementary schools, rooms in the building used for in-school suspension, for as little as an hour up to several days and without the need for paperwork.[7]

Metal detectors, school police, exterior door programs, uniforms, cameras, not to mention suspensions and expulsions, are not the real answers to student misbehavior. Good early childhood programs, high expectations, quality teachers and administrators, and strong professional development are the answers to creating safe and secure schools. Successful students become successful adults, workers, and citizens, thus reducing the social and financial costs of adult crime and violence.

## DECENTRALIZING DECISION-MAKING

### School-Based Decision-Making

As educational units become smaller and more accountable, they also need to be given more authority. It is exceptionally difficult to be a community and accept responsibility for one another and for every child's performance if all that you are allowed to do is carry out the directives of other people.

School-based decision-making, like other components of school reform, is not a silver bullet. Many districts in the late 1980s and early 1990s tried to implement a form of decentralization, without producing any real evidence that it improved achievement. The mistake was to pick out this one strategy to carry the burden of success by itself. But it is an important component of an overall standards-based reform. Authority (assuming capacity) and accountability (assuming adequate support) vested in a small school setting can further enhance teamwork and interaction among school staff, parents, and students.

The board and the superintendent, after consultation with other educators and the public, should decide what students should learn and be able to do; they should design and implement the districtwide assessment system and the accountability system; they should define and deliver on the opportunity to learn standards and retain authority for decisions to ensure equity for all students. All other decisions—how education takes place, where it takes place, who teaches and who teaches whom, and the time frames within which it occurs—should rest at the school level. School-based decisions should fall into six categories.

### Budget Decisions

Budget decisions, within an allocation determined centrally (to ensure equity), belong at the school level. Decisions about book purchases; how many of what kind of staff; and expenditures on extracurricular activities, cleaning supplies, and professional development must be made at a level at which the decision-makers can be directly familiar with the strengths and weaknesses of resources in an individual school or small learning community.

The most radical decentralization of budget decisions has occurred in the state of Victoria in Australia and the city of Edmonton, in Alberta, Canada, where more than 90 percent of the funds are placed under the control of the school. Even such services as curricular consultants, district psychologists, professional development, marketing, and warehouse items are purchased by local schools. Many central office service centers in the Australian and Canadian districts had no centrally allocated funds available. They existed (or did not) based on a purchase of their services in a competitive manner with non–school district providers or even from services that school-based personnel decided to provide themselves.[8] All accounts suggest it has worked well.

### Instructional Strategy

Instructional strategy decisions belong to the principal and her teams of teachers. Assuming access to information about effective practices, and the data to make informed decisions, they, better than anyone else, know the capacities of the team members. One size does not fit all.

### Disciplinary Measures

Disciplinary measures, within equity boundaries, belong with the school and parents. Equity boundaries would include corporal punishment and use of suspension and expulsion. Very importantly, decisions about actions to be taken *before* punitive measures are taken should be the responsibility of school staff. Prevention is a far more important part of the disciplinary code than what happens after school staff has failed with the student(s).

### Extracurricular Activity Policy

Extracurricular activity policy, including academic and behavior guidelines governing participation and the use of school facilities by the community, should be determined in large measure at the school level.

### School Staffing Decisions

School staffing decisions including selection and assignment of staff within the school belong to the school council and principal. The decisions must be framed, however, within district policy ensuring equitable distribution of highly qualified teachers.

### Student Assignments

Student assignments within the school must be determined by those who know them best, the teams of teachers and principal, within district policy frameworks that maximize heterogeneity.

### Philadelphia

From the beginning, radical decentralization was one of the central tenets of *Children Achieving*. It probably was also the one on which we made the least progress. There were three big reasons—the district's prior experience with school-based decision-making, the culture as exemplified by, but not limited to, the unions, and lack of capacity at every level.

### Previous Experience

Prior to my arrival in Philadelphia, Superintendent Clayton had made initial efforts at decentralization and school-based decision-making. Encouraged by the Philadelphia Schools Collaborative, which was seeking additional autonomy for charters, and by the business and educational trends at that time, she reached a School-Based Management/Shared Decision-Making agreement with the union, decentralized a number of central office staff to the six regional offices, and, finally, created the capacity for schools to make their own budget decisions, within the parameters of the law, court decisions, and the contract.

Some schools made effective use of this new authority and flexibility, but the road was very bumpy, and many regarded School-Based

Management/Shared Decision-Making as a failure. One big reason was that the budget flexibility was granted in a year when schools had to make large cuts. It was perceived by some as simply a way for the central office to avoid responsibility for hard decisions about what to cut.

### Culture

Despite these efforts at decentralization in Philadelphia, the culture of the district, like that of most large urban districts, was in general extremely top-down. It was so ingrained that even when a leader like Superintendent Clayton really wished to transfer some authority, there was a tendency to see this as a ploy, a trap, a "this too shall pass" fad. In general, people were comfortable with having decisions made for them.

During our attempts to further decentralize, this general resistance was exacerbated by the leadership of the teachers union. The union leadership's position on accountability made them opponents of school-based management since the two go hand-in-hand. Also, the union's own highly centralized organization was much easier to run when the district administration made decisions centrally. Therefore, the union membership participation in school-based decision-making was discouraged.

This is not to say that no school successfully implemented school-based decision-making. As teachers realized that participating in the school council gave them voice in decisions about areas like school budget and professional development, their involvement gradually increased. In the best cases, there was significant implementation.

### Capacity

Changing from a top-down system to a decentralized one requires new skills, new processes, new ways of thinking, at all levels of the organization. School personnel have to understand budgets, pricing systems, and the requirements about how various funding sources may be spent. They need to match budget decisions with instructional priorities. Principals need skills in consensus building. Central office budget systems and staff must be able to handle and process individual budgets and provide data for every school. The central office must undertake a mind-shift to be responsive to what schools perceive as their needs. Making such shifts does not happen automatically.

## ADEQUATE FACILITIES

Buildings that are suitable for the instructional program can make a big contribution to student learning. A walk through most suburban schools makes it clear that we know this. A walk through many urban schools shows that, collectively, we do not choose to act on that knowledge. The physical condition of many schools in our urban centers is shameful.

### Philadelphia

When we launched *Children Achieving* in Philadelphia in 1994, many of our schools—particularly in the highest-poverty neighborhoods—were plagued by broken windows, leaks, peeling paint, and faulty plumbing and heating systems. Some had insufficient space; there were waiting lists even for half-day kindergarten programs, and some classes were taught in adapted spaces such as auditoriums or hallways. Some lab sciences had no lab.

Far too much of the time of principals, whose primary function should be instructional leadership, was of necessity devoted to making their buildings usable. School facilities need not be luxurious to provide the necessary conditions for teaching and learning, but they must be safe, kept at a comfortable temperature, and well-maintained. The condition of the school buildings in Philadelphia not only was an impediment to learning but also conveyed disrespect to our teachers, students, and parents.

We conducted what many described as the only comprehensive facilities audit in the school district's history. We determined what it would take to bring the existing buildings to code—to make them sufficient for instruction, though not state-of-the-art. Even with these minimal standards, the news was not pretty. The average building was over sixty years old and had many problems due to poor maintenance. Not surprisingly, the buildings in the worst state of disrepair were most likely to house our lowest-income students. The projected cost of simply bringing all our buildings up to code was well over one billion dollars.

Thirty years of insufficient construction and deferred maintenance—the consequence of a very modest capital program for twenty-eight years between 1972 and 2000—led to these abysmal conditions. During the 1970s, the district was not even in the capital market for financing, and in the eleven years before I became superintendent, the district dedicated only $431 million to the capital program. Recognizing decades of neglect, we stepped up the capital program, creating capital obligations of nearly $800 million in the six years of *Children Achieving* (School District of Philadelphia Draft Financial Plan, 2001, p. 219).

We increased space by building eleven "Little School Houses" that served 360 young children each, renting space from the Archdiocese and purchasing and refurbishing five other former Archdiocesan schools.

Adding new space addressed only one part of our facilities problems. Maintenance needed urgent attention. We dramatically increased the number of building maintenance projects in the district. The district owned 300 buildings (260 schools, and 40 buildings used for administration, warehousing of supplies, etc.), and the challenge to stay on top of maintenance needs was enormous. Requesting, prioritizing, and monitoring work orders was still a paper-based process. Back orders numbered in the thousands; some were over ten years old. Principals often pointed to maintenance problems to illustrate how ineffective "downtown" was in supporting schools. Within three years of computerizing the system, the number of work tasks accomplished in a year went from 51,000 to 85,000, despite overall cuts in maintenance staff during those years (School District of Philadelphia Draft Financial Plan, 2001, p. 219).

Balancing the infrastructure requirements of key instructional reforms with the realities of tight budgets often required considerable ingenuity. Our decision to implement full-day kindergarten and smaller classes in kindergarten through third grade provides a good example. We were told that these changes would be impossible because they would require the construction of hundreds of millions of dollars of new schools, which were beyond the capacity of the local construction companies to provide even if we had the funds. These criticisms would have been valid had we approached the challenge in the traditional way. We solved the problems differently.

We decided that in six months, full-day kindergarten would be implemented in all 150 schools housing concentrated numbers of low-income students. The remaining twenty-five elementary schools would implement full-day kindergarten a year later. Under the leadership of Patricia Harris, a former regional superintendent with a reputation for her determination, we worked with principals to examine how they could better use their space.

We consolidated activities in rooms that were underused. In many instances, we turned out art and science teachers from their rooms and had them work from movable supply carts to create space for the kindergartners. In schools where such reorganization did not provide enough space, we brought in portable classrooms for the older students. This compromised the instruction of the older students, as the long, narrow shape of the trailers was far from ideal for teaching and learning, but we made this decision because full-day kindergarten was our highest priority. Results justified our decisions.

Later, we had the opportunity to use federal funds to lower the student to adult ratio from 30:1 to 17:1 in the early grades. Space again became an issue, since, in effect, this meant we would need twice as many classrooms for these grades if we approached this in traditional ways. We simply didn't have that much space, so we either had to give up the idea of lower class sizes or think of an innovative approach to the challenge.

My chief of staff, Germaine Ingram; associate superintendent, Katherine Conner; and central office instruction leader, Allie Mulvihill, reviewed research and best practices regarding reduced class size. They concluded that reduced class size improved outcomes not because of reduced numbers per se, but because they made different kinds of instruction possible.

In classrooms with fewer students, the teacher was able to work with struggling students one-on-one and in small groups more often, and to do so at the moment the student(s) needed help. This practice was key, for example, to the Reading Recovery program, and to the instructional systems developed by Bob Slavin, both very successful. The research further demonstrated that such immediate, personalized interventions were especially important for at-risk children.

One way to facilitate these interventions was to hire more teachers and build new classrooms for small groups of students. In our case, this was not possible. We decided that an acceptable alternative was to have a second teacher assigned full-time within an existing, regular-sized class, to specialize in providing one-on-one and small group instruction to children who needed extra help, while the regular teacher handled the ongoing instruction.

But this innovative idea created a new problem. As in all large urban districts, we faced a serious shortage of teachers, especially in the middle grades. Most middle-grade teachers had elementary certification. We were concerned that if the newly created elementary positions were made available to middle-school teachers already in the district, many would flee the middle schools, worsening an already untenable situation for our students in sixth, seventh, and eighth grade. Furthermore, we did not want new applicants for teaching jobs, our major resource for filling the middle-school vacancies, to choose the elementary positions instead of our understaffed middle schools.

We needed to enlarge the applicant pool. To accomplish this, we created a special class of teachers called Literacy Interns. We reached out to liberal arts graduates with strong academic records but without certification. Most were recent graduates and others were career changers, but all had strong academic records, enthusiastic recommendations, and lots of motivation. Their starting salaries were slightly below those of other starting teachers, and, in an agreement with the union, we used the difference to provide year-round professional development and college credits toward certification for this cadre of teachers.

In a sense, the approach was comparable to that of Teach for America or Urban Teaching Fellows programs, except that we were limiting our focus to the early grades and to the teaching of reading.

The Literacy Interns led to reading gains for our struggling students. There were other benefits as well. The interns were unusually fresh and enthusiastic, and their attitudes improved the atmosphere in many schools. In several schools, principals also reported that in the classrooms with interns, in addition to seeing reading progress, they were seeing reductions in disciplinary problems. They also became an outstanding pool of individuals from whom regularly certified teachers began to emerge.

## INSTRUCTIONAL MATERIALS

One of the necessary tools to an effective instructional program in which all students achieve to high standards is up-to-date quality instructional material in sufficient quantity.

### Philadelphia

In 1994, Philadelphia fell far short of meeting that standard. We did not have enough books, even old books, to allow all students to have their own textbook. It was not unusual in the upper grades to have only one set of books per teacher, for use with five or six classes of thirty to thirty-five students each. Since the books could not be taken home, teachers were forced either to give no homework or to spend valuable class time allowing students to copy down assignments.

In addition, the few books we did have were often of unacceptable quality. It was not unusual for the basic text in a class to be ten or more years old. In a science or history class, teaching recent developments and perspectives depended on the individual teacher. In many instances, learning strategies and even illustrations were seriously out of date or just plain wrong. An example that stands out in my mind was a biography of Nelson Mandela shelved in one school library, claiming that he was already dead.

Further, in any self-respecting school, the library should be a centerpiece of learning, but many of ours could not be kept open for lack of staff. Underresourced schools were forced to make Hobbesian choices about where to spend their meager resources, choosing, for example, between a librarian and a reading resource teacher or another teacher allowing a reduction in class size or another math teacher when the school was weak in math.

And, of course, to create good teaching and learning conditions quality schools require many instructional materials beyond books. Our schools had few graphing calculators, for example, and we had an insufficient quality of lab materials for science classes. When necessary materials aren't available or, as is often the case, the teacher regularly purchases materials out of her own pocket, it is clear that the state, city, or district is not meeting a fundamental obligation.

The school district was rightly criticized for these conditions by the city council. Books and other instructional materials should rank at the top of the expenditure list even in the absence of sufficient funding. The issue became a cause célèbre, since the deficiency was so obvious to public officials and to parents. It was quickly apparent that we had to deal with this issue on its merits and to get it off the front pages, since it masked the other good things that were going on.

To deal with this problem, we allocated millions of dollars to the purchase of books, doubling the instructional materials budget within one year. This created a significant budget deficit for us, but we considered it a necessary step. Despite our best efforts, a lack of instructional materials persisted in many of our nine thousand classrooms. Often, we found out about these instances from the press. To learn directly about these problems, we set up a parent hotline that anyone in the community could call to let us know where reality was not conforming to our intentions that no child should be without his/her own set of books.

We also obtained a state waiver that allowed all Title I schools in the district to be schoolwide project sites, a category which gave them greater flexibility with the use of federal funds, and loosened restrictions about the purchase and use of instructional materials. In addition, we changed budgeting rules to enable schools to carry over funds from one year to the next, so they could aggregate the dollars to buy, for example, a whole new series of a textbook at once.

All of these, however, were stopgap measures. School systems, rich and poor, need to be able to provide books, computers, and a range of other instructional materials in every class for every child. No school district should have to select the quantity or quality of instructional materials based on the constraints of an insufficient budget, rather than based on the best interest of students. To be forced into a position of doing otherwise is wrong and it should be illegal.

## TECHNOLOGY

Technology is becoming more and more important to education. As I have noted elsewhere, *what* children learn must be defined by what is necessary to equip them to function as effective adults. *How* children learn, *when* children learn, *where* children learn, and *who* teaches them are the variables of instruction. Technology can broaden the options we have regarding these variables. Indeed, technology has become an essential tool for children to meet the standards they need for success in life.

People learn in very different ways, and different subjects are best taught with different tools and strategies. Technology greatly increases the variety of teaching approaches available, and enhances pedagogy. Audio and video equipment can change the learning process to help students meet their needs. Software permits powerfully instructive simulations. Technology also creates powerful new opportunities for students with disabilities: readers for blind students, head-mounted pointers that enable a child who is quadriplegic to use a computer, tech-enabled voices for those unable to speak, even simple tools that extend the reach of students who are wheelchair bound.

Technology extends the reach, depth, richness, and breadth of the teacher. If we have technology, and teachers trained to use it, we have access to the most learned, the most skilled, the most experienced, and the most culturally diverse experts in their fields. The world can be our teacher.

### Philadelphia

Unfortunately, in Philadelphia we were in no position to take advantage of the capacity of technology as a vehicle for transformative reforms in instruction until we had created something as basic as the necessary wiring infrastructure and increased student access to computers and teacher skill in their use. This basic work consumed most of our effort and funds.

## NOTES

1. Marian Wright Edelman conveys the plight of the poor child in this country eloquently by describing them as America's Fifth Child in a family in which four of the children are secure, well-educated, healthy, loved and the fifth is left out with all the ravages of poverty unnecessarily being their lot.

2. A full description of Family Resource and Youth Service Centers in Kentucky can be found at www. childrenachieving.com.

3. A full description of these alternative placement opportunities can be found at www.childrenachieving.com.

4. In addition to requiring each school to have a formal partnership with a congregation, we also required a partnership with at least one community organization. I mention this in a footnote, not because it is less important, but because it was more routine and because the relationship to congregations often became more extensive.

5. In November 1999, in partnership with the National Council of Churches and the U.S. Department of Education, the national conference focused on expanding "the coordination, cooperation and collaboration concept to faith communities and public schools." An incredible array of keynote speakers included Rev. Dr. Charles Adams, Dr. Charles Haynes, Rabbi David Saperstein, Rev. Jeremiah Wright, Professor John Dililio, and Christopher Edley Jr.

6. One of the highlights of my year was to attend the annual St. Christopher Hospital's event when students from Olney High School (generally considered one of the lowest performing in the city and one that was at the center of a very controversial reconstitution effort—see the chapter on accountability) would be honored by their mentors, the outstanding president of St. Christopher, Calvin Bland, and the district. It was quite extraordinary as accolades were handed out and skills learned in the program were demonstrated.

7. "Early Warning, Timely Response: A Guide to Safe Schools," which can be obtained from the U.S. Department of Education.

8. A full description of these alternative placement opportunities can be found at www.childrenachieving.com.

# 13

# Resources

An investment in education always pays the best interest.

Benjamin Franklin

If all of the rich and all of the church people should send their children to the public schools they would feel bound to concentrate their money on improving these schools until they met the highest ideals.

Susan B. Anthony

Many would argue that the learning condition most lacking in urban schools is money. It is not accidental that the chapter on resources comes toward the end of this book rather than at the beginning, nor is it accidental that I use the term *resources* rather than *money*. Money is not *by itself* the answer to creating the conditions in which all students, including those with whom we historically fail, achieve to high levels. In phasing in a comprehensive reform agenda, large infusions of additional cash should not be the first, second, or third element of changing the system. Indeed, if such a large infusion is the first element, real change may be delayed or might not take place at all.

A number of examples serve as poster children for the proposition that money by itself is not the answer. In the early 1990s, in response to a long-running court battle in New Jersey (*Abbott v. Burke*) over funding equity that extended back to the early 1970s, Governor James Florio courageously and successfully proposed increasing taxes for education by more than a billion dollars. He lost the next election. But more to the point, he bought little for the money. There was no change in the expectations of students. There was no change in accountability. There were no changes in educator work rules as defined by union contracts. There was no requirement that the money be spent based on best-practice evidence. The billion-dollar investment simply created a system in which the poorest districts had as much money as the wealthiest districts. Unfortunately, more money by itself did not contribute to better education and higher achievement. Basically, it only bought higher priced poor performance.

Other good examples of the proposition that money alone is insufficient are places like Washington, DC, and Kansas City, Missouri. For years, there had been a tendency to pour money into the schools in the nation's capital. Performance did not improve.

In Kansas City, two decades of brilliant legal work by my old law firm, Hogan and Hartson, resulted in two billion dollars being made available, largely from state coffers, to the school district. Unfortunately, the educators were not as wise as the lawyers. The educators spent the money largely on buildings, constructing more than a dozen new schools and renovating more than four dozen. They did not undertake initiatives like quality preschool for all or a strong educator accountability system. Performance did not improve very much.

This book is about the elements that are necessary to create the conditions for high achievement among all children. The first conversation must be about those elements; the resource decisions must then flow from what is needed to put those elements in place. Some of them are costly. Others are not. This is particularly true of the necessary underlying belief system or at least the willingness to behave as if one believes that all children can learn to high standards. Money is not a silver bullet; it is simply one necessary feature needed to do many of the things that will result in higher achievement. It is the classic necessary, but not sufficient, element of reform.

The analysis of fiscal resources has three components. The first is good stewardship. How does a district spend the money it already has? Is it deployed most effectively and efficiently? The second is the role of private and philanthropic dollars. Is the district's thinking sufficiently creative to attract these funds? The third component of a comprehensive fiscal analysis is adequate government support. Are the various levels of government providing sufficient funds to enable the on-going support of the educational practices that research suggests will best raise student achievement?

## STEWARDSHIP

### Philadelphia

*Background and Context*

When I arrived in Philadelphia in 1994, there was a widespread perception that the district had much more money per pupil than other districts in the area, and that it was spending these funds wildly and unwisely. The prevailing myth was that our teachers and administrators were better paid, that administration rather than instruction got the lion's share of the money, that union contracts sucked up funds with no apparent impact on educational outcomes, and that we spent money on things like luxury cars and drivers for board members rather than on children.

In fact, most of this was wrong. Most devastating was the reality that teachers and administrators were seriously underpaid in comparison to the southeastern Pennsylvania marketplace within which we competed for personnel. The starting salary for a teacher in Philadelphia in 1994 was roughly $30,000, versus an average of $33,000 in the nearby suburbs. Our teachers were being asked to teach large classes of children with significant challenges arising from poverty, and to do so in buildings more than sixty years old, without enough books for their students, and with less support from professionals like librarians and counselors. They were being asked do all this for a salary 10 percent lower than what they could earn by teaching in the suburbs.

The salary differences were even greater for experienced teachers. For those teachers with fifteen years of experience, the difference grew to more than $10,000 per year, on average. The gap between salaries for city and suburban teachers was even greater in the most affluent suburbs, which could pay their most experienced teachers as much as $35,000 more per annum than we could in Philadelphia. Because of the extra challenges our teachers faced in the classroom we should have been paying more, much more, than the districts in the suburbs. Contrary to popular opinion, we were not. No wonder many of our best teachers eventually left us for the greener pastures outside the city.

The same was true for administration. In a sense, Philadelphia had become a de facto training ground not only for suburban teachers, but for future suburban principals. Routinely, a suburban district would offer one of our principals $25,000 to $35,000 more per annum to cross district lines. I did not blame either the suburban district or the principal.

The suburban district wanted the best they could find. The principals who accepted such offers often had children about to go off to college and needed the extra income.

This flight of talent and experience from the city was the fault of the governors and legislators who knew the votes to secure their re-election came from the suburban elite and not the urban poor, and the fault of the citizenry who thought their tax dollars were wasted in the schools that educated black and brown kids and who did not want to pay more in taxes.

Philadelphia's education expenditures were 7.9 percent lower than the national average, lower than the Pennsylvania average by 25.7 percent (which included hundreds of rural districts with low expenditures themselves) (School District of Philadelphia Draft Financial Plan, 2001, p. 18), and about 30 percent lower than the average in the surrounding sixty-one school districts. We wanted more. We needed more. We just didn't have it.

Michael Masch, former finance director for the city, state budget secretary, and now back at the district as chief business officer, was in the late years of my administration one of the school board members in Philadelphia. He observed that the high level spending of which I was accused was aspirational—that is, what I wanted to do—rather than reality. We just didn't have the money to fund everything we needed to do for our children.

In addition to the fact that total school expenditures in Philadelphia were well below local, state, and national averages, as a district we had to battle the public perception that what money we did have was spent on things other than instruction. At least in a relative sense, in this category Philadelphia actually performed better than the surrounding sixty-one school districts and better than the average in Pennsylvania. Contrary to the public perception, we were being better stewards of our financial resources than other districts, especially when one considers Philadelphia had many significant noninstructional costs, most notably those related to student health, safety, and security, that other districts did not have (School District of Philadelphia Draft Financial Plan, 2001, p. 6).[1]

Between 1996 and 2001, revenue per student actually declined when adjusted for inflation. Another important contextual factor specific to Philadelphia is the fact that, unlike other large cities in Pennsylvania, Philadelphia is simultaneously a city, a county, and a school district. The Greater Philadelphia First (GPF) committee carried out an analysis to determine whether this affected the amount of funding that was available for education. They compared the tax and expenditure structures in Philadelphia with that in Pittsburgh and Allegheny County (of which Pittsburgh is a subdivision).

A 1999 independent study by the Pew Charitable Trust found that the GPF

> study clearly demonstrates the fiscal "bind" that Philadelphia is in. Residents of both *cities* support relatively the *same* total per capita "tax expenditure"—a little over $1,500. However, Philadelphia spends more than twice as much as Pittsburgh on *county-provided functions*, because in Pittsburgh the costs of those functions are paid for in part by taxes on its suburbs in Allegheny County. This means that Philadelphia must spend proportionally less on other city functions, including schools.
>
> Moreover, Philadelphia's tax base is considerably *weaker* than Pittsburgh's in terms of both resident income and property value, meaning that Philadelphia's tax *burden* was 11 percent higher on property and 36 percent higher on incomes than Pittsburgh's. Indeed, Philadelphia's overall tax burden as a percentage of resident income is roughly twice that of its suburbs, while its tax expenditures on education as a percentage of resident income are actually *higher* than the average of communities around the state. (Whiting, 1999, p. 21)

The point is that the politics of rich and poor, black and white, Latino and English-speaking, and city/rural and suburban, resulted in long-term structural inadequacies and an unjust system that forced Philadelphia Public Schools to try to do more and more with less and less.

### Management and Productivity

As we announced in the *Children Achieving Action Design* in 1995, we decided early on that we would establish a Management and Productivity Task Force. Comprised largely of members of the Philadelphia business community, it would examine all aspects of the district's management and make recommendations about opportunities for us to reduce costs in certain areas, to enable us to shift funds to instruction that would contribute to better achievement by more students. Richard Smoot, the head of the PNC BANK in Philadelphia, and Emma Chappell, the head of United Bank of Philadelphia, the largest African American–controlled and managed bank in Philadelphia, co-chaired the task force.

The Management and Productivity Task Force identified several dozen areas in which cuts and savings were possible, including union contract work rule changes for employees responsible for facilities, energy use reductions through new incentive programs in which the schools shared in the savings they individually generated, the elimination of bus attendants and the outsourcing of more than five dozen of the bus routes we ran every day, the organizational consolidation of a number of management information system units, the termination of our historic practice of stockpiling supplies, changes in sick-leave policy and changes in sabbatical leave policy, and changes in the mailing systems (School District of Philadelphia Performance, 1998, pp. 28–29).

We left no stone unturned. The task force projected $46 million in savings or cost avoidance in five years. We actually achieved $47 million in three years. The outcomes were verified by the on-going work of the task force itself.

One of the things that significantly helped ensure that the task force recommendations were actually carried out was my appointment of two senior aides, to oversee implementation.[2] They operated with my full backing. Moreover, they were not restricted to implementing the Task Force recommendations but were expected to look for additional initiatives that we could take. This created the cultural conditions to facilitate change, despite internal opposition and anxiety both from those who resisted change and from those who, with the best of intentions, sought to "save me from myself."

We made additional improvements in productivity and stewardship through our successful efforts to reexamine the manner in which we distributed money to schools. Examples include:

- Realignment of almost $4 million in Title I funds to schools with higher concentrations of low-income students, and a district requirement to devote 10 percent of Title I budgets to staff development and 1 percent to parent involvement.
- The elimination of financial incentives to overidentify special needs students and of disincentives to serve students in the least-restrictive environment that meets their needs.
- Realignment of desegregation funds to provide incentives for schools to recruit for diversity.
- Resources to permit all special admission and vocational schools to provide services to English-language learners.
- Elimination of historic favoritism-based allocation of funds to certain schools. (School District of Philadelphia Performance, 1994–1998, p. 29)

Conceiving the funding formulas to achieve these goals was carried out as part of the equity function of the Office of Standards, Equity, and Services. These initiatives obviously caused controversy because they resulted in the movement of money from schools that had come to rely on it—which tended to be in communities with more political connections—to schools that needed it more and that tended to be in communities with less political clout.

However, the schools on the receiving end were those of whom the most achievement progress was being demanded by our commitment to all children learning to high levels, and hence by our accountability system. It required an intense educational effort, to help first the board, and then the schools and the public, understand both the rationale and how to make best use of the funds. But we were determined that while fighting for equity in Harrisburg, we would practice what we preached inside the system. In too many school districts across the country intradistrict funds distribution can be as big a problem as interdistrict distribution.

Key players in the efforts were Katherine Conner, associate superintendent; Diane Castelbuono (now Pennsylvania's commissioner of basic education), at the time a young staff member whose combination of intelligence, business skills, ferocity, and an intuitive understanding of how to translate equity into spreadsheets made her especially effective; and Terry Dellmuth, my chief of staff, who brought us a lifelong activist commitment to equity, the benefits of management skills, and his long experience with funding formulas and budgets in the governor's office and with the Pennsylvania Department of Education. Clay Armbrister, managing director, also provided consistent support as he worked to bring along the staff of the finance office, who were unaccustomed to having budget funding formulas reconceptualized for instructional purposes.

Another stewardship initiative we took was to sharpen our focus as we set priorities. When I first became superintendent and we announced *Children Achieving*, every proposal, every letter, every e-mail we received was filled with descriptions about how the subject matter was related to *Children Achieving*. We soon realized that under an expansive definition, almost any program or initiative could be related to some aspect of the *Children Achieving Action Design*. Therefore, during budget development we insisted that it was not sufficient for something to be merely *consistent* with *Children Achieving*; rather, to be included in our budget, a recommendation had actually to *be Children Achieving*. This standard not only freed up resources for essential initiatives, but also freed up time for school and central office to focus on their implementation.

There were efforts that we undertook that did not work out as we expected, and ones that we wanted but were never able to do. The best examples of the former were two of our outsourcing initiatives. In the first year I was superintendent, we bid out custodial work in ten schools. We were able to get the work done very cheaply. We also got ten dirty, poorly maintained schools. We abandoned the effort and negotiated higher productivity standards with the union to which our maintenance people belonged. Our objective was not just "cheap"; we wanted the least expensive, but consistent with quality performance.

One of our primary failures in the area of good stewardship and productivity, and an area related to our limited success in moving decision-making out of the central office and into schools, was our desire to turn many central office services into self-supporting service centers.

We wanted individual schools to decide whether to buy goods and services from the school district itself or whether to buy from some other vendor. We recognized that there were probably some areas, like school construction and major parts of the transportation system, where it made no sense to give schools block sums of money and let them purchase the services. But we wanted to examine instructional program support, information management and technology support, and all areas of administrative support to determine what needed to be managed centrally and what could be decentralized and made subject to purchase of service.

We knew major inroads could be made. The Edmonton School District in Alberta, Canada, and systems in Victoria, Australia, had made major strides in similar efforts. But we were never successful, for two reasons. First, there was little enthusiasm for such a system on the part of many managers—some self-serving, others genuinely worried that the system would not be effective. Second, a precondition of such a system is the capacity at the school level to make the necessary decisions. While some principals and staffs were capable of making wise, evidence-based decisions, too many were not yet at that point.

We had limited success in moving decisions down the bureaucratic pipeline into the schoolhouse. It may be that we would have been more effective if we had treated the freedom to purchase services as a reward for those schools making the most progress, though piecemeal implementation of such an initiative would have been logistically very difficult. If I were in a similar position again, this is one area in which I would exert great effort to succeed.

### Charter Schools

As is always the case in the real world, our efforts to increase productivity through good stewardship took place in a setting where the rules were constantly changing, and where political factors produced many curve balls. One good example is our experience with charter schools. In theory, charter schools are a great invention. They should free people—students, teachers, administrators, communities, and parents—to be more creative, to chart new courses, to innovate. They should be free of the constraints of the bureaucracy and the union. And, they have the potential not only to offer choices to students and parents but also to function as laboratories for the development of instructional strategies that could eventually benefit children in non-charter public schools.

At the same time, in order not to further disadvantage the students who remain in the regular schools, they should be established in a way that is financially[3] neutral to the rest of the district, and should have a proportional share of the students who are most challenging to educate. Finally, they should be rigorously evaluated.

The details of the charter law in any state are critical. In Pennsylvania, charter schools were not at all financially neutral, for a number of reasons. First, Pennsylvania state funding was not based on a per-pupil allotment, so it did not increase proportionally when district population increased. The charter law is built on the silly premise that charter students will come only from public schools, not private or parochial ones, thus creating no increase in total district population; however, as many as a third of the students entering charter schools in the period of my superintendency came from parochial schools. Thus, the already inadequate funding was being spread even thinner than before.

Finally, the law assumes that students will leave a given school in groups of about twenty-five so that their former teacher can be laid off or otherwise absorbed. According to this premise, their part of the school buildings need not be heated since they won't be there, the debt on the part of the building they occupied need no longer be paid since the students are gone, the buses they formerly rode can be sold, and so on. These premises are, of course, ridiculous—except to the legislature, which acted as though they were true.

The Philadelphia Board of Education approved thirty-eight charters by the time I stepped down. We did so both because we believed in the theory of charters and because the politics of the situation forced us into it.

We had hoped to establish ten to fifteen charters and then allow time for a serious analysis of their progress. However, the pressure from politicians was immense. Virtually every major Philadelphia legislator seemed to have "adopted" a charter school as his or her own. With all the teachers and parents connected to each school, they became a major new source of patronage where political factors, not instructional ones, too often dominated. I hope making the criteria for granting charters more explicitly related to education makes this degree of political influence impossible by charter laws in other states.

How much did this cost the noncharter public school students in Philadelphia? In March of 2001, the school board expected to spend $79.2 million on charter schools. The net cost of charter schools for the fourteen thousand projected enrollment to the Philadelphia school district was estimated to be $66.5 million for FY 2001, including nearly $24 million payments to charters for students not previously enrolled in any district school (School District of Philadelphia Draft Financial Plan, 2001, p. 159).

I would be the first to argue that if that extra $66.5 million resulted in a significant improvement in achievement for those fourteen thousand young people, and if those students were representative of the overall student population, it would be money well spent. However, on average, student achievement did not increase in Philadelphia's charter schools, compared to regular schools with the same demographics. Sadly we now know from repeated experience in Philadelphia and elsewhere around the nation that charter school students perform about the same as their regular public school counterparts—sometimes a little better, sometimes a little worse, but on the whole about the same.[4]

Thus, I contend that the $66.5 million would have been much better spent on one thousand teachers to reduce class size in our early grades, or any of a number of other purposes related to meeting our opportunity to learn standards. The state-mandated charter schools interfered significantly with our ability to responsibly steward the scarce resources available to us.[5]

### Lessons Learned

Lessons learned in the context of trying to be good stewards of the resources we had available can be summarized as follows:

- Examine every administrative and management practice, allowing none to be sacrosanct, and engage outside and independent assistance in the examination process so that practical improvements will not be overlooked due to either politics or familiarity.

- Examine whether instructional dollars can be better and/or more equitably spent.
- Examine rigorously the work rules, contractual or traditional, of employee deployment and practice, ensuring that employees are working at maximum efficiency and effectiveness. This also requires sensitivity to the employee's working conditions, and it requires their support.
- Investigate, with appropriate skepticism, new approaches to management such as outsourcing and competition to determine if there are genuine benefits.
- When deciding on new areas of expenditure, use real evidence that the new areas will contribute to improved achievement.

## PHILANTHROPY AND COMPETITIVE GRANTS

I include philanthropy and competitive grants in the discussion of resources since they can play an unusual role in the educational arena. Every organization needs to be constantly reflecting on its outcomes and practices, and experimenting with ways of achieving better results. This costs money. I believe that routine exploration and evaluation of new strategies should be incorporated into the definition of providing adequate funding.

Though we know far more about what actually works to improve student achievement of all students than we currently implement, schools and districts should always be pushing the edges, exploring new ways of accomplishing or implementing presently known strategies. However, since we are so far from achieving a permanent status of school funding adequate to address the continuing explosion of knowledge and workplace need for upgraded skills, there is a long-term need for outside funds to push the envelope. That is where philanthropy and competitive government grants come in. Money from grants is often used to support projects that operate on the margins of a school system, above and beyond the regular school activities.

### Philadelphia

In Philadelphia's case, philanthropy and competitive government grants played a crucial role. However, the $150 million plus that we raised from such outside sources over the six years of *Children Achieving* was not used for projects on the margins. Rather, it was very much part of our overall implementation of the ten-point agenda and the opportunity to learn standards.

Having determined what was needed to help all children achieve at high levels, and created a budget for those costs, we then directed the grant funds to the parts of our planned activities that were the most transformative (for example intensive professional development, implementation of new best practice instructional programs, and improvement of assessment instruments to make them more inclusive and fair).

This enabled the grants to play their usual "change agent" role within the context of a systemic, rather than individual program reform. While the grants were written for targeted activities, and the funds were tracked separately, the implementation was inextricably intertwined with our overall efforts to implement *Children Achieving*.

This strategy of embedding grant funding within a whole-system effort is very unusual. People would often ask me how much money we had available for *Children Achieving*. My answer always was, "$1.6 billion" (the total amount of our budget). They would look at me quizzically and I would follow up with the observation that *"Children Achieving* is the Philadelphia School District. It is not a project. It is not a pilot. It is the way we do business."

This section describes the process and sources of our fund-raising for *Children Achieving*, and then compares and contrasts our systemic approach with other grant-funded change strategies.

### Raising the Funds

Foundations have lots of money, and it is relatively simple to receive a share of it. My first venture in raising money occurred in 1966 when I was director of the Philadelphia Tutorial Project (PTP) and discovered I had been hired to lead an organization that did not have a dime to its name.

The proverbial "mother of necessity" led me to the 3 x 5 card catalog at the now defunct Health and Welfare Council where the names of all known foundations were kept. I went through them and picked two hundred that had given funds to education-related ventures. I convinced the pharmaceutical firm Smith Kline & French to print one hundred copies of my proposal. I sent it blindly to the first one hundred of the two hundred names on my list. Eventually eleven of them gave me grants. In less than two years PTP had a funded budget of almost $700,000, sixty employees, and thirty-five hundred volunteers.

From that early experience I learned that if one asks for money for a worthy cause, and has both a plan of action that indicates that the venture is doable and the objectives achievable and qualified staff to carry the plan out, foundations will be likely to give their support. This is especially true at the beginning of a venture, although securing sustained funding year in and year out is much more difficult. In Philadelphia, we followed this tried and true formula.

The driving philanthropic force was a $50 million grant we received from the Annenberg Foundation. In 2004, Ambassador Walter Annenberg had decided to spend $500 million across the nation to improve public education. Fortuitously, Philadelphia (Lower Merion) was the ambassador's hometown. At the time Vartan Gregorian (then the president of Brown University and now the president of the Carnegie Corporation) was a good friend of the ambassador and, along with Brown professor Ted Sizer, a key advisor to the ambassador on grant-making decisions. In turn, the ambassador and Mayor Rendell were close, and Ralph Smith (my closest colleague and confidant during my first two years in Philadelphia, and now at the Annie E. Casey Foundation) was a very good friend of Gregorian.

Hometown affection and the fact that Philadelphia was the fifth-largest district in the nation would have eventually resulted in our successfully landing a grant. But the network of relationships connecting us to the grantmakers certainly expedited the process. This was particularly true given that the Philadelphia proposal was different from the others entertained by Annenberg. The district itself, rather than an outside organization, was the moving party and the proposal revolved around a whole district effort.

Another unusual aspect of the Annenberg grant to Philadelphia was that we were required to match the grant two-to-one, when most other Annenberg grantees only had to produce a one-to-one match. I never objected to this condition because I was confident we could meet the more rigorous requirement. Moreover, we could use the match as leverage, and when we succeeded we would have 50 percent more money than if we settled for a one-to-one challenge.

Match it we did. We had raised 97 percent of what was required ($97 million) in less than a year, and we raised the complete match before other Annenberg grantees. The two largest donors were the Pew Charitable Trusts ($16 million+), where the CEO Rebecca Rimel and program officer Robert Schwartz[6] were terrific supporters, and the

William Penn Foundation ($13 million+), where Janet Haas and her brother David were pivotal.

Terry Larsen, CEO of CoreStates Bank, and the bank's president Rosemarie Greco, along with IBM CEO Louis Gerstner Jr., were the people responsible for the largest corporate gifts—$2 million from each company. Together these grants accounted for a quarter of all the money we raised from corporations.

The single largest competitive government grant was a $15 million grant from the National Science Foundation to support the *Children Achieving* work in math and science. More than half of our match came from these five sources. We received many, many smaller grants, ranging from $50,000 to $1 million.

During my last two years at the district we formed a district development committee, which I chaired and which met regularly to examine and set priorities among grant opportunities. Since we were so shortchanged by regular state government sources, we put a great deal of successful effort into raising money from private sources and through the competitive public grant processes at the state and federal levels.

### Systemic versus Targeted Approaches

The most typical approaches to using grant money to implement changes are "piloting" and "phasing in." Piloting usually involves trying out a new approach in a limited number of sites, hoping that it will prove effective, and that the sites can then serve as centers for demonstration and dissemination. The underlying assumption is that individuals, schools, and districts will recognize effective programs when they see them, and will then change their practice.

As logical as this sounds, there are few examples of a pilot approach leading to a large-scale educational change. In fact, in most cases the pilot sites gradually return to former practices once their extra funding is removed and/or the individuals who spearheaded the change are no longer there.

Phasing in is a strategy for initiating a system change by beginning with a portion of the system, and then adding successive cohorts until all schools are participating. This approach is a sensible one where (1) the resources to implement systemwide are foreseeable, but not available in the first year; (2) the changes are significant enough that it pays to try out some of them and work out the kinks before moving to a larger scale; and (3) there is a need to develop more capacity to assist schools in making the changes (for example, training more people able to do professional development required for implementation of the new program).

Philadelphia's fundamental approach was systemic, aimed at all students and all schools. Within that approach, we used a one-year phase-in, starting with one-third of the schools and clusters and then adding the rest in the next year.

The decision to limit the phase-in to one year was controversial among my staff, across the schools, and in the broader community. More than a few people felt that we should "demonstrate" that the program would work in the original six clusters for several years before moving the effort beyond them. They argued that this would permit us to concentrate resources on these students, and would increase the likelihood that the community would see the district and the *Children Achieving* agenda as credible.

I disagreed, for a number of reasons. First, I was skeptical of pilots, and of long phase-ins, for the reasons described above. Second, even during the year we pursued this course we began to get negative (and justified) feedback from schools, parents, and communities that had been left out asking us why they had drawn the short straw. Philadelphia already held second-class status in Pennsylvania and I was determined that we could not accomplish a quality education for all students if we created at our own initiative a second-class of schools and students inside the city itself. Third, it was clear that we were on our way to creating a second central office within the district, with redundant and competing offices; this could in fact be an interesting change strategy, but it was not one we could afford.

In the end, the decision to expand initiatives to all schools turned out to be the right one. The achievement gains over the years of my administration cut across the entire city.

### Bang for Our Buck

We took the money available to us from our good stewardship and from our success in pursuing philanthropic and competitive grant dollars and found ways to stretch it so that we could redirect resources to the most important programs. Some of the most notable areas of increased expenditure that helped us move achievement up substantially and to improve the on-time graduation rate significantly are listed below.

Our more efficient use of resources allowed us to

- Provide full-day kindergarten to every five-year-old.
- Support tens of thousands of new and more effective staff development hours, enabling us to include five thousand more teachers in extended development sessions in the summer alone.
- Hire well more than one hundred instructional coaches to work at the school level.
- Purchase enough new computers to move from a thirty-to-one student-to-computer ratio with largely outdated computers to a ten-to-one ratio with up-to-date machines.
- Wire every school for the Internet.
- Improve security with additional school police, cameras, and scanners.
- Recruit fifteen thousand school volunteers.
- Double the budget for books, allowing us to provide current editions of textbooks to every child.
- Reduce the student-to-teacher ratio for grades K–3.
- Build a new and more effective criterion-referenced system of assessment.
- Develop new programs for English-language learners.
- Increase the number of high school students participating in internship programs with local businesses.
- Boost payments to private schools for special-needs children.
- Start several new alternative programs for high school students returning from incarceration or who otherwise did not do well in a traditional setting.
- Create special opportunities for pregnant teens and their children.
- Provide new training programs for principals.
- Open 35 new district-sponsored after-school programs, 117 programs in partnership with the Recreation Department, and 13 family centers.

## Outcomes

So far this chapter has focused on how much money we received, how much we spent, and what we spent it on. The real issue is whether shifting funds from old expenditures to new and different expenditures resulted in achievement improvement. The answer is a resounding *yes*. From 1996–2000, scores went up by an average of 42 percent on more rigorous tests in reading, math, and science, despite the fact that we very significantly increased the pool of students taking the tests by including at-risk students who had been historically excluded from testing. Also, we improved the on-time graduation rate by more than 16 percent. That's the real meaning of good stewardship, the real definition of productivity.

## ADEQUATE GOVERNMENT SUPPORT

Pursuit of adequate government support has been a battleground in which I have been involved my entire professional life. One of the first examples was the unsuccessful twelve-year attempt to make the Maryland system of funding education a more adequate and equitable one when I was state superintendent. A highlight of that era was joining Senator Clarence Blount in handing Governor Harry Hughes, on whose cabinet I sat, petitions with nearly one hundred thousand signatures that I had helped to collect, asking the governor to provide school funding leadership. He chose not to do so.

The other highlight was the unforgettable experience of serving as one of the plaintiff's key witnesses in an equity lawsuit against the state of Maryland in which I, as the state superintendent of schools, was the named defendant (*Hornbeck v. Somerset County Board of Education*). I testified that the plaintiff's claims were right. The plaintiffs won at the trial level in a wonderful decision by Judge David Ross, but the decision was overturned on appeal by the highest Maryland court, the Court of Appeals, which was a Montgomery County (one of the nation's wealthiest counties) dominated court. As noted below, Maryland more recently distinguished itself by adopting a bold, ambitious and, in my view, adequate funding plan without a push from any court, the only time I know of that this has happened.

Another singular experience was the opportunity to help design the Kentucky Education Reform Act, which arguably still stands as the most comprehensive change in state funding and education practice in the history of American public education reform. It is the best example in the country of addressing curriculum, funding, and governance issues in a comprehensive, simultaneous, and systemic way.

A fourth experience has been the continuing effort to alter the funding landscape in Pennsylvania. My first exposure was during my tenure as executive deputy secretary of education from 1972–1976 under Secretary John Pittenger and Governor Milton Shapp. While it was hardly perfect, that period was the time in modern history during which the state picked up the largest share of education costs (about

54 percent, in contrast to less than 40 percent when I was superintendent; since Ed Rendell became governor, the proportion has moved above 40 percent).

Twenty years later, as Philadelphia's superintendent I joined the present Pennsylvania governor, then Mayor Ed Rendell, as a moving party in one of the only adequacy/equity lawsuits in the country in which a state's highest court declined to render a substantive opinion. It was also during that time that Rendell and I filed a Title VI race discrimination case against the state.

Following my resignation as superintendent, I founded and raised the money for Good Schools Pennsylvania, a grassroots organization that works for quality education for all students in Pennsylvania and helped lay the groundwork for Rendell's election. That resulted in hundreds of millions of new dollars for public education in Pennsylvania, investment in early childhood education, new accountability measure and, finally in 2008, the adoption of a new funding formula through which about $6 billion is projected to be invested in schools, over six years, with emphasis on districts with concentrations of at-risk children.

These experiences have given me a rich and unusual perspective on adequate government support.

## Philadelphia

The heart of our financial difficulty in Philadelphia rested in this third element of the resource analysis, government funding. Education funding in Pennsylvania did not begin very auspiciously. The basis for free public education was established in the Constitution of 1790 with the words, "The Legislature shall, as soon as conveniently may be, provide by law for the establishment of schools throughout the State, in such a manner, that the poor may be taught gratis" (Pennsylvania Constitution of 1790, Article Seven, Section 1).

It proved not to be "convenient" for another forty-four years. In 1823 a law passed providing for free public education for three years but was repealed three years later. Finally in 1834 a law providing for free public education passed both houses of the legislature with only three dissenting votes between them.

However, there was an immediate negative outcry from citizens. A petition to repeal the law was signed by 32,000 people, and backpedaling from the members of the legislature began immediately. In early 1835, the Senate voted to repeal the legislation by a vote of nineteen to eleven. Thirteen members of the new majority had voted for the free public education only months before. It looked like it was going to certain defeat until House member Thaddeus Stevens rose on the floor of the lower chamber, delivered an eloquent defense of the law, and defeated the move to repeal:

> He said the repeal act should be called:
> "An act for branding and marking the poor, so that they may be known from the rich and the proud. . . . I know how large a portion of the community can scarcely feel any sympathy with, or understand the necessities of the poor; the rich appreciate the exquisite feelings which they enjoy, when they see their children receiving the boon of education, and rising in intellectual superiority above the clogs which hereditary poverty had cast upon them. . . .
> When I reflect how apt hereditary wealth, hereditary influence, and perhaps as a consequence, hereditary pride, are to close the avenues and steel the heart against the wants and rights of the poor, I am induced to thank my Creator for having, from early life, bestowed upon me the blessing of poverty."
> He urged the legislators to ignore the misguided petitions and to lead their people as philosophers, with courage and benevolence. After he finished he limped back to his seat to the cheers of the entire assembly. The House suspended the rules and amended the Repeal Bill into an act that actually strengthened the original Free School Act and passed it. (Thaddeus Stevens College of Technology)

Where is such wisdom and courage in the halls of the General Assembly today?

There has been a form of free public education in the Commonwealth since. But this ignominious early half century, in some ways, foreshadowed the centuries to come. The citizens of Pennsylvania have failed repeatedly to insist that their elected officials provide quality education to all. Elected and corporate leadership have repeatedly failed to lead in that direction until recently under Governor Rendell's leadership.

Every state and major city is different in the details of their school funding, but they are usually similar in important ways. The rationale for the funding base is only partially related, if at all, to improving student achievement. Funding decisions are instead intensely political; thus poor children are seriously disadvantaged by the fact that their poor parents vote in smaller numbers, don't have PACs, and can't make large contributions to reelection campaigns.

Until 1992, the formula for distributing education dollars in Pennsylvania represented an attempt at fairness. Different student needs were taken into account. The wealth of a district was considered. The ebb and flow of enrollment was counted. The concentration of low-income children was considered relevant. Intensely rural or urban districts (sparsity and density) received special attention. Tax effort was weaved in.

The primary flaw in that formula—and the flaw was huge—was the base from which the rest of the formula built. In 1992, the base amount was $2,550 (Epstein, 2000), while the average per pupil expenditure in 1991–1992 was $6,347 (Education Commission of the States Note, 2004). This meant that almost all of the $3,797 average difference had to be supplied at the local level. In a wealthy district, that was easy. In a place that had little wealth, it was difficult to raise even an inadequate amount. If the $2,550 had been related to reality, it would have been a pretty good formula. As it was, it was simply better than what was to replace it in 1993.

The Democratic governor, Bob Casey, abandoned the formula. In 1993, the amount of state education aid was frozen. In 1994, the state legislature added some poverty and growth money to the amount each district had gotten in 1992. In 1995, 3 percent was added across the board, unrelated to anything other than the determination that politics required that something be added and the revenue picture permitted 3 percent without too much pain.

From 1997 through 2001, under the Republican governor Tom Ridge[7] state aid was sometimes frozen (except for some of Ridge's pet categorical programs, such as the addition of a lot of technology). Sometimes the budget included a percentage increase or a fixed-dollar increase (distributed in arbitrary and highly political ways), and it occasionally provided something for poverty or for the growth in student population.

This system cost Philadelphia huge sums of money when measured even against the grossly inadequate funding produced under the Equalized Subsidy for Basic Education (ESBE) formula that had existed through 1991. In 1992 ESBE resulted in Philadelphia receiving $548.5 million. Because of the freeze, the same amount was received in 1993. If it had not been frozen, district estimates based on previous practice were that Philadelphia would have received $586.2 million. Cumulatively from 1992 through 2001, the Philadelphia school district estimated that it lost $656.2 million in revenues that would have been received if the ESBE formula had remained in place.

Other poor districts, rural and urban, suffered the same fate. Thus, in an era of rising costs, poor districts faced a steady decline in the per-pupil funding which had been so inadequate in the first place. And the responsibility for this immoral reality was bipartisan, started under a Democratic administration, accelerated under a Republican administration, shared between the politicians who legislated it and the citizenry who tolerated it.

Without a formula, nothing was rational. Districts could not plan on anything. In Philadelphia, the trick was to get the mayor, through his chief of staff David Cohen and the city lobbyist Joe McLaughlin, to work the backrooms of Harrisburg to see what scraps might fall off the table for Philadelphia's children.

The district was told by Harrisburg to do more with what we had (the stewardship section above demonstrates that we agreed that we had that obligation), to look to the city for more money, despite the fact that Philadelphia already taxed itself at a higher rate than any other jurisdiction in Pennsylvania (and at one of the highest rates in the United States), to be grateful and quit bellyaching, and to make the cuts necessary to balance our budget.

It is important to note that our tenure did not begin with complaints. I went to Harrisburg shortly after Tom Ridge's first term election and had what I thought was a good conversation, sharing our plans, including our strong emphasis on student performance–based accountability. I had similar meetings with the leadership in both the Senate and the House.

Later, I privately proposed to David Girard diCarlo, a Ridge confidant and major fundraiser, that we work out a system through which we would receive the money we needed in exchange for agreed on changes in the union contract with the teachers and in exchange for explicit improvements in student achievement. I proposed that if we did not deliver, the legislation providing the funding should be written so that the additional funding would be automatically stopped.

What we received in return were computers (the categorical technology grant program the governor sponsored), charter schools that actually cost Philadelphia students tens of millions of dollars, and repeated proposals for vouchers (accompanied at one point by the insulting offer to give the Philadelphia School District $10 million if we would not object to vouchers).[8]

After a year of deep cuts, which built on cuts that the previous district administration had been forced to make, we did indeed begin to "bellyache" in response to this persistent mistreatment of our children by Governor Ridge and the legislature. We filed state and federal lawsuits. The state case was based on the premise that the funding system in Pennsylvania was not thorough and efficient as the constitution required. The federal lawsuit was a Title VI suit accusing the state of race discrimination.

It was based on facts such as the state funding system paying $52 less per student in districts where there was a concentration of poor and minority children. We also developed a strategy, in collaboration with the mayor and the president of city council, of refusing to make further cuts, and we began to implement the supports called for by *Children Achieving* in the hope and belief that this would force the state to address the issue of providing adequate funding. The eventual result instead was a cynical state takeover of the school system.

## ADEQUACY AND EQUITY

Defining justice and fairness is not a complex problem. It is just and fair to provide the same opportunity to achieve educational success and to access the American dream for children who are disadvantaged by poverty, disability, language, or color as we provide to children who enjoy the advantages of affluence, white skin, English as their first language, and freedom from disabilities. Some believe that "equal" opportunity means funding all schools at the same level. Others point out accurately that what is equal may not be equitable; differences in the advantages children have when they come to school mean that some youngsters need more resources than others do to produce the same level of opportunity. To provide equal dollars to the poor and the affluent will not create equitable opportunities for success. Adequacy or equity rather than simple equivalence is the relevant concept.

### States and Funding

Current responsibility for education is firmly rooted at the state level. Every state constitution assigns direct responsibility for education to the state, though there are a variety of interpretations of what that responsibility means.

In Pennsylvania, the Constitution provides that, "the General Assembly shall provide for the maintenance and support of a thorough and efficient system of public education to serve the needs of the Commonwealth (Constitution of the Commonwealth of Pennsylvania, Article III, Section 14). The courts in Pennsylvania have declared that public education is a matter for the legislature to determine and, thus, they have refused to interpret this provision in the Constitution.

States have responded to their constitutional responsibilities related to funding in many different ways. In forty-three states, there is some process to weight funding based on need. Most often students who are low-income, have disabilities, or are English-language learners generate extra money through the weighting process. Forty-eight states have categorical programs, which direct funds to specific programs like gifted and talented or special education or expenditure areas like technology or school construction, as well as a general funding stream. Many times these are directed toward the same categories of students as weighting; sometimes the categorical programs are designed around content or services such as technology or early childhood, and sometimes there is a student equity factor inside of the categorical programs.

In thirty-one states, taxes or fees are earmarked for education. In twenty-four states lottery money is at least partially earmarked for education. In thirty-five states there is reliance on local revenues. On an additional note, forty-three states enacted tax cuts in the boom of the 1990s when lower rates produced more money. Few have reversed them as the boom has stagnated and revenues have gone down, thus again (Olsen, 2005, p. 14) artificially creating the illusion that there is not enough money to go around. There is not enough only because of decisions about tax policy. If the same tax rates were in place as those before the boom 1990s, there would be a great deal more money.

In the decade following the 1989 Rose decision in Kentucky, plaintiffs won about two-thirds of all lawsuits related to school funding (Rebell, 2002, p. 228.) The concept of adequacy increasingly emerged as a powerful tool in these lawsuits. This is particularly true as standards became more and more important. If a state is going to establish standards with the underlying premise that they represent what a child should know and be able to do to function effectively as an adult, then it is incumbent on the state to give each child an equitable opportunity to attain the standards as the part of the definition of "thorough," "efficient," "uniform," or whatever other language relating to fairness is used in the state constitutions.

Money is not the only component of education reform, but sufficient funds are essential in order to provide the opportunity for students to achieve success and be promoted to the next grade, graduate from high school, and fully participate in the economy and in civil society. The opportunities we provide for all children should permit them to achieve what we want for our own children.

### Defining Adequacy and Equity

The substantive issue has become adequacy for every student. Mike Rebell, the executive director and counsel of the Campaign for Fiscal

Equity, Inc., says that "'adequacy' is a prudent judgment concerning the basic educational opportunities that a child will need to take his or her place as a functioning adult in contemporary society" (Rebell, 2002, p. 49). That is the legal equivalent of the so-called prudent-man standard that has been used for a very long time in the field of torts in the law.

We must ask ourselves: What knowledge and skills should every child have the opportunity to develop? What knowledge and skills must we provide each child to ensure that every generation has a better quality of life than the one before? What knowledge and skills are all children entitled to because it is right and moral to provide them, so that each of our children and grandchildren can do fulfilling and productive work, function as effective citizens, be good members of a family, and have the opportunity to be happy? Once we have answered these questions we will be in a position to determine the cost. Adequacy is defined as the resources necessary to create the conditions in which all children have the educational opportunity to reach whatever standards society has determined are appropriate such as being college-, career-, or citizen-ready.

Chapter 6 described the process through which Philadelphia defined the opportunity to learn standards that needed to be met in order for students to achieve the academic standards we expected. Having defined what was needed, we quantified each of the elements in two more ways. We identified what would be implemented in each school year through the 2007–2008 school year, phasing in various pieces of each of the eight program categories. We projected the amount of funding that would be needed through 2004–2005. We did not cost it out beyond then for two reasons. One was that planning more than five years in the future becomes unreliably speculative. The other was that we believed that if we followed through with our plans through 2004–2005, we might in fact be able to begin to reduce some of the intervention costs as students became more successful.

There are a variety of ways to approach the determination of what constitutes adequacy and "costing it out." Some would approach it through a Successful Schools model, in which one analyzes practices in a state's best performing schools, assume that other districts and schools could achieve similar results with similar practices, and cost it out.

Another approach is the Professional Judgment model, in which one looks to educators to determine what practices will result in the desired objectives, and costing that out. Although we did not label it,

I suppose one would characterize our Fair Opportunities to Learn approach as close to this model.

Still another approach is Evidence-Based. In this approach, research is used to identify successful practices, and the costs to implement them are then extrapolated. Another approach is called Cost Function. Here economists use complicated statistical analyses to examine the relationship between current spending and student achievement. They then determine what it would cost to bring all students to a particular level of performance, after accounting for differences in student and district characteristics (Hoff, 2005, p. 32ff).

How to approach costing out is merely a technical issue. The most important decision is deciding to adequately serve the education needs of all students. The most important step in making this decision is creating the necessary public and political will. Kentucky and Maryland are good examples of different approaches to this problem. Kentucky had the good fortune to have the Prichard Committee tilling the soil of school and financial reform for more than a decade before the Rose decision was handed down. Thus, public opinion and political will was open to having the court render its remarkable decision in 1989. Both the legislature and the governor embraced the responsibility.

In Maryland, the legal framework was quite different. While plaintiffs seeking adequate and equitable funding won at the trial level, the Court of Appeals in Maryland in the 1983 *Hornbeck v. Somerset County* decision became one of just a handful of courts over the past thirty years to rule in favor of the state defendants who argued that Maryland's system of school funding was constitutional.[9] Later, the Bradford school funding lawsuit in Maryland resulted in a consent decree involving the state and Baltimore City that provided a modest increase in state funds for the city and a change in the governance of city schools, but not fundamental funding change throughout the state. The fundamental change finally came from legislative and citizen leadership enacting the $1.3 billion six-year increase without a court order behind it. Maryland is alone in making such a large increase without being forced into it by the courts.

The resolve to act must come through a combination of legal pressure, public pressure, and/or political leadership. Then, there must be some way to establish the cost. Next, the legislature must adopt a funding formula motivated by a commitment to adequacy and based on standards and the cost study. It must reflect adequacy in the amount and equity in raising and distributing the funds.

### The Federal Role in Adequate Funding

Provisions for low-income children in Title I of the Elementary and Secondary Education Act (ESEA) and federal and state laws related to disabled students are all based, in part, on the premise that it costs more to provide the same opportunities to disadvantaged children. But even with these laws, it is widely acknowledged that the funds available are inadequate.

Congress had provided that for students with disabilities, federal dollars should provide 40 percent of the excess cost (those costs over and above what is spent on children without disabilities). In the thirty years since passage of the Education for All Handicapped Children Act, through its successors and now the Individuals with Disabilities Education Act (IDEA), the proportion available from the federal government has never exceeded 12 percent.

Similarly with ESEA, in the context of the No Child Left Behind legislation, the difference between what was authorized—presumably what Congress thought was necessary to help children achieve the standards that law establishes—and what has been appropriated are many billions of dollars. Moreover, Title I funds flow to a state even if the state's provision of state dollars is not equitable (or even equal). In Pennsylvania, during my superintendency, the five dozen school districts surrounding Philadelphia had an average of as much as $2,000 more to spend on each of their children than we did in Philadelphia. We received roughly $900 annually for each of our Title I eligible children. In this case, although Title I was supposed to "compensate" for the great challenges faced by disadvantaged children, it made up less than half of the funding difference between Philadelphia's poor children and their more affluent suburban counterparts.

The proportion of public school funding coming from the federal government has never exceeded 8 to 10 percent of the total, and in recent years it has dropped below 5 percent. Periodically, there have been proposals for the federal government to assume a third or more of the cost. William Taylor and Diane Peche, longtime civil rights lawyers, have repeatedly put the proposition in front of the nation, noting that children in Mississippi need to know algebra as much as children in Massachusetts so the issue is a national problem. Similarly, members of Congress like Philadelphia's Chaka Fattah have proposed legislation, with assistance from justice advocates like my first boss, Tom Gilhool, that would go a very long way toward making educational opportunity more financially equitable within states and between states.

It is not at all conceptually difficult to change the federal funding scheme.

- Resurrect the long-time proposal that the federal government pay for 33 percent or more of the education bill and distribute the money in a manner that actually results in helping those in less wealthy states more than those in wealthy states, and/or
- Require states themselves to meet certain equity and adequacy standards as a condition of federal funding for education or even other major federal domestic programs (health housing, employment, welfare, etc.) on which education impacts.
- Create a system in which the federal government determines what level of funding would be adequate and redesigns the present system so that states would meet some minimum level of adequacy and equity, taking the state's relative wealth into account. Title I could be revised to close the remaining gap. This is the premise of states with the best funding formulas as they seek to provide adequate funds, equitably distributed.
- The federal government could also integrate several programs related to health, early childhood, and welfare, framing them synergistically so the power of the whole would be greater than the sum of the parts, a federal form of the Children and Family Authority (see chapter 12).

## CONCLUSION

The challenge is not in system design or in education questions. We have the knowledge to create a funding system that is both adequate—ensuring enough funds for a quality education for all—and equitably distributed—ensuring more resources to those students who will need more support in order to reach standards. The challenge is a political one or, more broadly, a challenge that confronts the nation's citizens and how we want to see our values as a democracy play out.

## NOTES

1. The district's school police constituted the fifth-largest police force in Pennsylvania, after the city of Philadelphia, Pittsburgh, the Southeastern Pennsylvania Transportation Authority, and the Pennsylvania State Police.

2. Both Monique Burns and Ben Rayer were young, very smart, passionate about the work, trained and experienced in business/management practices, and not at all captured by the bureaucracy.

3. I leave aside the issue of how charters may or may not impact on schools programmatically. The theory is that they will be open on a first come/first serve basis and, thus, should have no appreciable impact on the schools from which they are coming. That, of course, even on its face, is false. It's commonsense that students who take the initiative to search out these new opportunities are much more likely in a poverty-impacted district, where most charters spring up, to have someone who is their advocate. So often one is taking the most advantaged of disadvantaged children away, further isolating the most disadvantaged, who remain behind. In addition, some group of people must take the initiative and do the hard work to set up the charter school. Often that includes a significant contingent of parents looking for a new school for their own children. Those children, not infrequently children who do not attend public school but want the advantage of free public education, make up an important part of the early student body of the new charter. Again, the program impact is not neutral. But I relegate these considerations to an endnote, because there are ways one could make the program impact more neutrally if the traditional public schools were treated in a way that led them to believe that charters were coming into existence for the benefit of all children, not just a handful of those with politically connected parents or those with natural advocates.

4. Actually in Philadelphia there are also another several dozen schools being run by private, for-profit groups as well. In at least the case of the Edison Schools, they receive more per pupil than is spent on non-Edison students (although not as much more as Edison wanted). They also generally have performed no better than the schools that were run directly by the school district under Paul Vallas's leadership, but it does reduce a bit further the funds available to the remaining student population after one takes out the charter school students.

5. Diane Castelbuono, who directed the charter office, was critical in our efforts to maximize the benefits, and minimize the harm, of the charter schools. She had the unenviable role of breaking new ground dealing with our board, the state bureaucracy, the district staff, and the charter directors, seeking to assure an honest and high-quality approval and monitoring process in a highly politicized atmosphere. She also carried out data collection and analysis that permitted us to have a clear sense of such issues as who was attending charters, whether the charters were carrying out their equity responsibilities, and the educational and financial impact of the program.

6. Bob Schwartz as the senior education program officer at Pew deserves significant credit for the growth of standards-based education across the United States. Not only did he support the work in Philadelphia vigorously but earlier he had supported the standards-based work—at the National Center on Education and the Economy (and its work with a dozen key cities and states in the National Alliance for Restructuring Education) and later as president of

Achieve, a partnership between Governors and CEOs in support of standards-based reform—before going to Harvard, where he is presently the academic dean at the Graduate School of Education.

7. Later appointed by President George W. Bush as secretary of homeland security.

8. Our objections to vouchers were threefold. First, we believed they were unconstitutional, since the slots for our students would have been almost exclusively in the parochial schools. Second, we were concerned that they would drain off our best-prepared students, leaving the district with an increasingly disadvantaged population. Finally, and ironically, we knew well that the Archdiocese of Philadelphia did not want our students in any case, due to fears of objections from the parents of current students.

9. This was the case in which I was the defendant in my official capacity as state superintendent of schools but, believing that the plaintiffs were correct in challenging the state education finance formula, I testified for the plaintiffs. When Governor Harry Hughes and others realized during depositions that was my position, they tried to persuade me to agree to withdraw as the defendant. I refused, thinking that there might be some advantage to the named defendant "pleading guilty." I spent twelve hours on the witness stand being questioned by "my lawyers" (the state's lawyers). The plaintiffs won at trial when Judge David Ross declared the system unconstitutional, but he was reversed on appeal to the state's highest court.

# The Choices We Make Determine School Effectiveness

The ultimate measure of a man is not where he stands in moments of comfort and convenience, but where he stands at times of challenge and controversy.

Dr. Martin Luther King

Never doubt that a small group of thoughtful, committed citizens can change the world; indeed, it is the only thing that ever has.

Margaret Mead

Every day is filled with choices that either create obstacles to or provide support for the achievement of high levels of learning by all students. For example, we know quality, developmentally appropriate pre-kindergarten programs are programmatically effective and economically efficient. However, only eight states have legislation that purport (unsuccessfully to date) to make such programs available to all for four-year-olds, and none even pretend to provide them universally to three-year-olds.

In the last year of former governor Tom Ridge's administration in Pennsylvania, an important segment of the business community decided to back early childhood programs. These business leaders included Republicans close to Ridge. After years of failure, early childhood advocates thought the timing and chemistry were right. They were wrong. As the story goes, in a meeting between the business leaders and Ridge, Ridge told them that he would either put as much as $25 million in the budget for early childhood, or call for a similar reduction in business taxes, but could not do both. Regretfully it does not take a genius to figure out what the business leaders preferred. It was more than two years later, during the Rendell administration, before the initial $15 million commitment of state funds for early childhood became a reality.

What an amazing difference between the choice made by Governor Ridge and Pennsylvania's business community and that made by Governor Dick Riley (SC). In 1983, with support he generated from the business community, the remarkable Governor Riley passed the nation's most comprehensive education bill until that time, which included not only early childhood education, standards, assessment, and accountability but a penny increase in the sales tax that raised $250 million.

The role of leaders and the choices they make cannot be clearer.

All children can learn to high levels, and the knowledge exists to create the conditions in which all children do so. When whole groups of children do not learn to high levels, then, it must be because we have made choices different from those that would result in all students achieving at high levels.

We make these wrong choices frequently. Achievement results tell us that every year. They also tell us that the children who do not achieve at high levels are disproportionately children of color, children for whom English is not the first language, children from low-income families, and children with disabilities.

What follows illustrates how Pennsylvanians and Philadelphians made choices that result in poor student performance. I contrast this with other places in the United States where more productive choices were made in similar circumstances. Major players in these stories include the newspapers, the mayors, the business community, the courts, and the unions. Many of these stories are frustrating, but other stories demonstrate that alternative choices always exist. It is never too late to reverse course. We must generate the public will to make the choices we know are right.


## NEWSPAPERS

Significant, systemic educational reform cannot be accomplished without public support. The media play a crucial role both in keeping the public informed about their schools, and in shaping the public's attitudes about them. The media should provide objective information about public schools. They should be a tool for holding schools accountable, whether by insisting on comprehensive and clear student performance data, or scrutinizing decisions involving taxpayers' money. However, responsible media will also help the public understand the challenges that schools face and the strategies they employ. They will focus more on progress toward long-term goals than short-term sensationalizing. Their decisions about how they frame their reporting, what they choose to emphasize, and even where they place each article have a substantial impact on how much support the public is willing to provide for education.

I begin this chapter on choices that affect education with the illustration of the choices made by the newspapers that covered the development and implementation of the Kentucky Educational Reform Act, and the two daily papers that covered *Children Achieving* in Philadelphia.

### Kentucky

The editorial decisions made by the *Louisville Courier-Journal* and the *Lexington Herald Leader* show the positive role that media can play in education reform. In the years leading up to and following the radical changes made to Kentucky's education system in 1990, the papers engaged in a positive, constructive crusade. They did their homework, and reported in a hard-hitting and unrelenting way. The problems and potential solutions were on the front pages, in the news, in the columns, and in the editorials day after day. The papers blasted the legislature and governors of Kentucky for not providing leadership. They praised the court decision that declared Kentucky's system of education to be unconstitutional and led the legislature to make necessary changes. They covered the work of the task force that was set up by the legislature to recommend changes. They praised the fact that the speaker of the House and the president of the Senate accepted responsibility by appointing themselves as chairmen of the task force, and had appointed the political leadership of the two houses as its members.

Because of their positive, engaged attempt to help create reform, the Kentucky papers helped change the course of history in Kentucky. Equally important, the *Courier-Journal* and the *Herald Leader* did not consider their work finished when the Kentucky Education Reform Act (KERA) was passed. Throughout the years since they have continued to help maintain the momentum of the reform. The payoff has been evident in Kentucky's jump from near the bottom of the rankings on the National Assessment of Education Progress, to a position in the top half. That is a huge accomplishment in one student generation, and it was unlikely to have happened without constructive media support and appropriate scrutiny.

## Philadelphia

The coverage of education provided during my tenure by one of Philadelphia's two daily newspapers, the *Inquirer*, was for a significant time period in the same tradition as the Kentucky papers. However, coverage provided by the *Daily News* stood in stark contrast. Knight-Ridder owned both papers, and both had the same publisher, Bob Hall. However, they treated education in radically different ways. The *Inquirer* had a productive, constructively critical view of the schools; in contrast, the *Daily News* chose to play a demagogic and destructive role.

The editorial pages of both papers tended to be supportive of our work. For example, the January 30, 1997, editorial in the *Inquirer* read,

> the city's most powerful Democratic state legislators have undermined David Hornbeck. . . . [Senator] Fumo . . . and [Representative] Evans each are concocting plans to revamp the city schools, stressing local control and accountability. . . . Funny, hasn't Mr. Hornbeck been struggling for three years to sell a . . . plan whose bywords are local control and accountability. . . . It would be nice if, for once, the city's Democrat heavyweights could resist the urge to freelance, and instead make a solid show of support for the ambitious school reform that's been on the table since 1994. . . . Some familiar stuff there, from anyone who's bothered to listen to Mr. Hornbeck.

This was fairly typical of the editorial page. So too was support from columnists such as Acel Moore. A long commentary by him a couple of months earlier was headlined, "Hornbeck Is Right: A Revolution Is Needed." The editorial page of the *Daily News* was also largely supportive and constructive. This included many wonderful and supportive political cartoons by the Daily News' gifted cartoonist Signe Wilkinson.

The difference between the two papers was not what was written on the editorial pages (toward the back of the papers)—it was largely what was written by the columnists and by the news reporters, and what was placed on the front page and in the early pages. At the *Inquirer*, columnists like Alexis Moore and Acel Moore asked hard questions and could be critical, but were not cynical about *Children Achieving*. There were also occasional supportive pieces at the *Daily News* from columnist Linda Wright Moore. However, the *Daily News* gave enormous play to a constant stream of vitriolic, often inaccurate columns by Dan Gerringer and the late Russell Byers.

The most destructive behavior by the *Daily News* began in 1996, two years into our administration. There was a series of front page articles that were thinly disguised as a summary and analysis of the progress of *Children Achieving*. In fact, they were the opening salvo of attacks designed to undermine confidence in the public schools and develop support for the voucher legislation repeatedly introduced by Governor Ridge. Like other tabloids, the *Daily News* always features a screaming headline that fills the front page; the headlines during this period began with "An 'F' For Flunking," and followed in that mold for four more days (given subsequent history, it's probably more accurate to say four more years).

Negative columns in direct support of vouchers were featured in the early pages (giving the impression of being "news," not opinion). They were embedded with a series of negative stories (e.g., "Failure at the Top"). More positive stories, such as "*Children Achieving* Is Far from the Snake Oil Byers Believes It to Be," by Linda Wright Moore, were relegated to the later pages that feature "opinion" rather than news.

Over the years, columns in the *Daily News* were augmented by often negative and sometimes false news stories, virtually all of which were placed near the front of the paper. In contrast, the *Inquirer* stories were largely tough, objective, balanced, fair, and accurate. Dale Mezzacappa, of the *Inquirer* (now writing for the *Philadelphia Notebook*), was an especially good reporter. She wrote well, did her homework, including researching other districts' reform efforts, and criticized us when warranted. She approached her reporting in a way that was constructive, rather than negative for the sake of being negative. She was probing, but not cynical.

The Philadelphia newspapers have a history of treating new superintendents like saviors for a honeymoon period, and then over time beginning to demonize them. This certainly happened in my case. In my first year, I was characterized as a national expert consultant from whom much was expected. The expectations were probably more than any one human being could deliver, but were all very positive and welcome nevertheless.

Later, both papers began to blame Harrisburg's unresponsiveness on my poor communication skills. I had been clear about what needed to be done when I was hired—indeed, I said that I did not want the job unless the city decision-makers wanted to pursue the ten-point *Children Achieving* agenda. My continuing commitment to that agenda was sometimes portrayed as rigid or bullheaded. My politically tin ear was evident, in their opinion, in the various ways we made the case that the Pennsylvania school funding formula was unfair.

I was cast as confrontational because I did not play the game the way it was supposed to be played. I did not hire people the pols wanted hired. I was blunt about state and city policy that put our children at a disadvantage, and for this, several editorials characterized me as messianic. One *Inquirer* editorial said that my approach was appropriate for a minister but not a school superintendent.

The papers' behavioral descriptions were largely accurate. The adjectives interpreting that behavior, in my view, were not. I believed then, and believe now, that I had an obligation as superintendent to make clear that the state system of education was discriminating against poor and minority children and had been doing so for a long time. In fact, I believe the media, elected officials, and civic and business leaders have the same obligation to speak out wherever such discrimination exists and persists. Moral positions should never be the reserve of ministers alone. If that made (makes) me impolitic, so be it.

The larger point is that the *Daily News* in particular, joined later by the *Inquirer*, made a conscious decision to make me the issue instead of the historic mistreatment of Philadelphia's children. They could have chosen in contrast to determine through their own analysis whether the things we were saying or doing were accurate instead of always portraying them as simply our opinion and, in the case of the *Daily News*, our erroneous opinion.

They could have chosen to educate the Philadelphia community about whether the strategies we were pursuing were best practice strategies taken in a national context rather than their practice of simply reporting what we said and what our critics said, leaving the impression that both were equally valid.

## MAYORS

Over the last two decades governance has emerged as one of the silver bullets to which some look as the solution for dysfunctional schools. In the late 1980s, for example, Illinois devolved most power in Chicago to school-based councils made up of elected parents. Vouchers, privatization, and charters are all about governance. For years, there has been debate about the merits and disadvantages of elected or appointed school boards.[1] Each is an attempt to find the decision-makers that will produce the best instructional decisions: parent councils (parents care most about the children); vouchers, privatization, and charters (market-based incentives will drive improvement); or elected versus appointed officials (election expresses the will of the people versus appointed boards attracting those with superior qualifications).

Increasingly, mayoral control is being touted as the silver bullet for urban schools. Three notable and relatively recent examples are Michael Bloomberg in New York, Richard Daley in Chicago, and Thomas Menino in Boston.

### Philadelphia

In Philadelphia, Edward Rendell became the appointing authority of the school board on his election as mayor in 1991. Since the mayor of Philadelphia appointed members to staggered terms, it took a mayor a full term to appoint a majority of the board.[2] In 2000, board selection procedures changed.

The City Charter was amended to provide that upon election, the mayor shall appoint a new school board, whose terms of office shall be concurrent with that of the mayor; the idea was that the mayor should have meaningful authority over the board. Less than a year after the change was made, however, a new state law stripped the mayoralty-appointed Philadelphia school board of its power and granted it to a School Reform Commission comprised of four members appointed by the governor and one appointed by the mayor. All of these changes were made amid significant controversy.

Mayors use their power quite differently one from the other and make different choices. Daley, Menino, and Bloomberg all eagerly and fully embraced the power and responsibility for the performance of the schools in their districts. In his 1996 State of the City address, Mayor Menino said, "I want to be judged as your mayor by what happens in the Boston public schools."

Mayor Daley, Chicago school CEO Paul Vallas, and school board president Gary Chico were known in some circles as the three musketeers of Chicago education reform. When Bloomberg was given control of the New York City School system by the state legislature in 2002, he echoed Menino's statement, saying, "I want to be held accountable for what happens in the New York schools."

All three mayors have run and won on their public school record. Daley won his fifth term with 79 percent of the vote, Menino won his fourth with 67.5 percent of the vote, and Bloomberg won his second election with 58.5 percent of the New York City vote. My point is not that mayoral accountability results in reelection. It is that wholehearted embrace of education responsibility does not hurt re-election prospects.

How did Philadelphia's Mayor Rendell compare in terms of his commitment to education? Rendell's commitment to comprehensive reform led to my hiring,[3] and without his support I could not have lasted six years.

Rendell was willing to make several courageous policy decisions that led to concrete benefits. The clearest examples of this are related to funding. Rendell supported my 1995 decision to refuse to cut any further funds out of school budgets, while knowing that this could lead to large and technically illegal budget deficits. Second, he suggested filing a state constitution–based lawsuit against the Commonwealth. Third, he supported the district's decision to file a federal lawsuit against the state, alleging race discrimination. All three were gutsy decisions.

Rendell's support was crucial to our work in *Children Achieving*. He helped ensure we had a supportive majority on the school board, and supported the extension of my contract so that we could continue our work. Had he not been mayor, it is highly unlikely that Philadelphia's children would have improved their performance in reading, math, and science by 42 percent, that the on-time graduation rate would have gone up from 48 percent to 59 percent, that full-day kindergarten would have become a reality for our students, or that other critical supports would have been put into place. As the students who benefited from these supports reach higher grades, Rendell deserves credit for the fact that their achievement continues to be substantially higher than that of earlier cohorts.

Nevertheless, Rendell missed several opportunities to use his mayoral power to beneficial effect. There was an initial commitment to reform, but too often it was not backed up with the necessary follow-through. Unlike Menino, Daley, and Bloomberg, he never made any pretense of wanting to be judged based on how the schools performed. His was quintessentially ambivalent behavior, blowing hot and cold, knowing what was right but not really believing at a gut level that major school reform could be successful.

Many superintendents would kill for the kind of support I got from Rendell. If my objective had been to keep my job, enjoy public notice nationally if not locally, and be pleased with moderate improvements in student achievement, then his support would have been enough. However, our objective was to become the first big American city where nearly all of the children achieved at very high levels. Part of the reason we could not accomplish this was Mayor

Rendell's unwillingness to put the full force of his political capital behind our children.

### Board Appointments

Rendell chose not to exercise his power over board appointments to provide stronger and more consistent support for the *Children Achieving* agenda in two main ways. First, the boards he appointed never supported the work of *Children Achieving* with more than a five to four margin. Second, he reappointed at least two board members whose behavior was particularly destructive to our efforts. It's inconceivable to me that he would have made the board appointments he made if he had embraced responsibility for the schools in the way Bloomberg, Daley, and Menino have.

We generally had five members who gave relatively consistent, if sometimes tepid, support to the reform agenda.[4] However, because the margin was so close that one vote could change the outcome, we had to spend a great deal of time and energy to ensure that every member was on board, particularly on ground-breaking issues. The mayor refused to appoint members that would give us a larger margin of success.

He did not seem to understand that even if a 5–4 decision gave us the same result as a 9–0 one, it at least took considerably more time and effort on our part to ensure it. On at least one occasion we had to specially transport an ill board member to the meeting to secure the majority vote. With almost half of the board voting against measures, more press attention was given to the negative views of those board members. And, of course, sometimes the positions that we put in front of the board were not as bold as they might have been if we had a greater cushion.

Additionally, despite Mayor Rendell's support for *Children Achieving*, he continued to reappoint board members who were vehemently opposed to our plan. Jacques Lurie and Thomas Mills were particularly vocal in their opposition. They also looked for ways to criticize, raise questions designed to cause controversy, and otherwise sought to publicly discredit the reform and the good results children were achieving.

In 1998, for example, over 140 schools had surpassed their achievement goals, making them eligible for the public recognition and other rewards due to them under the accountability program. We arranged a ceremony and invited each of the schools to send a small team of the principal, teachers, parents, and students to come on stage, shake hands with the board members and the superintendent, and receive a banner.

Lurie and Mills refused to sit on the stage, claiming that they didn't believe the results were valid. (It should be noted that Lurie made it a point in the back of the room to shake the hands of the teams from the schools that he saw himself as representing—those that generally had the fewest minority students and the least poverty.) Instead of focusing on the achievement of the students, teachers, principals, parents, and schools exclusively, a major focus of press around the event became, not surprisingly, the protest by these two men. So when good news was called for, the children and the district got mixed news instead.

Lurie and Mills also constantly attacked the integrity of the accountability program. They called for an independent panel of experts to investigate the program, planting seeds of doubt with their mere suggestion. The board rejected the suggestion as costly, time-consuming, and unnecessary. A few months later, Harcourt Brace had to revise some of the numbers they had reported due to a mistake they acknowledged making. These revisions were very minor, and did not change the results overall or the results of a single school. However, in the heated atmosphere that surrounded our work, this gave Lurie and Mills the opening they were looking for.

Anticipating this, I proposed a panel that would examine all the questions the two of them had raised, and would also serve as an ongoing independent group of experts, meeting several times a year for an indefinite period to provide us additional expert advice in this mostly uncharted area of a rigorous accountability system. The panel was chaired by Andrew Porter, University of Wisconsin–Madison, and consisted of many distinguished members.[5] The members were approved by the entire board. Several months later, after first examining all of the questions that critics had raised, they issued a report asserting that Philadelphia was quite consistent with standards of practice; and that on more than a few fronts they characterized our practices as leadership practices.

Despite the fact that the attacks were baseless, the board critics eroded confidence in the accountability system we had established. A panel report months later could not undo that erosion entirely. In the meantime, we lost months of momentum. Neither Lurie nor Mills ever acknowledged they had been wrong about the system. They simply moved on to other areas of attack. In my view, due to their lack of the belief that all children can learn, and to their political agendas, they made many destructive choices.

In 1999, Lurie's term was up. I repeatedly recommended, both through Rendell's chief of staff and in writing, that he not be reappointed. Nevertheless, Rendell reappointed him. He continued his destructive and relentless campaign against *Children Achieving*. The mayor could have made a different choice.

### Public Displays of Support

Mayors Menino, Daley, and Bloomberg routinely appeared and met with their superintendents in regular demonstrations of support and respect. Mayor Rendell was not ready to spend his considerable capital with the public in this way. Although *Children Achieving* delivered achievement growth from kindergarten through the twelfth grade, as good as the best big city and better than most, he sought to avoid the controversies and the difficulties of public education. He did not even show up to announce the good results.[6]

I think the mayor worried that *Children Achieving* might not work. He wanted to believe it would work. He liked it that I believed it; to him it was a primary selling point of my candidacy to be superintendent. But he stopped short of taking many of the strategic positions necessary to help make it work. Rendell also failed to provide timely public support in relation to my contract extension. While he ultimately supported the extension, he refused to do so early on, and he supported a two- instead of a three-year extension.

Contract extensions are often used as expressions of confidence. Because of Rendell's popularity, it would have been enormously helpful had he supported *Children Achieving*'s education agenda with a meaningful extension of the contract early on. It would have encouraged the people who were dedicated to working in the schools, turned some people "on the fence" into supporters, and dampened the ardor of the critics. Rendell's refusal to discuss the issue until the lame-duck end of his term was clearly a statement that his support was lukewarm. It was another choice and missed opportunity to support the agenda.

Rendell didn't need to play it safe. As some people put it, Rendell may be the best "retail" politician in America. He won his second term with nearly 75 percent of the vote. The records of Bloomberg, Daley, and Menino demonstrate that you can also win big while embracing responsibility for education.

When John Street was elected mayor in 1999, I was very hopeful. He had a history of activism; his constituency was more North Philadelphia than Society Hill or Chestnut Hill. Street started his tenure by holding a public meeting in each of the twenty-two clusters openly supporting *Children Achieving*. Ten thousand people turned out for these meetings with strong support from the school system. When he had the opportunity, he chose not to reappoint Jacques Lurie. Not surprisingly, we were encouraged by these choices. That hope was short-lived. Street reverted to traditional politics around education. He slipped into the conventional wisdom that conciliation rather than confrontation with Harrisburg would produce more equitable outcomes for students, even though that mode of operation was one that had historically failed our students.

Street could have decided to make different choices than the ones that Rendell had made. Unfortunately, he made the same old tired choices, certainly not demonstrating any more a profile in courage than Rendell. Soon the state took over city schools.

In 2006, six years after I resigned, the district's resources had not changed significantly. The district faced a $70 million "surprise" budget deficit. Appeasement as a strategy simply has not worked. Although Rendell, a much more pro–public education governor than mayor has been elected, many of his early bold initiatives were stymied by conservative Republicans who controlled both houses of the legislature through Rendell's first term as governor.

Happily, in his second term, and with a Democratic majority in the state House, the governor's strong leadership resulted in passing a historic increase in funding and, more importantly, a change in the school funding formula that is fairer to districts with concentrations of poor children. A cost of education study initially opposed by the governor but pushed by Good Schools Pennsylvania and other advocates helped set the stage. In addition, strong leadership from the governor's secretary of planning, Donna Cooper (former executive director of Good Schools Pennsylvania), and commissioner of basic education, Diane Castelbuono (my special assistant in Philadelphia), played a strong role in this outcome.

## THE BUSINESS AND CIVIC COMMUNITIES

### Kentucky

Kentucky's comprehensive reform initiatives have enjoyed remarkable support from the civic and business communities as well as the government and the courts.

The Prichard Committee for Academic Excellence emerged in the early 1980s as a powerful voice for change in Kentucky. Business has, from the beginning, played an important role in their work. Prichard's intense, patient labor, led by its outstanding executive director, Bob Sexton, made the conception and the delivery of KERA possible. After KERA was passed, Kentucky's business leadership was satisfied with the content of the law, but recognized that passing the law was only the first step. Implementation was critical. So, they formed the Partnership for Kentucky School Reform, initially under the umbrella of the Prichard Committee and with significant early leadership from Sexton.

The business leaders organized groups of supporters, funded the work of a new partnership organization, and provided critical support when some in the state were expressing resistance to reform. They also put up substantial sums to create a very creative series of television ads supporting public education in general and KERA in particular. Through the partnership, with leadership from Oz Nelson, CEO of UPS, John Hall, CEO of Ashland Oil, and David Jones, CEO of Humana, business helped shepherd the new day in Kentucky public education through fragile times.

Kentucky's 1995 gubernatorial election demonstrates the powerful effect of business support. KERA's critics were pushing for a change of leadership in the state capital. Business leaders, including lifelong Republicans led by Oz Nelson, were more committed to the education of Kentucky's children and future workforce than they were to political party allegiances. When the Republican candidate refused to support KERA, they put together a sizable sum that was poured into media in the last days of the election on behalf of the Democrat who had come out in favor of KERA. The Democrat won by 51.1 percent to 48.9 percent, a margin easily explained by the business community's support.

### Philadelphia

Philadelphia's business community made different choices. At best, they were fair-weather friends of the reform effort; at worst they were outright obstacles to change. Some business people, to be fair, were strong supporters of change. Rosemarie Greco, at the time president of CoreStates Bank, chaired the business group that interviewed candidates and endorsed my appointment as superintendent. Rosemarie continued her strong support of education. She served on various committees associated with the reform agenda. She was always available for consultation and advice. Along with her boss, Terry Larsen, she ensured that CoreStates was a strong supporter of the schools, including an early commitment of $1 million, later raised to $2 million to meet the Annenberg Challenge.

When Ambassador Walter Annenberg awarded Philadelphia a $50 million grant for *Children Achieving*, he required (as with all other awardees) that it flow through an entity other than the school district. I asked Greater Philadelphia First (GPF), the group of about thirty-five of the biggest employers in Philadelphia and its environs, to be the conduit. They agreed, and a committee of GPF was established to work with us, chaired by Tom Donovan, who headed Mellon Bank in Philadelphia.

At my recommendation, Vicki Phillips, with whom I had worked when she was a senior aide to Commissioner Tom Boysen in Kentucky and later as deputy director of the National Alliance for Restructuring Education, was chosen to be executive director of the *Children Achieving* Challenge. Vicki, one of my most substantive and trusted advisors, was one of two people whom I invited to sit on my executive committee at the district who were not school district employees; the other was Warren Simmons, the executive director of the Philadelphia Education Fund, now head of the Annenberg Institute at Brown University.[7]

Vicki is exceptionally talented and played a large role in the success of *Children Achieving*.[8] Through her good work, the relationship between the district and the GPF was productive, although as the months and years unfolded, it was clear that it was really the work of the Challenge (Vicki and her staff), not the business community, that made it productive. The Challenge received little support from the business leaders themselves or from the GPF.

We were extremely successful in raising the match of two-to-one required from Ambassador Annenberg. There is some perception that the GPF played an important role; in fact the role was relatively modest. The $100 million match required $50 million from private sources and permitted the rest from public sources. Most of the private money came from foundations, led by Pew at about $16 million and the William Penn Foundation at $13 million.

The total raised in the business community toward the $50 million in private funds was disappointing—about one-third of the required private match.[9] In only one instance was I even accompanied by one of the GPF CEOs to call on one of their peers. In that instance, the CEO's "ask" was one-half of what we had agreed to ask before the meeting.

Another very great exception to the generally miserable business support was Richard Smoot, the president of PNC Bank in the

Philadelphia region. Dick's involvement arose from two sources: his view that the economic health of the city and region depended on the health of the education system, and his conviction that offering equal opportunity to children was the right thing to do. As a consequence, he was the point person in the single most helpful contribution from the business community during my tenure, when he agreed to lead a management productivity study of the district.

We placed a lot of early emphasis on good stewardship of our (inadequate) resources. I asked Dick, along with Emma Chappel, CEO of the United Bank, to co-chair the effort. Dick contributed huge amounts of time and thought. We wanted to identify every dime that we were spending inefficiently so we could shift those funds to instruction. We wanted to do this for both fiscal and political reasons, to prove that we were using the money we had as best we could before we asked for more. From doing the analysis to publicizing the results, Dick stayed with this effort in one form or the other for my entire tenure as superintendent.[10] Later, as the Greater Philadelphia First's tepid support began to wane after Dick's presidency of the group, he continued what became fairly unpopular support within the business community of *Children Achieving.*

After Dick's presidency of GPF, the pretense of their support faded rapidly. The CEO of Crown Cork and Seal, Bill Avery, replaced Dick. Bill never hid his disdain for public education. He was a great supporter of Governor Tom Ridge, Archdiocesan schools, and voucher programs. While GPF paid occasional lip service to support for public schools, their real support was for the religious and private schools and the governor's repeated and failed efforts to push vouchers through the state legislature.[11]

Comparing business leadership in Kentucky (and Washington State, Delaware, and Alabama, among others) with that in Philadelphia and Pennsylvania makes it clear the choices made in this arena matter. The business community in Philadelphia and Pennsylvania clearly chose to live with a mediocre education system. Their lack of support for change helps maintain, or even worsen, the status quo.[12]

## THE COURTS

Contrasting cases in Pennsylvania with cases in other states shows the critical effect that the courts can have. In the past three decades, there have been lawsuits concerning the financing of public education in at least forty-five states. The suits began in California with the 1971 *Serrano v. Priest* case, and in New Jersey with the 1973 *Robinson v. Cahill* case. In the early years, plaintiffs tended to prevail. After a few years of victories for defendants, plaintiffs have again begun to enjoy success. In November 2004, according to Michael Rebell, plaintiffs' lawyer in a New York adequacy suit, twenty-five of the previous twenty-seven decisions had favored the plaintiffs, including all of the last six. In Pennsylvania, however, the decisions of the highly politicized Supreme Court have been shameful.

Pennsylvania is one of few states in which the Supreme Court refused even to rule on school funding. In *Pennsylvania Association of Rural and Small Schools v. Ridge* (originally Casey), filed in 1991, the Commonwealth Court, upheld by the State Supreme Court in 1999, found that the issue of whether the Pennsylvania school finance system was unconstitutional was nonjusticiable: that only the legislature could decide whether the system met the constitutional standard. Similarly, the Pennsylvania Supreme Court in *Marrero v. Commonwealth of Pennsylvania*, the adequacy suit filed by, among others, Mayor Ed Rendell and the school district, also determined that only the legislature could decide the definition of adequacy.[13]

I once observed in a school board meeting that we should probably alter the curriculum for middle school social studies because of these court decisions. We had always taught that there were three branches of government, the legislative, judicial, and executive. With the ruling in the PARSS and Marrero cases, the Supreme Court had, in effect, eliminated the judicial branch, at least for poor children in public education.

In four of the five states contiguous to Pennsylvania—Maryland, Ohio, New Jersey, and West Virginia—the constitutional requirement is, as in Pennsylvania, that the state provide a "thorough and efficient" system of education. New York's constitution provides that New York provide for the "maintenance and support of a system of free common schools." In three of the four bordering states that have "thorough and efficient" in their constitutions, the highest courts have ruled in favor of the plaintiffs in funding cases. Maryland is the exception, where, without the prodding of a high court opinion, the legislature passed a schools finance plan that is adequate and equitable. The fifth contiguous state, New York, also had a landmark lawsuit *CFE v. State of New York*, handed down in 2001. The ruling was also for the plaintiffs.

Again, courts, for political reasons, make very different choices, even when the language and facts in different states are very similar.

## TEACHER UNIONS

There is an important role for responsible, professional unions in education reform, and there are many examples of union leaders who personify this.[14] The behavior of the union leadership in Philadelphia resulted not from the inevitabilities of labor dynamics, but from their consistently antistudent choices.

A number of union leaders demonstrate the potential for a more productive labor relationship. Roger Erskine is one. As president of the Seattle Education Association, he said, "Our imperative is student achievement and we don't have time for wars between adults. Schools must become more productive places." Pursuing this idea, under Erskine's leadership the Seattle school administration and union entered some years ago into what they called a Trust Agreement, not a contract. A system of meaningful school-based decision-making and accountability processes were adopted.

Roger is not alone among union leaders who seek to bring a different set of choices to the table. Al Shanker took a back seat to no one in his defense of teachers and their well-being. As a New York labor leader in the 1960s, he led strikes and confronted the powers-that-be. He, more than any other teacher union leader, created a new definition of unions, properly decrying lousy wages and working conditions. But the same strength, wisdom, and brains recognized changing requirements over the years. He became a spokesperson for still new definitions of responsibility as union leaders.

In the spirit of Shanker, a new breed of union leaders is trying to make their way. Members of several dozen unions around the country comprise the Teacher Union Reform Network (TURN). Established in 1996 under the leadership of Adam Urbanski (longtime president of the Rochester, New York, union) and the late Helen Bernstein (then president of the Los Angeles union), these leaders want to be agents of reform. They are exploring how teacher unions can develop new union models and provide the kind of leadership that continuously improves teaching and results in all children learning. The unions have included the leaders from many of the big cities—New York, Chicago, Los Angeles, Miami-Dade, Cincinnati, Seattle, Portland, Cleveland, Denver, San Francisco, Pittsburgh, and others. It never included Philadelphia's leadership.

### Philadelphia

The Philadelphia union leadership repeatedly made choices that worked against the interests of children. Their refusal to accept, or even talk about, any semblance of accountability has already been described in chapter 8, as was their attempt in 1996 to sandbag the reconstitution provision that they had agreed to two years before. Elsewhere I describe their intransigence during negotiations on other important issues. However, the examples I describe here are included because they demonstrate the fundamental attitudes and choices of the union leadership, and their stonewalling in the face of efforts to improve the relationships between them and the district.

At one point Mayor Rendell thought that perhaps he could help facilitate productive discussions between the district and the union. He organized meetings between union president Kirsch, board of education president Pedro Ramos, Shanker's AFT successor the late Sandra Feldman, and me. The five of us met for an hour or more at least twice. For decades, seniority was determinative in teacher assignments in Philadelphia. If there were a vacancy in a school and a teacher with more seniority and proper certification wanted it, she got it. The principal, the staff, the nature of the school's program, and the quality of the more senior teacher were not taken into consideration. I said that this was a problem; we wanted to allow the school staff and principal to have a significant role in making staffing decisions, and we wanted student need to play a dominant role. I knew that Feldman, when she had succeeded Shanker as president of the United Federation of Teachers in New York City, had negotiated provisions of the contract related to seniority that were far more intelligent and reflective of student need than ours in Philadelphia.

I proposed that we adopt the same seniority provisions that Feldman had negotiated in New York. I observed that Feldman did not seem to think them pernicious to teachers. She certainly was not a union leader with the reputation of being soft on management. If the proposition were accepted, the kids and schools were winners. While the far less desirable alternative, at least if Kirsch rejected it, it would make clear to the other meeting participants that these issues were hard because the union leadership would not even entertain movement on them.

Feldman, of course, responded with the typical national position that the decision was up to the PFT, since the national AFT didn't get into local bargaining over particular issues. We turned to Kirsch whose only response was to say that in Philadelphia, seniority was a difficult issue. I think both Rendell and Feldman realized that future sessions would prove to be equally worthless. We did not meet again.

It was not the last external attempt to bring rationality to our relationship with the union leadership. Someone proposed that Jim Martin of the Philadelphia Area Labor Management committee facilitate meetings with Kirsch and me. Martin, who came out of the labor movement, was considered to be a neutral and objective party. We believed that he would be evenhanded and that, perhaps, given his background, he might be able to change the conversation between the PFT and the district, between Ted and me, to a different and more productive place. I readily agreed, as did Ted.

We met monthly. Both Kirsch and I would submit suggested agenda items to Jim. Jim would determine the agenda. The meetings went nowhere. We would discuss an issue; Jim would ask a lot of questions to try to get everything on the table; typically he would, at some point say, "Well, what shall we do about that?" I would often make some sort of a suggestion, which Kirsch would reject. Along the way, I thought it was clear that if I made a suggestion, by definition, he had to oppose it. So I ceased making suggestions, leading to Kirsch being specifically asked by Martin to make a suggestion. He never did.

After some months, Jim concluded that the meetings were a waste of time and called them off, though a few months later we decided to try them again. It was suggested that we add to the group two people who got along relatively well: Jerry Jordan, the chief staff person at the PFT (now president of the PFT), and Germaine Ingram, the number two person at the district. The hope was that adding them to the mix might change the dynamics and make the conversations worthwhile. It did not. The meetings ended again.

Reforms in the compensation system negotiated in 2000 again illustrate how the Philadelphia teachers union leadership choices were obstacles to implementation. The compensation reforms had been part of the proposals developed during my superintendency, though the contract was not actually settled until several months after I had left. The new features of the compensation included, in addition to bonuses for teachers willing to work in our most challenging schools and in subject areas where we had the highest vacancy rate, significant steps for moving the basic compensation scale from one based on seniority and degrees to one based on demonstrated skills and knowledge.

The contract included a broad outline of the new system and called for a committee of both the PFT and the administration to further develop and implement it. It also included a process for outside arbitration of differences. Within a few weeks of the contract settlement, Jack Steinberg, a PFT vice president, publicly stated that the system would never be implemented. Despite the fact that the members of the committee worked well together and developed a pilot program for implementation in year two of the contract, he was proven right. The acting CEO and, later, Paul Vallas and the union diluted it significantly, and the administration eventually dropped it altogether.

The union leadership in Philadelphia made very different choices than the leadership in dozens of other cities.


## CONCLUSION

A different choice by any of these major players—newspaper policy, decisions by the mayors, a different orientation of the business community, less political courts, or more enlightened union leadership— could have made a huge difference in outcomes for children.

In 2005, the president and the Congress cut taxes for the rich by as much as an additional $60–$95 billion (on top of trillions previously cut), while cutting Medicaid and food stamps. More recently, they've said that they have to cut such social programs in order to pay for relief aid for the victims of hurricane Katrina, while simultaneously spending billions of unbudgeted dollars for the war in Iraq. Such thinking had also led to the "reform of welfare as we knew it," requiring mothers to work in order to receive welfare payments, but declining to provide child care or other supports that make working possible. The United States is experiencing the biggest economic meltdown since the depression because of mortgage and credit choices made by business inside deregulatory choices in economic policy made by the federal government.

The conditions that result in low achievement by poor children and those with disabilities and English-language learners and children of color are not preordained. These outcomes are not inevitable. Those of us who have political, policy, and civic power make specific decisions that can be named that result in such disastrous consequences. But all of us are complicit. Even if we don't have the direct responsibility, we tolerate the choices made in election after election.

The good news, of course, is that just as we make the terrible choices that disadvantage children, we can make different decisions, and when we do, the performance of America's children will be radically different.


## NOTES

1. During my tenure as Maryland's state superintendent, roughly half of the Maryland boards of education were elected and half appointed. Over that twelve-year period, about 25 percent of them, for one reason or another,

changed their method of selection and, if memory serves me correctly, one of them actually changed and then changed back. I am skeptical whether a single child read better as a consequence of these machinations.

2. Interestingly, the power to appoint school board members had moved from the Court of Common Pleas to the mayor just prior to Rendell's election.

3. I should add that his was not the only decisive voice in my becoming superintendent. Both Father Paul Washington, my board chair twenty-five years earlier when I was executive director of the Philadelphia Tutorial Project, and David Richardson, a state legislator in 1994 and a young, very effective activist leader in the late 1960s with whom I worked at that time, stood up for my candidacy. And, of course, the very independent-minded Ruth Hayre, who cast the fifth and deciding vote for me was crucial. Their being African American and highly respected in the African American community made it possible for me, a white man, to have credibility in a school district that was 80 percent minority.

4. There was one interesting period when the balance of votes was 4–3 against *Children Achieving*. On at least two important decisions, when we were about to lose votes, I called the mayor in the middle of a public board meeting and told him we were about to lose the vote. He asked me to call a particular one of the four oppositional board members to the phone. In each case, she changed her vote so that *Children Achieving* prevailed. Having to resort to such tactics, when it could have been wholly unnecessary, hurt the reform effort.

5. The other members were Lloyd Bond, University of North Carolina, Greensboro; Tom Corcoran, Consortium for Policy Research in Education, University of Pennsylvania; Sylvia Johnson, Howard University; Robert Linn, University of Colorado, Boulder; and Walter Secada, University of Wisconsin–Madison.

6. A fascinating and ironic postscript is that during the gubernatorial election that he won in 2002 both his primary and general election opponents tried to attack him on education grounds, especially as education became the number one issue in the campaign as a result of Good Schools Pennsylvania's relentless work (see chapter 15). He could not avoid addressing the record of the Philadelphia schools during his tenure. As a consequence he discovered what Philadelphia's children had accomplished was a strength that stood up under scrutiny rather than a weakness from which to hide.

7. I had first met Warren when he was thirteen and lived in East Harlem, where my wife and I were working at the East Harlem Protestant Parish. Warren was a member of a local group with whom we worked called the Enchanters. We rediscovered this part of our past in 1992 at a Clinton inauguration event in DC after having worked together for several years. I also worked with Warren at the National Center for Education and the Economy. He remains one of the nation's outstanding voices for systemic change in education practice.

8. After leaving the Challenge, Vicki became an outstanding superintendent in Lancaster, Pennsylvania, where student achievement improved significantly.

When Rendell became governor, he appointed Vicki secretary of education. She later moved on to several productive years as superintendent of schools in Portland, Oregon. She is now head of education grantmaking for the Gates Foundation.

9. As indicated, $2 million came from CoreStates (Terry Larsen and Rosemarie Greco), $1 million from PNC Bank (Dick Smoot—see below), and $2 million from IBM nationally that I was able to raise because Louis Gerstner, IBM's CEO, believed deeply in the standards-based and accountability-driven systems change that *Children Achieving* represented. There was also a $1 million contribution from Mellon Bank, whose Philadelphia leader Tom Donovan chaired the GPF *Children Achieving* Oversight Committee. Arco gave another $1 million. Later, after numerous on again–off again commitments, the Philadelphia Electric and Gas Company made a pledge of $1 million that was the only one of the corporate gifts heavily restricted in its use.

10. The Management and Productivity Task Force, its work, and its results were covered in chapter 13, as we discussed stewardship as the first priority for generating adequate resources for the system.

11. The Philadelphia Chamber of Commerce played virtually no role. While the president of the Chamber, Charlie Pizzi, greeted me warmly enough and introduced me with enthusiasm, I cannot remember a single substantive thing the Chamber did for public education while I was superintendent. Today, the president of the Chamber is Mark Schweiker, the former governor, hardly a friend of public education, and Greater Philadelphia First actually went out of business in 2001. Regretfully, Philadelphia has become largely a branch office city augmented by accounting and law firms. It does not provide the kind of business leadership exemplified by people like Oz Nelson and other Business Roundtable leaders in the early 1990s.

12. Recently, David L. Cohen, chief of staff to Mayor Rendell, on his election as chair of the Greater Philadelphia Chamber of Commerce, said that business had to place education on its A-list of issues, making it comparable to lowering business taxes as a lobbying priority. Governor Rendell has taken the same position. They recognize the tepid, photo-opportunity type of support that is characteristic of most business involvement will not result in the tough changes in education policy that is required. Business must step as much out of character on financing policy as unions must on compensation and accountability policy. Neither as general rule have understood that.

13. In Alabama the courts have also denied review or otherwise closed the courthouse door to poor children seeking judicial redress for school finance schemes. Even there, the Alabama Supreme Court originally affirmed the trial court's finding that the Alabama system was unconstitutional, and affirmed the remedy that was fashioned. Then over the years, they reaffirmed the underlying decision four times. However, in 1997, they vacated the remedy order. In a bizarre turn of events in May 2002, at their own initiative and years after their appellate jurisdiction had expired, with no request from any party to do so, the Alabama Supreme Court reopened the case and then dismissed it. I would have to agree that as appalling as the Pennsylvania courts' decisions

have been, to decide a case, affirm it four times, and then reopen it in order to dismiss it wins the ultimate prize for political rather than rational decision-making.

14. My early and very positive views can be found in "Improving Educational Services through Statewide Bargaining," in *Handbook of Faculty Bargaining*, by George W. Angell, Edward P. Kelley, et al. (San Francisco: Jossey Bass, 1977).

# 15

# The Public Will to Make
# Different Choices

A different world cannot be built by indifferent people.

Horace Mann

It is not just newspapers, politicians, courts, union officials, business-people, and school district officials who make choices that make a difference in the lives of children. The wider citizenry also makes fateful choices; indeed, in a democracy, citizens make the core choices from which all others flow. The officials we elect have made policy decisions that create and maintain an intolerable, ineffective, unjust educational system. They do so because they think it is what the public wants, because our actions and our inactions have tolerated the status quo. We must send a different message, replacing our indifference with resolute insistence that all children have the conditions they need to learn to high levels. This requires building a movement in support of children state by state and nationally that ensures a quality education for every child.

Many of those in power got there by learning to accommodate the status quo. Even policy-makers of good will are unlikely to change the status quo radically enough from inside; it is too risky and too difficult. Change also requires outside demand. Those decision-makers who want to preserve the status quo need to be pressured by the risk of defeat if they stay set in their ways. At the same time, those decision-makers who seek change need to be actively supported by the electorate with votes and with public support.

In Philadelphia, despite resistance from many politicians, union officials, newspapers, business leaders, courts, and local and state legislative bodies, we put together teaching and learning conditions that resulted in a 42 percent jump in student achievement in reading, mathematics, and science for all tested grades between 1996 and 2000. We also increased the on-time graduation rate substantially, from 48.9 percent to 56.9 percent. But we failed to generate enough public will to pressure the politicians into providing sustained support for several critical and controversial features of the agenda, most notably:

- Educator accountability.
- Adequate funding, equitably raised and distributed.
- Comprehensive, simultaneous implementation of all required components.

The type of citizen action that builds and sustains the political and public will to support social justice—in this instance, quality education for all children and youth—is different from the normal concept of public engagement. Traditional public engagement in education includes activities such as participation in the parent-teacher organization, assistance with fund-raising events, and other school volunteer activities. Activist citizen action, on the other hand, intends to change the status quo. Obviously, there is a continuum from public engagement to citizen action. Nevertheless, the basic distinction between the two types of involvement is very real.

## BUILDING PUBLIC WILL IN PHILADELPHIA

### Supporting Grassroots Organizing

Citizen action was an integral part of *Children Achieving* from the beginning. When I went to Philadelphia, one of my goals was to stimulate community organizing that would challenge the district, city, and state with the reality that we were not doing the right thing, or at least not doing it well enough or fast enough. We could not fully succeed in our schools without a partnership with the community. The residents of many neighborhoods in Philadelphia had very little political power. Thus, we allocated more than $4 million over five years to the Alliance for Progress, an independent coalition of community organizations, for independent community organizing.

According to our plan, the Alliance for Progress would employ one organizer in each of the twenty-two district clusters, an average of one full-time organizer for every dozen schools. The alliance would invite proposals from existing community organizations in each cluster. The local organization would select the organizer. We wanted to build local community capacity; then the twenty-two could work together under the direction of the alliance, wielding significant aggregate power, and governing themselves, since the alliance board would be made up of representatives from the twenty-two organizations.

It didn't work out that way. Within the first year, the alliance began to fall apart. It employed a lead organizer who changed the alliance from a coalition of community groups to a freestanding organization, the Alliance Organizing Project (AOP).

Although I respected the lead organizer, I was not at all happy with these developments, but I decided not to intervene. I did not know whether they would develop into a powerful community force, but it was clear that they had to develop into whatever lay ahead by virtue of their own work and decisions. They were either going to be independent or they were not. Despite my misgivings and that of others, for the next four years we maintained our $4 million financial commitment to them.

This venture was a failure. While some parents at some schools provided some leadership, it did not develop into the large-scale advocacy group that Philadelphia needs. A case can be made that devoting as much money to the project as we did corrupted the process. On the other hand, without money, the predecessor alliance was equally inconsequential. The AOP officially closed in 2004.

### Public Information Campaign

A second major effort to build public will was our relentless campaign to fight misinformation about district finances. We wanted to make it clear to residents of the city and the state that Philadelphia schools, contrary to what most people believed, were spending less per child than the state average and far less than our regional neighbors, and that teacher salaries were not close to competitive.

This message was difficult to get across in the surrounding counties; even citizens who followed local news tended to be aware of the Philadelphia public schools only when there was a major short-term crisis. In addition, there was a kind of collective denial of the funding gap because of its potential tax implications. Nevertheless, our occasional opinion polls showed that over the years, public awareness on this issue grew substantially, it helped create the foundation for organizing work that became Good Schools Pennsylvania.

### Approaching Harrisburg

For decades, the district had avoided confrontations with Harrisburg, preferring to work through back channels and make do with what they could get. The steady decline in our per-pupil funding was clear evidence that this strategy was a failure.

On my arrival, I made it clear that though the district would eventually need far more resources, before asking for them, we would first improve our stewardship of the resources we already had, establish high standards, create a staff accountability system, and show increases in student achievement. By the spring of 1996, all of this had been done.

As soon as Tom Ridge was elected governor in November 1994, we met with him and his secretary of education, Eugene Hickock. In my naïveté, I thought our proposal of accountability for dollars would be of interest to the governor. It was not. At no time did the Ridge administration entertain any proposal that included fair funding for the poor children of the state. They obsessed instead about vouchers throughout their tenure.

## Confronting Harrisburg

### Desegregation Lawsuit

For decades, Philadelphia had been involved in a desegregation lawsuit. The original consent decree committed the district to a voluntary desegregation plan; this decree was later modified, at the district's request, to add focus on improving learning conditions and achievement in racially isolated schools.

Just prior to my arrival, Judge Delores Smith of the Commonwealth Court had become impatient with the slow progress and ordered that a specific set of actions be accomplished within a given timeline. To its credit, the board of education had decided not to appeal this ruling. While the judge and I often differed over the particulars of implementing her order, the overall framework she established was similar enough to *Children Achieving* that we were able to use the order to bolster our efforts to provide more for Philadelphia children and reinforce our claim that more money was needed.

For years, the district had argued that it could go only so far in its school-improvement effort without additional state funds. For years, Judge Smith had responded that the district could and would have to go further before she would consider the issue of resources. Finally, in late 1995, the judge determined that the district's efforts under *Children Achieving* were strong enough that it was time to reopen the question of resources.[1] Hours upon hours of preparation, testimony, and depositions led to a ruling that Philadelphia's children were entitled to hundreds of million of new dollars per year from Harrisburg. As part of our campaign to increase public and political will, we made massive efforts to be sure the public was made aware of these developments. However, Judge Smith's decision was later overturned by the Pennsylvania Supreme Court, which ruled in September 1996 that Judge Smith had no jurisdiction over funding and remanded the case to her to deal with the issues without regard to funding.

## Refusal to Cut Budgets

The next strategy for building public will developed during the state and the city's budgeting process. The process for developing the annual district spending plan had been in place for years. During the fall of each year, the various budget units—from the teacher to the central office—submitted "wish list" budget requests. Then the central office required all schools and offices to submit multiple projected spending plans in addition to the original wish list.

Often, these spending plans were required to maintain previous funding levels with no adjustment for inflation; sometimes the multiple plans had to include various levels of budget cuts. Actual funding numbers from the state were never made clear in a timely way. Projections were always a shot in the dark. Nevertheless, the district was required by law to present a balanced budget based on the funds that were projected (never accurate) as of June 30.

The district would be forced to reduce the number of positions in schools to correspond to the then-current state budget limits, resulting in the least senior teachers and staff being sent layoff notices, as the union contract required, to allow those who received notices time to look for jobs elsewhere. Teachers with low seniority would also lose their position in a particular school. Morale plummeted as the uncertainty of this annual ritual played out. In August, as Harrisburg finalized the actual budget allocations, some people began to receive rehiring notices and could select from the vacancies then available, wherever they might be. This insane process was often incomplete when the school year started.

The final craziness did not occur until late October or early November when "leveling" would occur. "Leveling" was the process through which teachers were transferred throughout the system to ensure that there were no more than one elementary teacher for every thirty elementary students and one high school teacher for every thirty-three high school students, limits set by the contract. This would minimize budget requirements since the system would have no more or no fewer teachers than the contract required as a minimum.

Thus, teachers did not know who their students would be and students didn't know who their teachers would be, and principals didn't know who their staff members would be, until about 20 percent of the school year was over. Absolutely nuts!

New to the job in the summer 1994, I observed this pernicious budget process based on the budget submitted by my predecessor, and experienced it directly the following year. We anticipated cuts not only from the operating budget, but also from federal funds. The clamor, as schools received their projected budgets, was very painful to hear. Even worse was witnessing the conflicts that developed within the system as schools, programs, and city regions tried to cannibalize each other for the biggest possible share of the far-too-small pie. I vowed that this spectacle would not occur again.

As we were to begin the budget process for the 1996–1997 school year, I met with Mayor Rendell and David L. Cohen, Rendell's chief of staff. I told them that if we expected radical school reform, supported by the wider community, we had to change the system of budgeting. We had to take the position that we would not make further dollar cuts, at least at the school level and vow that we were not going to lay off any more teachers only to bring them back, and that we were going to budget for the cost of "leveling" earlier in the year.[2]

Rendell unhesitatingly made a two-pronged commitment that he honored consistently for the rest of his term. First, he agreed to support the district in its refusal to make any more cuts at the school level, and to support a sane budgeting process that permitted some measure of advance planning and respect for school teams, parents, and children. This meant that the district, with the mayor's support, would sooner or later be in violation of the state law requiring a balanced school budget.[3]

In addition to being a more intelligent approach to management and budgeting, the intention was to use this to focus public attention on the issue, and to pressure the state into taking the responsibility it had been ducking for so long.

**Bringing Lawsuits**

The mayor's second commitment in our late-night meeting was to join the district in seeking fair funding through the courts. Few states have made dramatic commitments to adequate and equitable funding outside of a court requirement. It was clear that step one should be a lawsuit against the state, making the argument that Pennsylvania's funding system did not meet the "thorough and efficient" standard set by the state Constitution.

We filed the suit. In the end it failed, when the highly political State Supreme Court ruled that only the legislature had the power to determine what "thorough and efficient means."[4] It should be noted that, in the many cases where school funding lawsuits have been brought, some have been won and some lost, but only in Pennsylvania and one or two other states has the court washed its hands of interpreting the standards of the state constitution in the name of politics.

Anticipating the perils of the Pennsylvania courts, the mayor also agreed with us that the federal courts could be a route to develop the political will to support a quality education for all students. While in the United States the individual states have responsibility for public education, they are nevertheless bound by federal civil rights legislation.

Our *Powell v Commonwealth* suit was filed in March 1998 against both the governor and the legislature, alleging that the state had violated regulations adopted by the U.S. Department of Education to implement Title VI of the Civil Rights Act of 1964. William Coleman, Nixon's secretary of transportation and longtime Pennsylvania education and civil right supporter, agreed to the role of lead counsel for us. Germaine Ingram, my extraordinary chief of staff and previously chief counsel, led the district's effort.[5]

The fundamental premise of the suit was that Pennsylvania's school funding formula discriminated against children of color who resided in school districts that were majority minority and poor. One of the best pieces of data supporting this was the fact that, "on average, for 1995–1996, for two school districts with the same level of poverty . . . the school districts with higher non-white enrollment received $52.88 less per pupil for each increase of 1 percent in non-white enrollment."[6]

At the time there were twelve school districts in Pennsylvania in which more than one-half of the students were minority. The defendants—the governor and the legislature—argued that the court should dismiss the case for failure to state a claim, and won at the district court level. However, when the plaintiffs appealed that decision to the Third Circuit, a three-judge panel unanimously overturned the lower court in a strong, almost blistering rejection of the defendant's position.

After John Street became mayor, he agreed to back off of this lawsuit as part of the ineffective conciliation strategy he decided to pursue with Harrisburg following my departure.

### Seeking the Mayor's Leadership in Grassroots Organizing

I made a serious effort to convince Mayor Rendell, and later Mayor Street, to provide leadership for the development of grassroots insistence on fairness. As early as August 1997, I persuaded Mayor Rendell to convene a meeting of the school board and district leadership, City Council President Street, and Chief of Staff David Cohen. In addition to legal and financial strategies, we discussed the need to dramatize the seriousness of the situation, but no specific decisions were made. Subsequently, I suggested a number of very specific activist tactics.[7]

My proposals fell on deaf ears.[8] In retrospect I should have realized that ambitious politicians like Rendell and Street, advised by self-proclaimed "realists" like Chief of Staff David Cohen and political pollster/advisor Neil Oxman, simply were not going to step that far out of the box. Filing lawsuits, making pronouncements, declaring education a priority, giving me the five school-board votes I needed to try to keep the substantive agenda marginally on track all fit inside the norm of big-time politics.

The type of dramatic activist proposal that involved rallies, marches, hunger strikes, countdown clocks, and the like was, in their eyes, my impolitic way of thinking and acting. Increasingly, I developed a reputation for being unrealistic and making over-the-top demands. According to my critics, I would not engage in "the art of the possible, and compromise was not in my vocabulary." My view was that it was not I who was unrealistic. Rather, it was unrealistic to think that we could provide equitable learning opportunities to poor children, largely children of color, many of whom did not speak English as a first language and a disproportionate number of whom were disabled due to poverty, with 25 percent fewer dollars per child than was being spent on children with multiple advantages.

### Seeking Compromise

In reality, I was more than willing to compromise and to demonstrate that I was not looking for large infusions of new money to continue to do the same old thing. I had offered proposals that exchanged accountability for money, as early as my first meeting with Governor Ridge. In April 1999, I took this concept several steps further. I met with David Girard diCarlo, a Philadelphia lawyer and a leader in Republican politics who was a strong supporter and advisor of Governor Ridge with the kind of access that ensured that his recommendations would be seriously considered. I made a specific proposal[9] to address the three big concerns the Commonwealth routinely expressed.

With respect to their concern about persistent low achievement, I suggested that we mutually define a minimum level of performance by students as a precondition to our receiving additional funds. Concerning stewardship and focusing on instruction, I proposed we choose an indicator like the percentage of each dollar spent on instruction (as determined by the State Department of Education) and require that we stay below the regional average. Regarding collective bargaining, I proposed that we consider statewide bargaining around wages, hours, and conditions of employment with market basket variations throughout the state.

In return for these radical changes, I proposed that we receive funding that would cover the structural deficit in our budget plus $388 million that would support the fair opportunities to learn we projected as necessary for our students to meet the very high standards of performance we had set for ourselves. While that seems like a lot of money, in fact, the $388 million was almost exactly the amount that would have closed the per pupil spending gap between us and the sixty-two surrounding suburban school systems.

In effect, we were saying give us what they have and we'll produce higher achievement gains than they do with our students having greater challenges. And if we don't produce, we will have built into the omnibus legislation a provision for the additional money to cease.

Despite repeated attempts to get an answer, we never even got an acknowledgment that we made the proposal. This confirmed for me that the issues of student performance, accountability, and the union contract were all contrived excuses by the governor to avoid being fair to poor kids of color in Philadelphia and throughout the Commonwealth. He simply had no interest in their success.

### Mayor Street's Involvement

City Council President John Street soon became the Democratic candidate to succeed Mayor Rendell. I was pleased with that development. Street had the reputation of being willing to act outside the bounds of accepted political niceties. In the early days of his career, he had been on protest lines, and he was noted for his advocacy for the poor.

During the series of meetings with Mayor Rendell when I had proposed an activist campaign, Street had pulled me aside to say that I had to understand that Mayor Rendell simply didn't have the stomach for it and, even if he did, David Cohen would not let him do those kinds of things.[10] I mistakenly took his implication to be that he would embrace the suggestions if it were up to him.

Shortly after meeting with him after his election, I sent him a proposal "Strategy for Public Education Advocacy in Pennsylvania." It laid out a plan that would extend from then until after the Republican Convention that was scheduled for August 2000. While the details were different, it embodied the same activist orientation as the previous proposal to Rendell.[11]

Shortly after the memo was sent, Mayor Street agreed to hold twenty-two cluster community meetings before the end of March. My hopes and spirits skyrocketed, since that was the first of the major activities in my proposal. I also set in motion the identification of 1,295 faith leaders (five per principal) and the 2,590 (ten per principal) parents by the 259 principals. More than ten thousand people showed up to standing room only meetings with the mayor. We collected all ten thousand names in anticipation of the mobilization that we hoped would develop.

I was wrong about Street. He stopped returning phone calls. I could not get meetings with him. He made it clear through the school board that he would not even support enough money to meet the modest Fair Opportunity to Learn Standards called for in that next year.

As a result, I proposed that we concentrate what money we had in the elementary schools, maintaining the student promotion requirements for that year's fourth graders but to suspend the promotion requirements for the eighth graders, since we would not have the ability to provide them with the help they would need to meet the standards. After a terrible battle with the board behind closed doors, in which several members sought to maintain the grade 8 standards even without the supports we had promised, the board agreed. That was in May 2000.

On June 5, recognizing that the mayor and the board of education had decided to renew the historic and failed strategy of conciliation instead of mobilizing the citizenry in an aggressive activist campaign, I announced my resignation. There was simply no way that I could continue to pretend that what needed to be done either was being done or could be done.

## MOVING ON: GOOD SCHOOLS PENNSYLVANIA

Mayor Street was frozen out by the state takeover of the district in 2001, with little to show for any efforts in education.

Rendell, the former mayor, was elected governor in 2002. As he entered the office, Governor Rendell, in his first budget, proposed major increases for education and pushed for them courageously and audaciously. However, saddled with a highly recalcitrant legislature with little interest in the achievement of poor children, rural or urban, let alone minority children, he was able to get only small increases passed. In the governor's second term, with a Democratic majority in the House, he has made significant progress. In the 2008 legislative session he was able to secure an additional $270 million. More importantly, there is language in the budget that calls for $2.3 billion more over the next six years to be disbursed in a more equitable manner. Through the governor's support and the activism of Good Schools Pennsylvania (see below) and others, Pennsylvania has the first chance in decades of meeting its constitutional and moral commitment to its children.

But this relative success is fourteen years after my arrival in Philadelphia, nearly eighteen years after Governor Casey permitted the last semiequitable formula to be dismantled, and more than three decades since the state was paying more than half of education costs under Governor Shapp. We have failed more than another entire generation of children, literally millions of children.

Through savvy and Herculean effort, what Rendell (and Donna Cooper) has achieved is outstanding in a world of low expectations and compared to previous years. It remains nowhere near adequate.

## BUILDING PUBLIC WILL TO MAKE DIFFERENT CHOICES: STATE PERSPECTIVE, 2000–2008

In 2000, after nearly thirty-five years in education, it finally became compellingly clear to me that the barriers we face in delivering a quality public education to every child are not educational. We have the knowledge to succeed with all children. The barriers are political ones, rooted in the absence of political will. Citizens have not provided the support that results in elected officials and other policy-makers having the courage to make the decisions necessary to ensure that every child will learn to high levels.

Since then I have spent most of my time seeking to generate this will through grassroots efforts, first in Pennsylvania and now at the national level. This section of the chapter describes the founding and activities of a state-level organization called Good Schools Pennsylvania, and the role it has played in supporting and demanding changes in state policies before and during Governor Rendell's administration.

As my tenure in Philadelphia had wound down, I had begun to explore the appetite for a grassroots activist campaign for public education in the state. I received support from a variety of education advocates and religious leaders. Key among them were Marian Wright Edelman, president of the Children's Defense Fund; Wendy Puriefoy, president of the Public Education Network; and Eileen Lindner, deputy general secretary of the National Council of Churches.[12] The campaign that became Good Schools Pennsylvania began to take shape.

We decided that before we could successfully run a three-year grassroots campaign in Pennsylvania, we would need to secure our funding. We calculated that we would need about $4.5 million. I sent out the first grant proposal in December, and by the following April we had raised the entire amount from ten different foundations.[13]

## GOOD SCHOOLS PENNSYLVANIA

In March of 2000 I asked Donna Cooper, Mayor Rendell's former deputy mayor of planning, and now Governor Rendell's secretary of planning, to serve as the executive director of Good Schools Pennsylvania. A few years earlier she had been unable to work with me on this kind of organizing because she had promised the mayor she would take on the challenge of placing several thousand women in jobs under what was then the new federal welfare law. By late 2000 she had largely completed the job-placement work and agreed to take on this new challenge. Donna is tough, smart, demanding, and very focused. She did a great job as executive director over the next two years.

Donna in turn hired about twenty others to staff seven regional offices throughout the state. Northeast Philadelphia served as headquarters, chosen because it was located two blocks from the home office of then Majority Leader John Perzel (R). We chose offices strategically, in areas of population concentration, in legislative leadership districts, and in districts where we thought the incumbent legislators were most vulnerable and, thus, susceptible to hearing us.

Our mission was focused on three areas, which research showed would lead to significant improvement in student education: mandating adequate funding, equitably raised and distributed; a reasonable, hard-edged accountability system for educators; and ensuring that schools and school districts used proven instructional practices.

We designed a six-part organizing agenda:

- Establish groups of ten people each, with each group meeting monthly to learn about education, to write two letters per member to elected officials, and to be the source of other activist activities.
- Establish chapters of Good Schools Pennsylvania on college campuses throughout the state.
- Organize high school chapters.
- Hold a monthly prayer vigil on the steps of the capitol in Harrisburg.
- Hold periodic large rallies to dramatize the crisis in public education and to serve as a recruitment ground.
- Make public education the number one issue of the 2002 gubernatorial campaign.

### Groups of Ten

The core strategy of Good Schools Pennsylvania was to establish groups of ten people each who were willing to become education activists.[14] During the initial three-year campaign we established about 350 such groups. Our effort centered around identifying people to be leaders of the groups, training them, and asking them to take the lead in recruiting others. The norm was for a group to gather at a home, spend the first hour learning more about public education, and then write two letters, one to a statewide official like the governor and a second to one of their own legislators in the General Assembly. Each month they followed the same pattern, writing to different officials at each session.

The basis for the study portion of each meeting was a nine-unit curriculum that we developed with assistance from Professor Ted Hershberg's Center for Greater Philadelphia at the University of Pennsylvania. The units included topics such as "What Every School Needs to Do," "The Impact of Inequity," "The Legislature," "A National Problem," "Where Money Matters," and "Standards and Accountability."

While we reached out to many different groups, faith communities comprised our primary recruitment ground. We would approach judicatory leaders such as bishops in the Episcopal, Methodist, and Lutheran churches, Executive Presbyters in the Presbyterian church, leading rabbis in Jewish congregations, and counterparts in other faith traditions and denominations, and ask each to pledge to a goal of establishing a number of groups of ten equal to 25 percent of the number of congregations within their sphere of influence.

More than twenty judicatory leaders ultimately pledged a total of more than fifteen hundred groups of ten. They ranged from a pledge of two groups from the state's Reconstructionist Jews to two hundred groups from the Western Pennsylvania Conference of the United Methodist Church. Three hundred fifty groups were established in the first three years; that was short of our goal, but, in retrospect, that was a function of an overly ambitious goal rather than a failure of the faith communities to produce. In this age of multiple obligations, to agree to actually give two hours a month to advocacy proved to be a significant commitment.

## College Students

A second strategy was organizing college chapters. Within three years we had twenty-three college chapters across the state. At least once a year we held a weekend training session for chapter leaders at one of the campuses. Chapter members and others they recruited attended rallies, and some attended the prayer vigils described below. College students particularly enjoyed the "phone slams." For these, we bought a number of cell phones and loaded them with minutes. Members of the Good Schools campus chapter set up informational tables to explain the issues to students, faculty, and campus visitors, who were then asked to call the members of the General Assembly representing the area in which the campus was located or, in the case of Pennsylvania residents registered as voters elsewhere, their own representative. These "slams" routinely would generate several hundred calls in a day.

## High School Students

A third strategy was organizing high school students. I was inspired to do this by my experience with the Philadelphia Student Union. This was a group that did their homework and were particularly creative in dramatizing injustice around education issues through skits, demonstrations, street theater, and other activities. Two of the major high school student events were Harrisburg demonstrations. Each involved more than fifteen hundred high school students from more than four dozen school districts across the state.

## Prayer Vigils

We held prayer vigils in Harrisburg once a month for eighteen months. Each month, we assigned responsibility to a particular faith-based group. The assigned group took the lead in recruiting participants, with their groups of ten playing a major role in producing people. The month's leader also led that month's program. At least three hundred people (up to fifteen hundred) attended each vigil. The frequency and size of the effort far exceeded the capital's usual diet of one to two small demonstrations per year for education. The Good Schools vigils were held on the steps of the capitol or in the capitol rotunda, depending on weather and the number of participants. Following thirty minutes of prayers, meditations, and speeches, the participants visited their legislators to urge them to give priority to education issues. Our dependability and persistence conveyed that we were not going to go away.

We seek to change hearts and minds, but where that is not possible, our goal becomes to change behavior. The biblical story that I think of as the basis for this strategy is that of the poor and persistent widow and the unjust judge. Luke describes her inspiring advocacy for justice in chapter 18. She went before the judge repeatedly asking for justice; she was repeatedly turned down. Finally the judge gave her justice, not because she turned his heart but because her persistence wore him down. My hope is that Good Schools Pennsylvania, Prepare The Future (described below), and all our allies will play the role of the persistent widow as we seek justice for all America's children and families.[15]

## Rallies

Rallies were our fifth strategy. A fun example began in a Lutheran church in Swarthmore with speeches and pep talks from people like Marian Wright Edelman, Congressman Chaka Fattah, and Methodist Bishop Peter Weaver. Also present were giant papier-mâché likenesses of gubernatorial candidates Ed Rendell and Mike Fisher, whom we addressed, since the candidates themselves were not in attendance. At the end of the church portion of the event, the one thousand people present marched from wealthy Swarthmore symbolically and literally across a bridge to the largely poor and African American town of Chester, where we held another rally in a park. With this, we dramatized the gap between the rich and the poor in a visual way.

The rallies served two purposes. They provided a time when supporters could come together and meet others who shared their commitment to justice. It was a time to celebrate the movement and the mission. The rallies had a second very practical function, as well. They gave us an opportunity to recruit more participants, as there were always several hundred new people who attended each rally.

## Gubernatorial Campaign

The sixth strategy was to make public education the number one issue during the 2002 gubernatorial campaign. Because there was no Republican primary, we focused our attention during the primary on the race between Mayor Rendell and the auditor general and future U.S. Senator Robert Casey. We challenged them to support an agenda of change that would not only provide adequate funding to our schools, but also ensure that districts used proven instructional practices. We also made clear that accountability was necessary. Both candidates supported education, but Mayor Rendell's response was clearer, stronger, and more aligned with our policy position.

The real test was to emerge during the general election between Mayor Rendell and Attorney General Fisher. We again urged both to make education their number one priority. Someone from Good Schools Pennsylvania was present at almost every campaign stop. We became politically savvy quickly. Both candidates pledged to make education their number one priority; however, again, Rendell was much stronger than Fisher in outlining his commitment to fair funding, accountability, and best practices, and to the elimination of the property tax as the basis for school funding. After Rendell was elected, he observed that Good Schools had carried the education ball to the five-yard line, that it was now up to him to carry it across the goal. We were thrilled, but it was not to be anytime soon.

## Stand for Children[16]

The monthly vigils, continuing as "Stand for Children," following the gubernatorial election, were organized during the important legislative session of 2003. The new governor had been elected; he hired our executive director, Donna Cooper, as secretary of policy and our chief superintendent supporter, Vicki Phillips, as secretary of education; he adopted and introduced legislation embodying much of our policy agenda.

Our three-year campaign was on track. We pledged to put a minimum of one hundred people in Harrisburg on every one of the scheduled fifty-seven legislative days. Over those fifty-seven days, missing three or four days due to weather, Good Schools mobilized more than seventy-five hundred people to participate in a persistent presence to remind legislators about the importance of public education. The effort culminated with more than twenty-five hundred citizens gathering on June 26 at a rally cosponsored by sixty organizations. A petition that had been signed by eighteen thousand people was presented to the governor and legislative leaders that day.

Stand for Children was a time of great hope. Using Good Schools material, the participants met with their legislators every day. They used creative "leave behinds." The York Pennsylvania delegation left York Peppermint Patties tied to notes that read, "Sweeten the possibility of equitable and fair funding for schools in Pennsylvania today." Bethlehem faith leaders left behind a star that read "Be a light for children. Stand for education justice." High school students presented a parody of "The Price Is Right," and other groups of high school students used an oversized blank check as a backdrop to pose the question, "What am I worth to Pennsylvania?" Mon Valley left ketchup bottles with a note reading "Please Don't Make Our Kids Play Catch-Up." It was a remarkable outpouring of passion and advocacy, imagination and fun.

### Outcomes

Though we did achieve positive results, they were not what we had hoped for. As we launched Stand for Children, Good Schools Pennsylvania was prepared to handle the logistical work, make arrangements in Harrisburg, help with buses and lunches, set up microphones, produce people on the legislative days, and even provide core turnout for the culminating event in June. We expressed the hope that as many as twenty-five thousand people would turn out in June—only twenty-five hundred did. It was clear from the beginning that to meet our turn-out goals we would require the open support of the administration, which never materialized. Those on the inside (not just the Rendell administration) rarely vigorously join in such advocacy efforts until it is clear that the tide is turning in favor of the advocacy goals.

During the legislative session, Rendell blew in like a lion, but went out battered. The legislature passed an early budget intended to embarrass him, with no additional funds for education; he boldly vetoed it. After several months of politicking, the constitutional deadline of June

30 for passing the budget came and went. The governor, demonstrating considerable resolve, made it clear that he was not going to sign a budget that did not have a substantial portion of his education package in it. The administration advanced school districts funds when they faced cash flow challenges in an effort to defuse rebellion from school districts themselves. It appeared that the governor was going to "hang tough."

Then there began to be signs of compromise. He agreed to a "back-end referendum" proposal that would require voter approval of increases in taxes beyond a certain point. Pennsylvania had never had that, and states that have used it have had detrimental results. He embraced gambling as a centerpiece to raise revenue despite widespread opposition from the faith community, diluting their support for the overall package while attracting no new fans. In the end, an agreement was struck that in any other year over the previous three decades would have been perceived as a great victory for education, but in this year was a modest improvement compared to the expectations which had been raised and to the real needs of the children.

I don't want to overstate criticism of Governor Rendell. He went considerably further than most politicians would, and certainly further than any Pennsylvania governor in recent memory, to advance the cause of education. The real problem was the leadership of the legislature, particularly president of the Senate David Brightbill from Lebanon County and Majority Leader John Perzel.[17] Many felt that if they had permitted a free vote unrestrained by their leadership, education and children would have won handily. However, the tight control of the Republican members of the legislature precluded such a vote and thus children were defeated.

The decision to be "realistic"[18] once again sentenced those without power to lives of poverty, racism, and despair as too many of the "good guys" seemed to shrug their shoulders and sigh that this is how the game is played and what we achieved was the best that was possible. To Rendell's credit, he has continued to make education a high priority, made incremental progress every year since until 2008, five years later, when there was a real breakthrough with more money and an equitable formula.

### Digging In

And so Good Schools went into a new mode. As Nellie Sepulveda, Donna Cooper's replacement as executive director, wrote at the end of the Stand for Children effort,

> The "campaign" phase of our initiative where we sought to achieve
> the maximum results in the shortest amount of time has come to a
> conclusion, and we must now adopt as our new motto, "We're in it
> 'til we win it." If we are to truly achieve comprehensive reform then
> we need nothing less than a sustainable movement dedicated to en-
> suring each child has access to high quality public education. (Good
> Schools Pennsylvania, 2004, p. 3)

The mistake we made with Good Schools Pennsylvania was in
limiting our scope to a specific campaign, rather than focusing on
building a permanent movement. We believed that an intense three-
year campaign would create the changes we sought. As it turned
out, we were wrong. Once again, persistence emerged as a necessary
quality.

Because Good Schools had treated the challenge as a campaign, we
did not pay enough attention to ongoing fundraising. As we neared the
end of our three years of funding, there was nothing new in the coffers.
I had left the state some six or eight months earlier to become CEO
and president of the International Youth Foundation and was not paying as much attention as the situation warranted.

Lou Anne Caligiuri, who had replaced Nellie as executive director,
and I quickly went to see Candace Bell at the William Penn Foundation, who maintained a strong understanding of and interest in the organizing work. We secured a new grant from William Penn, augmented by another from the Surdna Foundation, thanks to Robert
Sherman's continuing support. Even with these two grants, we had to
cut salaries, lay off several people, and shift others to ten-month positions to continue our work. Good Schools survived, and has reframed
its work for the long term. Annual funding has continued to grow with
particularly strong continuing support from the William Penn foundation and outstanding leadership from Janice Risch.

In 2006, with Good Schools leadership, the General Assembly and
Governor Augenblick agreed to conduct a "costing out study." John
Aguenblick, with whom I had worked in Kentucky, was selected by
the Pennsylvania officials to do the work. While some thought a costing out study a waste of time, they were wrong. The study determined
that the state was underfunding its schools to the tune of about $4 bil-
lion using "adequacy" as the standard.

In 2008, with powerful leadership from Governor Rendell, staff
work by the first Good Schools executive director Donna Cooper, now
the secretary of planning, and Diane Castelbuono, one of my special
assistants in Philadelphia, now commissioner of basic education, and
strong advocacy by Good Schools and the Education Law Center, the

2008–2009 budget contains an unprecedented $275 million down payment toward adequacy and, perhaps most importantly, a new formula for the more equitable distribution of funds (for the first time in nearly two decades).

The 2008 legislation requires that an "adequacy" target be established for each school district and that it be met by 2013. The formula distributes money taking into account the number of students in a district, incidence of poverty, English-language learners, and geographic cost differences among other factors. It links accountability, receipt of funds, and strategies to improve student achievement.

Much work remains in monitoring further implementation of the formula and best practice education strategies, but it is clear Good Schools Pennsylvania has been a success. These major advances would not have happened without the organized public will it played a leadership role in producing.

## A NATIONAL EFFORT

The type of infrastructure building that GSPA engaged in is an essential component of building a movement for children to ensure quality education conditions for all children throughout the fifty states.

There is so much evidence of what we need to do to create those conditions. Foundations have engaged in hundreds, if not thousands of pilot projects that have been successful. There are hundreds of schools and thousands of classrooms in which quality teachers and administrators with the right tools and conditions provide education that produces strong outcomes. There are major program initiatives such as early childhood education that research and decisions by affluent people about opportunities for their own children tell us are effective. We are missing the public will and political resolve to require our leaders to create those conditions.

A movement is required. We also know that movements are possible. We see the power of movement building in the past fifty years in the civil rights movement, the women's movement, the gay rights movement, the peace movement. Over the last twenty-five years, a Christian right, politically conservative movement emerged that was pivotal in electing George Bush twice. Since Howard Dean's candidacy for president in 2004, movement building has changed with much greater reliance on web-based networks. Barack Obama raised such movement building to an artform in the 2008 election cycle.

Quality public education does not have the sophisticated advocacy movement base that other "issue" groups have developed. We will not be able to create the learning conditions necessary for all children to achieve at high levels until we do.

After a couple of false starts in trying to move forward toward such movement building, I took two steps backward and decided some serious design and planning needed to be undertaken. In early 2006, with support from Marshall (Mike) Smith, head of education at the William and Flora Hewlett Foundation, and his outstanding colleague, Kristi Kimball, Hewlett provided the funds to do the necessary design and planning work to build a public voice on the values of fairness, trust, responsibility, and strong caring communities, and powerful enough to insist successfully that every child in America have a quality public education.

Mike served as dean of the Stanford School of Education, as chair of the Pew Forum for School Reform, and as undersecretary and then deputy secretary of the U.S. Department of Education under the visionary Richard Riley. He is now a senior adviser to Secretary of Education Arne Ducan. No one understands better than Mike that we have the knowledge we need to succeed with all children and, simultaneously, that we haven't had the political muscle to get the job done. Hewlett provided three years of planning and design support for what we have come to call Prepare The Future.[19]

The design is built on the premise that we know what works to deliver a quality education to all children, and that the barriers are ones of public will and political resolve. If the barriers to preparing our children for life are the lack of public and political will, the solution is to build that will.

If we are able to raise the funds, Prepare The Future will employ three key organizing strategies.

## Action Tree Organizing

Building Action Trees is web-based organizing. I sometimes refer to it as the Mary Kay or Amway approach to social justice. The Action Trees are designed to grow from existing organizations, such as a diocese or presbytery, community organization, local education fund, large congregation, sorority or fraternity, community foundation, or any other organization enlisting forty people from among its staff, board, active members, and volunteers. Each of the forty will make four commitments: (1) commit to the values and children/education agenda of Prepare The Future, (2) commit to one action at least quarterly, (3) commit to an annual donation of $20 or more to help support the organization, and (4) commit to find five friends, neighbors, or family members who will make the same four commitments.

If the five-friend multiple is extended through three levels and a final level is added in which the commitment is to find one additional friend to make the first three commitments, the result is a network of 11,240 people. Prepare The Future will service and support the Action Trees electronically. As this is written, there are 141 organizations, half of which are faith based, that have pledged good faith efforts to build an Action Tree once we raise the funds to staff the work. Fully successful that would translate into more than 1.5 million people.

## Small Group Advocates

The design envisions the establishment of large numbers of small groups (reprising that strategy used so successfully in Pennsylvania) in at least two states in each of the first five years of operation. This will be the core on-the-ground organizational base in each of the target states.

In addition to advocacy activities like those in Pennsylvania, we will ask each small group to build a mini–Action Tree. Unlike in the larger Action Trees, each small group member will be asked to find only two friends each and extend the invitations to three additional levels. Not only can these mini–Action Trees be activated for the larger issues in a city or state, but they can also be activated at the neighborhood level by the small local groups generating them. They will provide a way for people to address problems at the local level that are of immediate concern. Not only will this allow issues to be addressed in a timely and effective manner, but it will also help maintain organization engagement so participants don't lose interest.

## Student Organizing

The design includes organizing high school and college chapters in each of the ten target states, including work with existing youth-led activist groups. Youth-led organizing is on the rise, and education is an issue these groups frequently address. Among other entry points, we will pursue partnerships with students already engaged in a variety of community service and service learning activities. We will also approach students through faith community youth groups, as many young people who are involved with their churches, mosques, and synagogues seek to make the connection between their faith, fairness, responsibility, and social justice. In addition to the chapters meeting regularly, we will invite college and high school chapters of Prepare The Future to participate in Action Trees and build mini–Action Trees as appropriate. We will emphasize technologies that have become extensions of the way young people communicate such as text messaging, blogging, and audio/video podcasting.

## DESIGN PRINCIPLES OF PREPARE THE FUTURE

Using California, Colorado, and Ohio[20] as our design states and after meeting with hundreds of individuals and organizational leaders in these and other states, Prepare The Future emerges, characterized by several key design principles:

### Values-Driven

Values, not technical policy solutions to education and other children/ family issues, will drive our efforts. We think of the core driving force of movement building as a moral imperative to do what's right for children, not, in the first instance, a commitment to policy positions on adequate funding or accountability. The latter are simply tools to achieve what's right. In southern California, for example, five of the initial Action Tree pledging organizations are the Episcopal Diocese of Los Angeles, Fuller Seminary, the Board of Rabbis, the Islamic Shura Council, and the leader of Hispanic evangelicals. None of the groups made their decisions as policy wonks. While they want to be confident that the policy positions of Prepare The Future are sound, they have committed to the effort based on the Prepare The Future values of fairness, trust, responsibility, and strong caring communities, knowing that policy positions will be supportive of these values.[21]

### Advocacy-Based Governance

Governance will be vested in the hands of those committed to building the grassroots base. At the national level, the design provides for national organizations pledging to build ten or more Action Trees having a representative on the national board. In addition, each of the ten target states will have a representative.

Target state governance will technically be in the hands of the national organization. However, practically, the key strategic and tactical decisions in a target state will be made by the state steering committee, comprised of representatives of the organizations in the respective states who are committed to building the advocacy base through Action Trees and small groups.

Those who produce the people will decide when and where to deploy the people. Prepare The Future is committed to building the capacity of its constituent organizations as much as in building its aggregate power. Each organization building an Action Tree and each small group or high school/college building a mini–Action Tree may activate its own network, using Prepare The Future technology and staff support, for its own issues. Each also has the right through its representation in the governance structure to ask the organization as a whole to act on an issue not originally on the larger agenda.

### Technologically Proficient and Sophisticated

We envision supporting the Action Trees, small groups, their attendant mini–Action Trees, and student organizing electronically, with sophisticated communication systems that are highly interactive. Our technology employs the principles of social networking used so successfully in networks such as Facebook, combining that innovative approach to creating networks with the social justice–focused use identified with Move On and other political/policy online advocacy initiatives. Other social justice and public policy efforts build their database through the use of hot button/front page issues. We do not believe that public education or other children's issues (unfortunately) have the "sizzle" to engage two or three million people based purely on the issues themselves. Thus, we are building the system to rely on people participating because their friends ask them to be involved.

### Grassroots, Not Just Grasstops

In education and other children, family, and human service areas, we have relied frequently on what some refer to as grasstops efforts to secure changes requiring political muscle. Given the evidence, a grasstops approach by itself does not work, in part because most leaders (grasstops) have some stake in the status quo (almost by definition). They often will find it impossible, without being pushed, to make the quality and depth of change that is required. Even those inclined to make major change often need support or grassroots cover to be effective.

### Well Funded

Focus on the Family has an annual budget of more than $100 million. Barack Obama's successful presidential race cost well over $600 million. Lobbying in Washington is a multibillion-dollar enterprise. State and local business advocacy expenditures reach corollary proportions. Chambers of Commerce and citizen antitax groups spend heavily to oppose school finance initiatives. Teacher unions frequently do the same in opposition to meaningful accountability efforts. Radically changing the single largest public domestic enterprise in the United States with broad and deep vested interests is not going to happen solely with a volunteer mom and pop effort.

As this is written we cannot know whether Prepare The Future will be successful. We presently have 141 organizations in the three target states and nationally that have pledged good faith efforts to build Action Trees once we raise the funds for staff to support the effort. Thus, we are optimistic. But the jury is out because we are only beginning to raise the initial $50 million we believe it will take. The financial meltdown will at least delay the effort. Whether Prepare The Future is successful, what is clear is that an unprecedented and powerful voice of ordinary people of the dimensions we seek is absolutely vital to creating the conditions in which every child has the opportunities for success that can only come through quality public education.

## NOTES

1. Judge Smith was involved in more drama in 1995. In early 1994 she had ordered the implementation of a number of programs to help Philadelphia's children, including full-day kindergarten. Her order was one of the reasons I decided to go to Philadelphia. I thought that we might be able to get done what needed to be done if we had a court behind us. Judge Smith focused on the district as the culprit, and ordered us to expand funds for kindergarten and other programs. We supported the programs, but argued that funding them was the state's responsibility, hoping the court would use its leverage to secure these funds from Harrisburg. We feared that if the district budgeted for these changes, taking funding away from other necessary programs, we would lose our leverage with the state. Smith threatened to cite me for contempt. During a highly publicized court appearance, she had several deputies standing by waiting to arrest me (I confess I found it a bit humorous that someone thought more than one deputy might be necessary). Last-minute negotiations between the district's lawyer and the court produced a compromise, and I was spared detention. It was a sad example of the all-too-common circumstances in which people who are all trying to provide quality education for poor children end up fighting with each other rather than directing the energy toward those actually responsible for the children's plight.

2. As I made my pitch, the "conversation" was repeatedly interrupted by the insistence of the mayor's dog Mandy on "playing ball" while we talked. My description of the dire circumstances and huge challenges we faced was

punctuated by this lovable dog constantly shoving a saliva-dripping ball back into my hand so that I could throw it again.

3. In order to avoid technical violation of the law, when we presented the unbalanced budget we would plug the gap with what was, in fact, projected revenue from the state or other sources (we made it up). Then we would get whatever we were given for the year and worked to bring the actual expenditure during the year within that amount. We ended every year with a small surplus, except my last, when we missed by only $300,000 out of a nearly $2 billion budget.

4. The end of that story was that the Pennsylvania Supreme Court several years later declined to reach the merits of the case; they said that the case posed "a political question" and, as a consequence, was within the exclusive purview of the legislature. Such an outcome had been predicted earlier by several people when a Republican candidate for the Supreme Court beat the Democrat the previous year (a good example why so many oppose elected judges).

5. Germaine was an amazing partner. She agreed to become chief counsel, one of my earliest senior appointments. Later she took Jeannette Brewer's place as the number two person in the district. From that perch, she was my right hand (and sometimes my left) in all matters. She helped direct legal strategy; she oversaw planning; in many ways, she was the chief operating officer in the district. When I would become frustrated and wrote cathartic letters to the mayor and others, she and my dear friend and special assistant Terry Dellmuth, would explain to me why I was not allowed to send them.

6. *Powell v. Ridge*, opinion of the three-judge panel of the Third Circuit Court of Appeals, 189 F.3rd 387, handed down on August 25, 1999.

7. The reader will find full descriptions of proposed tactics at www.childrenachieving.com.

8. After I sent the memo, there were no subsequent meetings on the subject and I never met with the mayor again one-on-one even though I sought meetings with him repeatedly. He continued to support a one-vote majority on my board; he also eventually, after months of delay, supported the extension of my contract by two years (though not more), but it became clear that any conversation about serious activism was over.

9. The text of the letter can be found at www.childrenachieving.com.

10. I had another reason as well for being optimistic about Street. Street, following Rendell's consistent support, had declared that he supported my continuing in office for at least two more years. Republican candidate Sam Katz had announced that he would seek my departure should he be elected. Katz's position surprised me a bit. I had known him since he was an intern in the secretary of education's office when I had served as deputy secretary. He had been a likeable fellow, seemed to support a progressive agenda, and indeed had been a Democrat until he determined that he could never go anywhere politically as a Democrat and therefore switched parties. Consistent with such opportunistic instincts, Sam asked that we meet. I always had mixed feelings about the meeting. I admired him for being willing to tell me to my face that he would not support me. On the other hand, his reason was that, despite his view that I was doing a pretty good job, I was not liked by members of his

party, and thus he had to take the position to remove me—another burst of courage from a Philadelphia politician. Katz took another shot at the mayoralty four years later, and lost again.

11. The details of the proposal can be found on www.childrenachieving.com.

12. When Bob Edgar became general secretary of the National Council of Churches, he became a strong supporter of Good Schools Pennsylvania. On one occasion, he even convened his Executive Board meeting in Harrisburg. These leaders of Protestantism, in full regalia, marched through the streets of Harrisburg to the steps of the capitol and engaged in a prayer vigil on behalf of the children of Pennsylvania. He is now president, Common Cause, and continues his vigorous support of public education, recognizing the pivotal role of education in the maintenance of democracy.

13. Annenberg, with Gail Levin's leadership, and the William Penn Foundation, with Janet Haas leading the way, gave more than $1.3 million each. Other contributors were the Clark foundation, the Fels Fund, Ford, Heinz, Mott, the Pittsburgh Foundation, Schott, and Surdna.

14. In the early days of planning we tried to think of a name that had more market appeal than Groups of Ten; we never did and eventually the name just stuck.

15. "In a certain town there was a judge who neither feared God nor cared about men. And there was a widow in that town who kept coming to him with the plea, 'Grant me justice against my adversary.' For some time he refused. But finally he said to himself, 'Even though I don't fear God or care about men, yet because this widow keeps bothering me, I will see that she gets justice, so that she won't eventually wear me out with her coming!'" Luke 18:1–5.

16. We borrowed the phrase "Stand for Children" from the Children's Defense Fund.

17. David Brightbill was defeated in the primary in his bid for reelection in 2006. John Perzel, while still in office, is now in the minority as a result of the House becoming Democratic by one vote in the general election of 2006.

18. I have earlier juxtaposed those who cite realism as the reason for inequitable funding with those of us who think it is equally unrealistic to think we are actually going to succeed with all children including those fighting the burdens of poverty, race, language, and disability—both positions are supported by the facts. However, I would add that in Pennsylvania in nearly any year in the last three decades it would have taken a shift in the votes of fewer than a dozen legislators to totally turn the financial equation on its head. That is quite doable and has been largely done in places like Kentucky. My point is that adequate funds, equitably distributed, can be provided by a handful of people making more just decisions. It is not a complex goal. It is a matter of choice in the legislature, by the governor, and by the citizenry who puts the elected officials into office.

19. A description of the design and planning process for Prepare The Future can be found at www.childrenachieving.com. Current information and joining information about Prepare The Future can be found at www.preparethe future.org.

20. Those who have pledged Action Trees in Colorado and Ohio met to determine the specific education agenda they wanted to pursue in their respective states if and when Prepare The Future becomes a reality. Their conclusions are quite far-reaching. Interested readers will find their proposals at www.childrenachieving.com.

21. Readers interested in understanding the greater organizing effectiveness of values-based organizing can find more on the subject at www.children achieving.com.

# 16

# Walk the Walk: Choosing Excellence and Equity in Public Education

Most things worth doing had been declared impossible before they were done.

Louis Brandeis

We must be the change we wish to see.

Mahatma Gandhi

As I began to write this book, I hoped that the reader would finish reading it with four clear convictions:

- That all children can and must achieve high standards resulting in their being equipped for success in postsecondary education, work, and as a citizen.
- That the knowledge exists to make the success of every child a reality.
- That when we leave children behind it is the result of choices made in the past and choices we continue to make every day.
- That each and all of us can and must build the public will to change these collective choices at the local, state, and national levels.

Toward that end, the early chapters focused on high expectations. That was followed by a description of the key action elements of a successful education system. Finally, I highlighted the ways in which each of us is complicit in the creation of the educational, social, and moral conditions that result in low achievement by so many of our children, and the ways in which each and all of us can choose to create solutions.

*Choosing Excellence in Public Schools* is based on research and experience but it is also value-laden and personal. Thus, it is appropriate that I end with personal reflections.

## REFLECTIONS

The reflections below are framed by three questions: whether, if I had it to do over again, I would choose to become superintendent in Philadelphia; what I would do differently; and what I am most proud of.

### Would I Do It Again?

The answer is an emphatic yes. Despite the stresses, the frustrations, the deep disappointments, the personal attacks, and the wrenching decision to leave, I will be forever grateful for having had that opportunity. I repeatedly saw many of my strongest beliefs and hopes come to life. Every student, teacher, parent, principal, and administrator who came to exemplify high expectations gave me renewed energy and deep pleasure, day after day. And, despite what many saw as the stubbornness of my vision, I found myself steadily learning from others the nuances of making the vision a reality.

Two very special people illustrate the point. The first is Jeanette Brewer, the educator's educator who had more than thirty years' dedicated service in the district as a teacher, principal, and regional superintendent. When I became superintendent, as a non-Philadelphian and nontraditional educator, I needed a deputy who was everything I was not. Many people extolled Jeanette's intelligence and deep knowledge of instruction. I asked her to come out of retirement to help for a year. Driven by her lifelong commitment to children and the potential of the *Children Achieving* agenda, Jeanette agreed. Then she stayed two years, making incalculably significant contributions to the design and initial implementation of the agenda. She did much to establish the credibility of our administration. She was also tough, smart, resilient, and a straight shooter.

When Jeanette left, I asked Germaine Ingram, who had been our chief counsel, to assume her responsibilities. I had known Germaine when we were in law school together from 1968 to 1971. When I interviewed her for the chief counsel position,[1] she asked me who my heroes were, trying to get at the values I was bringing to the job. I told her two were Father Paul Washington, the extraordinary rector of the

Church of the Advocate, whom I knew she knew, and Bill Webber, my mentor and senior thesis advisor in seminary, who had founded the East Harlem Protestant Parish where Becky and I had worked for two years. I started to tell her about him.

She interrupted to say, "Oh I know Bill; I have Thanksgiving dinner with him every year and I know why you would hold him up as a life-shaping influence in your life." I think we both knew in the question and the answer that we were values-driven soul mates and so it proved to be. For six years, Germaine framed both our legal work, including our school-funding lawsuits, as chief counsel, and her management of the district as chief of staff, around her commitment to the proposition that all children can learn to high levels.

The skills, energy, courage, resilience, and sense of humor of both these colleagues and friends were crucial to the successes of *Children Achieving*. They are also prototypes for so many other wonderful staff in Philadelphia.

## What Would I Do Differently?

Across the chapters of this book, I have mentioned examples of things I would do differently. Some of these examples were products of history beyond our control; some were miscalculations or mistakes; still others reflect instances where we tried a strategy but failed, or at least fell far short of the goal. Some that stand out are highlighted below.

### Miscalculations

Along with much of the nation, I underestimated in the spring and summer of 1994 the changes in the political climate that would result from the November election. When I arrived in Philadelphia, the Democrat Party controlled the White House and both houses of Congress, and the Pennsylvania governorship and both houses of the Pennsylvania legislature. When we woke up on November 8, all of that had changed except the White House. Pennsylvania had elected a Republican governor and the Republicans controlled both the Pennsylvania legislature and the U.S. Congress. Many Republicans are firm supporters of education, and of poor and minority children; nevertheless, the years following proved that the road to fairer opportunities to learn was suddenly much steeper after that election.

I also miscalculated how much I could count on elected officials to lead organizing or political efforts designed to generate the pressure for change. Many big city superintendents would be properly jealous of the level of support I did receive from Mayor Rendell, and from John Street at the beginning of his term. Ironically, it was partly this support that led me to hope for more from each of them. These are men who have been creative and courageous in many venues, but even they did not feel they could take the risks that were necessary to succeed in our mission. As governor, Ed Rendell has grown enormously in understanding the significance of education and how important expending political capital on its improvement is.

I overestimated the support that would be provided by the business community. The business leadership stated strong support in the early days of our administration, happy to hear about high standards and hard-edged accountability. However, with the exception of a few exceptional individuals, they bailed out as they began to realize that we were serious about opportunity to learn standards. Rather than putting their muscle behind getting the resources we needed to help all students learn and prepare the kind of workforce they were demanding of us, they chose to act based on their short-term interests, avoiding any commitment to increased resources for the district that might have translated into more taxes. Thus, they cast their lot with Ridge's voucher approach, mistakingly persuading themselves that this would be a cost-free way to achieve better education.

Despite many warnings, I underestimated the resistance that would come from the union leadership. Having spent much of my career helping various parties bridge differences and find win-win solutions or at least workable compromises, I believed that despite all I had heard about the Philadelphia Federation of Teachers, we would be able to find ways to work together. We tried many approaches—to no avail. Other than simply giving up central features of the reform agenda, such as all parties accepting responsibility for the product of our work (accountability), or the idea of the best teachers teaching the neediest students (seniority) I cannot imagine a strategy that would have worked with that group of union "leaders."

I underestimated the difficulty of changing the culture of the parts of the administration that were not directly related to instruction. Finance, technology, personnel, building, and grounds were accustomed to functioning as fairly independent bureaucracies, rather than as seeing themselves in service of the instructional responsibility of the district. Embedded in this was the reality that in many ways these operations were a white boys' network, often resistant to pressures from instructional staff who were more likely to be female and/or people of color. While I believe conscious racism and sexism were seldom present, both were clearly operating at an unconscious, institutional level.

This was true even during the tenure of Clay Armbrister as managing director. Clay was easily one of the smartest, most talented members of my administration, African American, and as committed to children, instruction, and institutional change as one could wish. It didn't make much difference. One big reason was that personnel in these offices often had independent relationships with board members, which undermined our efforts at efficient implementation and transparency. We made progress on all of these issues during our administration, but there was still a long way to go.

## Mistakes

Many will argue that my biggest mistake was confronting political leaders with their failure to fulfill their responsibility to the children of Philadelphia. However, that is not something I would change if I had it to do over. The politic, "realistic" strategies had been tried for years before I came, and have been tried again since my departure—and have failed miserably. Behaving as if we are asking favors when we advocate for adequate and equitable public education is neither appropriate nor effective. My mistake was in not being more aggressive. I should have taken more direct ownership of grassroots organizing. Even without mayoralty leadership, I should have undertaken activist campaigns of the kind I recommended to them. I should have provided more leadership in mobilizing the faith community as we did in Good Schools Pennsylvania and as we hope to do on a national basis.

While I reject the charge that my being "impolitic" was a mistake, there are many mistakes that I do own. One of my biggest was the failure to secure the widespread support and confidence of the teachers. I mistakenly decided to work toward that goal through the union, as representatives of the teachers. Looking back, I should have worked directly with teachers on issues of instruction and educational policy, neither of which were directly contract-related.

I should have been as strategic in approaching teachers as we were in other areas. From day one I should have developed a districtwide body of teacher instructional leaders with whom I consulted regularly. I should have asked for and implemented five or ten genuinely meaningful things that teachers advised me would make my support and respect for teachers and their work clear. I should have considered a council of teachers in every cluster whose advice I sought and used routinely. I should have started every day in a classroom chosen by the teacher advisors to illustrate things they wanted me to see. This could have been done while still maintaining a commitment to changes that had to be made in the accountability and seniority systems—indeed, one of the things we should have done with teacher advisors was to seek their advice about these most controversial and difficult issues.

Discussing such hard issues would not have been easy. None of this would have been easy in the teachers union political atmosphere. No doubt the union leadership would have filed an unfair labor practice, charging me with "direct dealing" (meaning, going directly to the membership on contractual issues, which is against collective bargaining law in Pennsylvania). However, if the relationship with teachers had been long-term and they had seen similar leadership exemplified by other administrative personnel and they had seen that at least some of their more meaningful recommendations were being implemented, it might have made a difference. If it had failed, so be it, but it was a serious mistake not to have tried for an extended period of time with careful attention to the detail of how we did it.

There were other mistakes. I was and am a strong believer in establishing goals, measures, accountability, and support systems, and then maximizing the flexibility for schools to design their own instructional programs. However, I came to realize that many schools lacked the capacity to make high-quality instructional decisions without more support than we were able to give. The lack of capacity could have many causes: lack of expertise on the part of the principal and other key staff, inability to form an effective school team, or overwhelming issues of staff turnover and school security. It was also most likely to be a problem with schools teaching the neediest students, though there were notable exceptions to this generalization.

We made various attempts to address the lack of capacity, including giving rating authority to the cluster leaders, providing everincreasing specificity in curriculum guides, and giving very specific mandates to the schools making the least progress. However, some of these actions would have been more helpful if we had begun them sooner and more robustly.

I should also have been more sensitive, earlier, to the need for both staff and the public to see more explicit attention to the issue of school safety. I do believe that we were doing enough in this arena. But we were ineffective in communicating what we were doing, starting from our failure to list safety and security as part of the ten-point agenda.

Like any other leader, I also made some mistakes in staffing decisions. I suppose this is inevitable, but was painful for me and for the organization. I appointed people I truly believed would be excellent in their positions. I never had to cave to political pressure in any major staff selection. However, sometimes I was wrong, despite high recommendations from people I respect, national searches, thorough reference checks, interviews with multiple staff members, and my own instincts. Fortunately, I recognized eventually, after repeated efforts at support, that some appointments were not working, and saw to it that the people moved on. But this was not without heartache and time lost in fulfilling the agenda (and on two or three occasions these decisions to remove people were delayed by political interference, particularly from board members).

### Efforts That Failed

A primary area in which our efforts failed was negotiating contracts that moved the instructional program forward to the degree I had hoped. I do not believe that all the responsibility for this falls on our shoulders; there were a number of undermining factors beyond our control, most notably political interference in the final hours before possible strikes. Perhaps I should have stared down the politicians and, if they persisted, taken a strike. Nor is it to say that we made no substantial progress. However, there was so much more that remained to be done.

There were other areas where we made progress but we failed to change fundamental structures or approaches to the way things were done. In technology, we wired every school and reduced the computer-to-student ratio from thirty-to-one to ten-to-one. But we failed to move many of the computers out of labs into routine and creative uses instructionally in individual classrooms. They remained an add-on, not an integral part of instruction.

We failed to increase the availability of three- and four-year-old pre-kindergarten; mental health services expanded relatively little; after-school programs were still more the exception than the rule. Despite a number of notable and successful efforts to leverage more and better nonacademic services for children and youth through coordinating and integrating services, in the end, we largely rendered service in the same old way and tended to argue that failure rested in an agency other than our own. We failed to establish a viable system of school-based decision-making.

The largest failure, of course, was the failure to secure adequate funding for our children. We so much wanted to have the opportunity to demonstrate not only how much more children can learn with better stewardship of current resources, but also that they can achieve at high standards given sustained, fair opportunities to learn. Even though this struggle remains far from over, I choose to see the many efforts we made as steps toward eventually reaching this goal.

Perhaps our efforts to communicate across the city, region, and state that we took standards and accountability seriously; that our district had substantially fewer dollars per pupil than those around us; that the Pennsylvania court system and the legislature went out of their way to create rationales for continuing the injustices of the school funding system; that inequitable funding is a civil rights issue—perhaps all of these laid the groundwork for the efforts, and successes of Good Schools Pennsylvania and victories achieved by Governor Rendell. I know the groundwork for designing a national grassroots advocacy was born in Philadelphia and in Pennsylvania. We'll have to wait and see how that unfolds.

I am struck as I reflect on our failures with the ironic connection of a phrase that I used early in my tenure that some said was connected to our failure to win the "hearts and minds" of teachers. To emphasize that outcomes are what counts, I said that "Trying hard isn't good enough. That may get you points in the next life, but in this one what matters is whether the students can actually read, write, and do arithmetic." I still believe that. I regret that some teachers and school administrators felt that my saying it meant I did not understand how hard they worked or how much they cared. To fail doesn't make one a bad person. To be a good person, one does not have to succeed. But one cannot make something a success by calling it that.

We tried excruciatingly hard to secure fair opportunities to learn for our kids, to deliver good mental health services, to change the contract so that it contributed to education improvement rather than distracting from it and on and on. But, in the end, trying hard simply was not good enough. We failed in these critical areas.

### What Am I Most Proud Of?

The first answer is easy and obvious: the achievement increases from 1996 to 2000 and the improvement in on-time graduation, across grades and subjects, were a remarkable testimony to what children, and schools, are capable of, and to the strategies we were implementing.

I am also very proud of the way these achievement gains have been sustained and built on in subsequent years. The class which made the largest gains while I was superintendent—the first cohort of students to experience full-day kindergarten, and to also benefit from increased professional development, staff accountability, reduced student-to-teacher ratios, and other supports throughout their elementary experience—has continued to lead the district's gains as they moved through middle school and high school. The initiatives that brought these gains have made a real difference in the life chances of these students and the classes that have followed them.

A major accomplishment was the system of standards, assessments, and accountability that we developed. They continue to provide a model for what districts, states, and the federal government should be doing to improve education and achievement for all students.

I am especially proud of our early and explicit pairing of opportunity to learn standards with achievement standards. The social contract we articulated was essential then; it is even more vital now, as NCLB raises stakes across the nation but is not meeting opportunity to learn standards, providing the resources to make accountability effective and constructive rather than punitive and destructive.

Our rapid implementation of full-day kindergarten, without additional resources, was a major accomplishment. Related to this is our creative use of funding sources in subsequent years to permit us to begin reducing student-to-teacher ratios in the early grades.

I am also proud of the many ways in which we increased time for learning. Lengthening the school year and the school day are obvious examples, as are summer school and after-school programs; we put all of these in place. In addition, there are many less obvious and more complex ways to make time productive. We improved effective learning time in high schools through our support of block rostering, in which students spend longer periods in each class; we piloted year-round schooling; we insisted on more teachers of English, math, science, and social studies in our high schools, some of which had more phys-ed teachers than math and science combined. Increasing learning time is not just a matter of quantity; it is also a matter of making sure the time available is focused on what is most important.

We pushed public education to the front of the agenda in Philadelphia and in Pennsylvania. We made major contributions in defining the agenda to include funding but going far beyond funding. During our six years, public education was the story.

Finally, I consider it a major accomplishment that *Children Achieving* developed and nurtured a large cohort of educators—and significant numbers of community members and even students—whose dreams are larger, sense of mission is stronger, and understanding of what it takes to have all children learn to high standards is clearer than before 1994. Some have retired since I left, but most are still fully engaged in seeking ways to help all children achieve, both in Philadelphia and beyond. I am proud of this legacy, and grateful to each of them.

## WALKING THE WALK

Educators are more aware than ever of what schools need to do to enable all students to reach high standards. I hope this book will serve as an important resource to them, as well as to the school boards and other institutions with which they interact. However, educators alone cannot win the struggle for excellence and equity. If we are really to leave no child behind, excellent and equitable education must become part of a shared value system, and a priority that leads people to speak out, give of their time, give of their resources, and sometimes take risks.

Each of us in leadership positions in urban education has encountered the well-meaning elected official or candidate or business executive or faith leader who peppers us with questions and then closes the conversation by saying, "It's so important—but it's just unsolvable." This challenge of educating all children to high standards is complex and difficult, but it is certainly no more unsolvable than the problem of slavery, or of women's suffrage, or of abolishing Jim Crow laws. It is, in fact, conceptually, historically, and ethically linked to all of those struggles. However, like them, it is deeply related to expectations, belief systems, resource distribution, and power relationships; like them, it will only be won through a widespread social movement that eventually forces political change.

The objective of public schools in America is a quality education for every child; thus, there is no alternative to creating the conditions in which all of the components are in place. They must move into place in reasonable enough proximity to each other that the synergy required between and among them takes place with the power to effect the results intended from each component in combination with each other one.

Each of us as individuals—teachers, superintendents, parents, elected officials, businesspersons, philanthropists, faith leaders, people who sit in the pews, students—decide what we believe and how we are going to act (or not) on our beliefs. But in the end it is how we act in concert with one another—as teacher unions, as school boards, as legislatures, as advocacy organizations, as institutions of faith, as foundations, as brokers of power—it is the choices we make that will determine the future of the democracy, the vitality of the economy, and the happiness of the grandchildren of all who are alive today. These grandchildren will live in a nation that is majority minority; a nation where a plurality of the population speak a language other than English at home; a nation comprised of a large plurality if not a majority of people who are no more than an ill-educated generation or two removed from poverty.

We know what to do and how to do it. The choices are ours. The consequences of the choices are the legacy we leave to our grandchildren.

## NOTE

1. A further indication of Germaine's commitment to our agenda is that she later told me that when I interviewed her, and she agreed to come to the district, she did not know what role I wanted her to play—just that she wanted to be part of the effort.

# References

*Abbott v. Burke*, 149 N.J. 145, 693 A.2d 417 (1997).

Abecediarian Educational Child Care Program. (2002, June 22). Chicago parent child center, Chicago longitudinal study, Issue 2. Retrieved November 2008, from www.fpg.unc.edu/~abc/.

Adelman, L. (2003). A long history of racial preferences—For whites. In *Race—The power of an illusion: Background readings.* www.pbs.org/race/000 _About/002_04-background-03-02.htm.

Baird, C., Pavelsky, N., Savage, B., & Valburg, K. (n.d.). Identifying and removing barriers to student achievement—Executive Summary. Retrieved February 2009 from faculty.fullerton.edu/lorozco/stlec-barriers.html.

BBC. (2001, July 2). Education promises a better life. Retrieved November 2008 from news.bbc.co.uk/2/hi/uk_news/education/1418645.stm.

Beez, W. V. (1968). Influences of biased sociological reports on teacher behavior and pupil performance. In *Proceedings of the 76th annual convention of the American Psychological Association*, vol. 3 (605–6). Washington, DC: American Psychological Association.

Bentley, T., Kaye, A., MacLeod, P., O'Leary, D., & Parker, S. (2004, May). A fair go: Public value and diversity in education. A paper prepared for the Education Foundation symposium *The Case for Change in Australian Schooling Arrangements: A Way Forward*, June 2004. www.educationfoundation.org .au/Downloads/Research/Education_Foundation_Demos.pdf.

Bikson, T. K. (1974). *Minority speech as objectively measured and subjectively evaluated.* Bethesda, MD: ERIC Document Reproduction Service No. ED 131 135.

Bolman, L. G., & Deal, Terrence E. (1995). *Leading with soul.* San Francisco: Jossey-Bass.

Bond, L. (1996). Ensuring fairness in the setting of performance standards. In William M. Sullivan, Anne Colby, Judith Welch Wegner, Lloyd Bond, & Lee S. Shulman (Ed.), *Proceedings, Joint conference on standard-setting for large-scale assessments*, vol. 2. Washington, DC: National Center for

Education Statistics. www.carnegiefoundation.org/about/sub.asp?key=10& subkey=248.

Bond, L., Moss, P., & Carr, P. (1996). Fairness in Large Scale Performance Assessment. In Gary Phillips (Ed.), *Technical issues in large-scale performance assessment*. Washington, DC: National Center for Education Statistics, NCES 96-802, U.S. Department of Education, Office of Educational Research and Improvement.

Boyer, E. (1991). *Ready to learn: A mandate for the nation*. Princeton, NJ: The Carnegie Foundation for the Advancement of Teaching.

Bureau of Labor Statistics. (2008). *Education pays*. Retrieved November 2008 from www.bls.gov/emp/emptab7.htm.

Caldwell, B. J. (1996). Principles and practices in resource allocation to schools under conditions of radical decentralization. In William J. Fowler (Ed.), *Developments in school finance*. Washington, DC: National Center for Education Statistics.

Caruthers, L. (1994). Power teaching: Principles of empowerment (Rev. ed.). Kansas City, MO: Mid-continent Regional Educational Laboratory. Retrieved February 2009 from www.mcrel.org/PDF/Noteworthy/Learners _Learning_Schoolig/loycec.asp.

*CFE v. State of New York*. (2001, January 10). Retrieved November 2008 from www.cfequity.org/decision.html.

*Children Achieving Action Design*. (1995, February 6). School District of Philadelphia. Available at www.childrenachieving.com.

Children's Defense Fund. (2001). The state of America's children. Retrieved February 2009 from www.amazon.com/State-Americans-Children-Yearbook -2001/dp/0807042153.

Constitution of the Commonwealth of Pennsylvania, Article III, Section 14. Pennsylvania Historical and Museum Commission. Archives. Retrieved November 2008 from www.portal.state.pa.us/portal/server.pt?open=512 &objID=2887&&level=1&menuLevel=Level_1&parentCommID=0&mode= 2&in_hi_userid=2&cached=true.

Cotton, K. (1989, November). *Expectations and student outcomes*. Portland, OR: Northwest Regional Education Laboratory.

*Current population survey and the national committee on pay equity*. (1967). Retrieved November 2008 from www.infoplease.com/ipa/A0882775.html.

Daniels, R. (2002). *Coming to America: A history of immigration and ethnicity in American life* (Second ed.). New York: Harper Collins.

Delgado, M., et al. (1999). *Principles, guidelines and procedures for developing fair assessment systems*. Pennsylvania Department of Education.

Dinkes, R., Cataldi, E. F., Kena, G., & Baum, K. (2006). *Indicators of school crime and safety, 2006*. Washington, DC: U.S. Department of Education.

Dolan, R. P., & Hall, T. E. (2001). Universal design for learning: Implications for large-scale assessment. *IDA Perspectives, 27*(4), 22–25.

Doskoch, P. (2005, November/December). The winning edge. *Psychology Today*. Retrieved February 2009 from www.psychologytoday.com/articles/index .php?term=pto-20051017-000003.xml&print=1.

Duckworth, A. L., Peterson, C., Matthews, M. D., & Kelly, D. R. (2007). Grit: Perseverance and passion for long-term goals. *Journal of Personality and Social Psychology, 92*(6), 1087–1101.

Edmonds, R. (1979a, March/April). Some schools work . . . and more can. *Social Policy.*

Edmonds, R. (1979b, October) Effective schools for the urban poor. *Educational Leadership, 37*, 15–29.

Education Commission of the States. (2002, May). *A guide to standards-based assessment.* No Child Left Behind Issue Brief. Available at www.ecs.org/html/Document.asp?chouseid=3550.

Education Commission of the States Note. (2004). *Full day kindergarten: An exploratory study of finance and access in the United States.* ECS study.

Education Trust. (2006) *Funding gaps.* Retrieved November 2008 from www2.edtrust.org/NR/rdonlyres/CDEF9403-5A75-437E-93FF-EBF1174181FB/0/FundingGap2006.pdf.

Education Trust. (2002–2003, Winter). *Education watch, key education facts and figures: Achievement, attainment and opportunity from elementary school through college.* www2.edtrust.org/edtrust/summaries2003/PA_statesum.qxd.pdf.

*Education Week.* (2003). "If I can't learn from you . . . ": Ensuring a highly qualified teacher for every classroom. *Education Week, 22*(17).

*Education Week.* (2005, January 6). Small change targeting money toward student performance.

Elmore, R. F. (2002). *Bridging the gap between standards and achievement: The imperative for professional development in education.* Washington, DC: Albert Shanker Institute.

Feagin, J. R. (1996). Reflections on education and race: Examining the intersections. In *Select addresses from the Public Education Network 1996 Annual Conference.* A PEN Occasional Paper. www.publiceducation.org/pdf/Publications/Public_Engagement/CAW_report.pdf.

Ferguson, R. F. (1998). Teachers' perceptions and expectations and the black-white test score gap. In C. Jencks & M. Phillips (Eds.), *The black-white test score gap* (273–317). Washington, DC: Brookings Institution Press.

Flynn, J. (1980). *Race, IQ and Jensen.* London: Routledge.

Good, T. L. (1981). Teacher expectations and student perceptions: A decade of research. *Educational Leadership, 38*(5), 415–22.

Good Schools Pennsylvania. (2004, January). *Stand for Children 2003.*

Gould, S. J. (1981). *The mismeasure of man.* New York: Norton.

Grissmer, D., Flanagan, A., & Williamson, S. (1998). Why did the black-white score gap narrow in the 1970s and 1980s? In C. Jencks and M. Phillips (Eds.), *The black-white test score gap* (188–227). Washington, DC: Brookings Institution Press.

Haycock, K. (1998). Good teaching matters: How well-qualified teachers can close the gap. *Thinking K-16, 3*(2).

Haycock, K. (2008, September 29). Raising achievement and closing gaps: Lessons from schools on the performance frontier. Tampa: Florida Department of

Education. Available at Education Trust, Inc., www2.edtrust.org/EdTrust/ Product+Catalog/presentations-archive-Sep08.htm.

Heifetz, R. (1994). *Leadership without easy answers*. Cambridge, MA: Belknap Press of Harvard University Press.

Herrnstein, R., & Murray, C. (1994). *The bell curve: Intelligence and class structure in American life*. New York: Free Press.

*High Scope/Perry Preschool Project*. Retrieved November 2008 from www .highscope.org.

Hochschild, J. L. (2005, Winter). Looking ahead: Racial trends in the United States. *Daedalus, 134,* 74–79.

Hoff, D. J. (2005, January 6). The bottom line, no small change targeting money toward student performance. *Education Week*, 32ff.

Hornbeck, D. (1990, February 15). Memo from David W. Hornbeck to Chairmen Karem and Richards, members of the Curriculum Committee, recommendations related to curriculum adopted February 15, 1990.

*Hornbeck v. Somerset County Board of Education*, 458 A.2nd 758.

Howard, J. The Efficacy Institute. Retrieved November 2008 from www .efficacy.org/.

Howe, M. J. A. (1997). *IQ in question: The truth about intelligence*. Thousand Oaks, CA: Sage Publications.

Infoplease. *Wage gap, by gender and race*. Retrieved November 2008 from www.infoplease.com/ipa/A0882775.html.

Jacobson, M. F. (1998). *Whiteness of a different color: European immigrants and the alchemy of race*. Cambridge, MA: Harvard University Press.

Kennedy, J. F. (1960, October 29). *Excerpts from a speech delivered at Valley Forge Country Club, Valley Forge, PA*. Retrieved November 2008 from www .presidency.ucsb.edu/ws/index.php?pid=74292 11/11.

Kent, M., Pollard, K. M., Haaga, J., & Mather, M. (2001, June). *First glimpses from the 2000 U.S. census. Population Bulletin, 56*(2). Washington, DC: Population Reference Bureau.

Kopp, W. (2000, June 21). Ten years of Teach for America: What we have learned. *Education Week*.

Laczko-Kerr, I., & Berliner, D. C. (2002, September 6). The effectiveness of "Teach for America" and other under-certified teachers on student academic achievement: A case of harmful public policy. *Education Policy Analysis Archives, 10*(37).

Leacock, E. (1969). *Teaching and learning in city schools*. New York: Basic Books.

Learning First Alliance. (2001, November). *Every child learning: Safe and supportive schools*.

Leithwood, K. A., & Riehl, C. (2003, January). What we know about successful school leadership, Division A of the American Educational Research Association, January 2003, p. 2. Retrieved February 2009 from www.ecs.org/ html/Document.asp?chouseid=4236.

Lichtenberg, F. R., & Lleras-Muney, A. (2002). *The effect of education on medical technology adoption: Are the more educated more likely to use new drugs?* Cambridge, MA: National Bureau of Economic Research.

Lleras-Muney, A. (2005). The relationship between education and adult mortality in the United States. *Review of Economic Studies, 72*(1), 189–222.

Lui, M. (2004, September 16). *Doubly divided: The racial wealth gap.* The Racial Wealth Divide Project. Retrieved November 2008 from www.racial wealthdivide.org/archives/byrwdstaff.html.

Marshall, R., & Tucker, M. (1992). *Thinking for a living.* New York: Basic Books.

Martinez, M. ( 2000). *The cultivation of intelligence.* Mahwak, NJ, and London: Erlbaum.

Mcbeath, A. B. (2001, May). Decentralized dollars and decisions. *School Administrator, 58.*

McIntosh, P. (1990). White privilege: Unpacking the invisible knapsack. Reprinted from *Independent School Magazine,* Winter 1990, National Association of Independent Schools, Washington, DC. Retrieved November 2008 from mmcisaac.faculty.asu.edu/emc598ge/Unpacking.html.

Menendez, R., & Musca, T. (1988) *Stand and Deliver.* Warner Bros. Pictures.

Merrow Report. (2000a). *School crusade: A tale of urban school reform.* Learning Matters PBS. www.pbs.org/merrow/archives/tv3.html.

Merrow Report. (2000b). *Toughest job in America.* Learning Matters PBS. Retrieved November 2008 from www.pbs.org/merrow/tv/tough/index.html.

Mezzacappa, Dale. (1996, September 1). Hornbeck chalks up a small victory. *Philadelphia Inquirer.*

Miller, C., McLaughlin, J., Haddon, J., & Chansky, N. (1969). Socioeconomic class and teacher bias. *Psychological Reports, 23.*

Morris, S. (2000). *America's work force after the baby boomers: The surprising role that immigration will play.* CED in Brief, A Policy Series from a Business Perspective.

National Association for the Education of Young Children. *Accreditation of programs for young children.* Retrieved November 2008 from www.naeyc .org/accreditation/.

National Center on Education and the Economy (U.S.). (2007). *Tough choices or tough times: The report of the New Commission on the Skills of the American Workforce.* San Francisco: Wiley and Sons.

National Center on Educational Outcomes. (1993, August). *Educational outcomes and indicators for early childhood (age 3).* The College of Education, University of Minnesota.

National Commission on Teaching and America's Future. (2003). *No dream denied: A pledge to America's children.* www.utofp.org/FormsandDocuments/ NoDreamDenied.pdf.

National Commission on Teaching and America's Future. (2003, January). *Summary report.*

National Democratic Leadership Council. (1999, September 13). *Rules of the road: Governing principles for the new economy; New economy task force report.* Progressive Policy Institute. Retrieved February 2009 from www.ppi online.org/ppi_ci.cfm?knlgAreaID=107&subsecID=123&contentID=1268.

Native Americans Library of Congress Website. *American memories.* Retrieved November 2008 from rs6.loc.gov/learn/features/immig/native _american.html.

NCREL. (1993). *Charter schools: A new breed of public schools.* NCREL Policy Briefs, Report 2. www.ncrel.org/sdrs/areas/issues/envrnmnt/go/93-2locl.htm.

Nisbett, R. (2009). *Intelligence and how to get it: Why schools and culture count.* New York: W. W. Norton & Co.

Oakes, J. (1992). Can tracking research inform practice? Technical, normative and political considerations. *Educational Researcher, 21*(4), 12–21.

Olsen, Lynn. (2005, January 6). Financial evolution. *Education Week.* www .edweek.org.

Parks, G. (2000, October). The High Scope/Perry Preschool Project. *Juvenile Justice Bulletin.* Office of Juvenile Justice and Delinquency Prevention. Retrieved February 2009 from www.ncjrs.gov/pdffiles1/ojjdp/181725.pdf.

Pelligrino, J. (2001, April). *Rethinking and redesigning educational assessment.* Education Commission of the States. www.ecs.org/clearinghouse/ 24/88/2488.htm.

Pennington, H. (2007, January). *The Massachusetts expanding learning time to support student success initiative.* Center for American Progress. Retrieved February 2009 from www.americanprogress.org/issues/2006/10/pdf/ extended_learning_report.pdf.

Pennsylvania Department of Education. (1996–2000). *Pennsylvania System of School Assessment, 1996–2000.* Office of Assessment. www.pde.state.pa.us/ a_and_t/site/default.asp (last viewed November 6, 2008).

*Philadelphia Daily News.* (1996, February 15), 4ff.

*Philadelphia Inquirer.* (1997, January 16), A16.

*Philadelphia Inquirer.* (1997, February 18).

Policy Studies Associates. (2007, July). Washington, DC, Teach for America 2007 National Principal Survey. www.teachforamerica.org/research/principal _survey.htm.

Raymond, M., Fletcher, S. H., & Luque, J. (2001, August). *Teach for America: An evaluation of teacher differences and student outcomes in Houston, Texas.* Center for Research on Education Outcomes (CREDO). credo.stanford .edu/downloads/tfa.pdf.

Rebell, M. (2002). Education, adequacy, democracy and the courts. In T. Ready, C. Edley Jr., and C. Snow (Eds.), *Achieving high educational standards for all conference summary.* National Research Council. www.tc.columbia.edu/ faculty/about.htm?facid=mar224.

Resnick, L. B. (1995). From aptitude to effort: A new foundation for our schools. *Daedalus, 124.* Retrieved November 2008 from www.institutefor learning.org/media/docs/AppitudeToEffort.pdf.

Richardson, K. (2002). *The making of intelligence.* New York: Columbia University Press.

Rist, R. (1970). Student social class and teacher expectations: The self-fulfilling prophecy in ghetto education. *Harvard Educational Review, 40*(3): 411–51.

Rosenthal, R. (1973, September). The Pygmalion effect lives. *Psychology Today, 56–63.*

Rosenthal, R. (1987). Pygmalion revisited. *Journal of Ed Psych, 79*(4): 461–64.

Rosenthal, R., & Jacobson, L. "Pygmalion in the Classroom." *The Urban Review, 3*(1) (September 1968): 16–20.

Rowe, M. B. (2004, November 5). "Payoff from Pausing." *Eastern Illinois University Science Education* (June 1995). www.eiu.edu/~scienced/5660/options/Op-4-R-6.html. Retrieved February 2009 from www.plainfieldnjk12.org/Departments/Curriculum/Math_Docs/Teacher%20Tools/Questions%20to%20Encourage%20Critical%20Thinking.pdf.

*San Antonio Independent School District v. Rodriquez*, 411 U.S. 1 (1973).

Sanders, W. L., & Rivers, J. C. (1996, November). *Cumulative and residual effects of teachers on future academic achievement.* Knoxville: University of Tennesee Value-Added Research and Assessment Center. www.mccsc.edu/~curriculum/cumulative%20and%20residual%20effects%20of%20teachers.pdf.

School District of Philadelphia. (1993/1994–1995/1996). *Summary of student achievement and demographic characteristics.* Office of Accountability and Assessment.

School District of Philadelphia. (1994–1998). *Performance.*

School District of Philadelphia. (1996, December). *Persistence information: Audenried Sr. High and Olney High School.*

School District of Philadelphia. (1998, June 29). *Reaching higher: Graduation and promotion supports and requirements, 1998–2003.* Adopted by the Board of Education June 29, 1998.

School District of Philadelphia. (2001, February). *Financial update.*

School District of Philadelphia. (2001, March 1). *Draft financial plan: Appendix B: Charter schools.*

Scott-Jones, D., & Clark, M. L. (1986). The school experiences of black girls: The interaction of gender, race, and socioeconomic status. *Phi Delta Kappan, 67*(7): 520–26.

Shanker, A. (1990, January 1). The end of the traditional model of schooling— And a proposal for using incentives to restructure our public schools. *KAPPAN, 344*–57.

Slavin, R. (1981). Synthesis of research on cooperative learning. *Educational Leadership, 38*(8), 655–60.

Slavin, R. (1983a). *Cooperative learning.* New York: Longman.

Slavin, R. (1983b). When does cooperative learning increase student achievement? *Psychological Bulletin, 94*(3), 429–45.

Slavin, R. (1991). Are cooperative learning and untracking harmful to the gifted? *Educational Leadership, 48*(6), 68–71.

Sloan, E. (1977). *Interventions designed to effect conscious changes in teacher behaviors that convey expectations.* Unpublished doctoral dissertation, University of Massachusetts, Amherst.

Sloan, E., & Schwartz, F. (1980). *The expectations project.* School District of Philadelphia.

Sowell, T. (1995). Ethnicity and IQ. In S. Fraser (Ed.), *The bell curve wars: Race, intelligence, and the future of America.* New York: Basic Books.

Steele, C. (1999, August). Thin ice: Stereotype threat and black college students. *The Atlantic.* Retrieved November 2008 from www.theatlantic.com/doc/199908/student-stereotype.

Sternberg, R. J. (1995). For whom the bell curve tolls: A review of *The Bell Curve*. *Psychological Science, 6,* 257–61.

Surgeon General. (1999). *Mental health: A report of the surgeon general.* www .surgeongeneral.gov/library/mentalhealth/summary.html.

Surgeon General. (2001). *Mental health: Culture, race, and ethnicity; A supplement to Mental health: A report of the surgeon general.* www.surgeon general.gov/library/mentalhealth/cre/.

Thaddeus Stevens College of Technology. *Thaddeus Stevens biography.* Available at www.stevenscollege.edu/301396.ihtml.

Tharp, R. G. (1997). From at-risk to excellence: Principles for practice. Washington, DC: ERIC Clearinghouse on Languages and Linguistics, October. #EDO-FL-98-01, October.

Tirozzi, G. N. (2002). Associations and the principalship. In M. S. Tucker & J. B. Codding (Eds.), *The principal challenge* (347–93). San Francisco: Jossey Bass.

Tucker, M. S., & Codding, J. B. (2002). Preparing principals in this age of accountability. In M. S. Tucker & J. B. Codding (Eds.), *The principal challenge* (1–43). San Francisco: Jossey Bass.

University of Pennsylvania. *GRIT study.* Positive Psychology Center. Retrieved November 2008 from www.ppresearch.sas.upenn.edu/.

U.S. Census Bureau. (1901–2000). *Education summary: High school graduates, and college enrollment and degrees, 1901–2000.* Table HS 21. Retrieved November 7, 2008, from www.census.gov/statab/hist/02HS0021.xls.

U.S. Census Bureau. (2008, August 14). *An older and more diverse nation by mid-century.* www.census.gov/Press-Release/www/releases/archives/ population/012496.html.

U.S. Department of Education. (1998). *Early warning, timely response: A guide to safe schools.* Washington, DC: U.S. Department of Education.

U.S. Department of Education. (2001). *Educational achievement and black-white inequality.* Center for Educational Statistics. Retrieved November 2008 from nces.ed.gov/pubs2001/inequality/3.asp.

U.S. Department of Labor. *Education pays.* Bureau of Labor Statistics. Retrieved November 2008 from www.bls.gov/emp/emptab7.htm.

Walsh, K. (2001). *Teacher certification reconsidered: Stumbling for quality.* The Abell Foundation. Retrieved February 2009 from www.abell.org/publications/ detail.asp?ID=59.

Whiting, B. (1999). Philadelphia: Prospects and challenges at the end of the decade. A report to the Pew Charitable Trusts. *The Pew Charitable Trusts 10*(1) (Spring 2007).

William Penn Foundation. (2001, August). *Evaluation report: Children Achieving.* www.williampennfoundation.org/usr_doc/children_achieving _web.pdf.

Wilson, J. J. (2000, October). *Juvenile Justice Bulletin.*, Office of Juvenile Justice and Delinquency Prevention.

Young, J. (2001, May). A system of building franchises. *School Administrator, 58.*

# Index

Abecediarian Educational Child Care Program. See early childhood education

achievement outcomes, 19, 59–65, 175
    by time periods, 61, 99, 233

accountability, xxv, 18, 60, 67, 91, 93–122, 130, 135, 136, 138, 141, 144–45, 147, 160, 163, 175, 176, 177–78, 185, 187, 201
    accommodations to, 88, 90–91 (see also assessment, accommodations in)
    accountability, system of, 23–24
    criteria for, 95–98
    criticism of, 108–10, 256
    groups for, 94
        central/cluster office accountability, 94, 99
        citizen accountability, 95, 97–98, 113–18
        educator accountability, 95–97, 105–13, 160
        parent accountability, 113–14
        student accountability, 98, 118–20
    measures, Performance Index calculated from, 105–7
    attendance calculated for, 108

graduation rate calculated for, 96, 101–2, 105
    participation calculated for, 96
    professional responsibility system for, 105, 199
    and NCLB, 77–78, 122n3, 123n4
    and opportunity to learn standards, 68, 71–73, 76–77, 115–18
    Philadelphia, development in, 98–120
    rewards, supports, sanctions for, 23, 94, 96, 97, 110–13, 118, 121, 138, 255
    school support process/teams for, 111–13
    targets for, 105, 108, 109, 112, 113, 119
    tests for
        alternatives, 119, 120
        high-stakes, 98, 147
        Stanford Achievement Test, SAT-9, 106
        untested students, 106–7, 110

action trees. See Prepare the Future
Adler, Majorie, 136
adequacy. See equity; resources
African American, 2, 5, 8, 28, 33–34, 45, 48–49, 197, 285
    See also color; expectations; immigrants; stereotypes

# About the Authors

**David W. Hornbeck** has spent forty-two years as an educator, community organizer, and activist. He served as Maryland state superintendent of schools and Philadelphia superintendent of schools. Among service on many boards and commissions at the local, state, and national levels, David was chair of the Carnegie Foundation for the Advancement of Teaching, Carnegie Corporation's Task Force on the Education of Early Adolescents, Children's Defense Fund, Council of Chief State School Officers, National Chapter I Commission, and the Public Education Network. David has been a partner in the Washington law firm of Hogan and Hartson, president of the International Fellows Program, codirector of the National Alliance for Restructuring Education, and senior education advisor to the Business Roundtable and the National Center on Education and the Economy.

Deciding that the major challenges we face in public education are political, not educational, when he stepped down as Philadelphia's superintendent, he founded Good Schools Pennsylvania, a grassroots advocacy organization and, arising from that success, has been working on the design of a national grassroots organization to build public will for quality public education for all children in America. David has two graduate degrees in theology (Union Theological Seminary and Oxford University) and earned his law degree cum laude from the University of Pennsylvania. He has been married to his wife Becky for forty-six years and has two sons, both inner-city principals, and four grandchildren, with three already in Baltimore City's public schools and the four-year-old on his way.

**Katherine Conner** spent her career in the School District of Philadelphia as a teacher, teacher coach, and administrator, finishing as associate superintendent for standards, assessment, and social services. Her persistent commitment was creating belief systems, instructional approaches, and strategies to build high expectations for those children least well served by our school systems, particularly those who are poor, nonwhite, have disabilities, or are English-language learners, through standards, assessments, research, accountability, and support systems that best serve all students.